D1069391

Collaborative Information Literacy Assessments

Strategies for Evaluating Teaching and Learning

Edited by Thomas P. Mackey
and Trudi E. Jacobson

Neal-Schuman Publishers, Inc.

New York   London

Published by Neal-Schuman Publishers, Inc.
100 William St., Suite 2004
New York, NY 10038

Copyright © 2010 Neal-Schuman Publishers, Inc.

Printed and bound in the United States of America.

The paper used in this publication meets the minimum requirements of American National Standard for Information Sciences-Permanence of Paper for Printed Library Materials, ANSI Z39.48-1992.

Library of Congress Cataloging-in-Publication Data

Collaborative information literacy assessments : strategies for evaluating teaching and learning / edited by Thomas P. Mackey and Trudi E. Jacobson.
     p. cm. — (Information literacy sourcebooks)
   Includes bibliographical references and index.
   ISBN 978-1-55570-693-7 (alk. paper)
   1. Information literacy—Study and teaching (Higher) 2. Information literacy—Study and teaching (Higher)—Evaluation. 3. Information literacy—Ability testing. 4. Academic libraries—Relations with faculty and curriculum. I. Mackey, Thomas P. II. Jacobson, Trudi.

ZA3075.C66 2010
028.7071'1—dc22
                                                          2009045950

Dedication

To Sue Faerman for being a great mentor
and for supporting the scholarship of pedagogy.
To Mom and James for encouragement and support
and to an inspiring next generation—
Jack Thomas, Shackleton, James,
Keene, Isabel, and Henry.

–Tom Mackey

To the dedicated and innovative instruction librarians
with whom I've had the pleasure to work
in the Instruction Section of
the Association of College and Research Libraries.
To John, who helps make all things possible.

–Trudi Jacobson

Contents

Part I: Business

Part II: Social Science and Education

Part III: Humanities

8. Many Voices, One Goal: Measuring Student Success through Partnerships in the Core Curriculum <span></span> 175

Becky Canovan, Anne Marie Gruber, Mary Anne Knefel, and Michele McKinlay

List of Figures, Tables, and Appendixes

FIGURES

TABLES

APPENDIXES

Foreword

It is a cool spring morning in the Pacific Northwest. Lilacs are blooming and rhododendron blossoms are poised to burst forth with color. I carry my kayak down to the shore, slide into the cockpit, and push off into the salt waters of Puget Sound. Paddling out a distance, I rest my paddle on the deck and float idly along with the subtle current to look around and take in the sights. But I find that on this particular morning it's the sounds that capture me. The birds are actively bantering, crows squawk at the eagle they are chasing, the wind ruffles the leaves, the tugboat horn sounds, the water laps on the rocks at the shore ... all sounds that ensure a viable system is operating. All sounds that would have otherwise escaped my notice had I not paused to listen.

Margaret Wheatley observed, "All change, even very large and powerful change, begins when a few people start talking with one another about something they care about ... And as an added joy, we also discover our collective wisdom. We suddenly see how wise we can be together" (*Turning to One Another*, 2002). And that is precisely what Trudi and Tom have done—listened to what was needed in our professional assessment conversations and creatively achieved it through the design and execution of this book. Through these assessment scenarios we have the opportunity to eavesdrop on key collaborations and deliberations and to benefit from learning in action. Many books have led us through the process of assessment—the focus and design, the creation of outcomes, the structure of assessments. But what the editors and the chapter authors provide for us in these pages are examples of collaboratively developing integrated assessments with discipline faculty, using student success as opposed to class time or content as the basis of those conversations, and deeply analyzing and engaging student work. These are the components that assure us a viable information literacy system is operational.

Trudi and Tom invite us into one of the most important dialogues we can have—listening to students through the avenue of assessment in order to understand and improve student learning. The assessment cycle provides us with the opportunity to communicate about learning and realize "how wise we can be together." It's now time for us to listen. It's time to be inspired to act. We couldn't ask for a more compelling resource to motivate us to dip into the water and take another paddle stroke forward.

Debra Gilchrist
Dean of Libraries and Institutional Effectiveness
Pierce College
Lakewood and Puyallup, Washington

Preface

Assessment of learning outcomes is a central consideration for faculty, librarians, and administrators, especially as colleges, universities, and accrediting agencies mandate this process. New courses and programs must consider assessment at the start of project planning, rather than after, and existing programs are being re-examined to incorporate an assessment component. The assessment of information literacy learning outcomes has matured with the expanse of these programs in higher education. Now that information literacy has been integrated into the curriculum at many institutions, in some cases built into general education programs, assessment of the information literacy curricula is a priority. We are especially interested in the role of faculty-librarian partnerships in the development of assessment best practices. This book explores assessment strategies designed by faculty-librarian teams from institutions at the forefront of this work in the United States, New Zealand, and the United Kingdom. This book presents eight innovative models for information literacy assessment in four main discipline areas: business, social science, education, and humanities. The methods explored in the book illustrate the relationship between assessment and collaboration in iterative course design and are portable to disciplinary perspectives and institutional contexts beyond those identified here.

In our first book, *Information Literacy Collaborations That Work* (2007), we presented faculty-librarian collaborations for teaching information literacy in multiple disciplines. We followed that project with *Using Technology to Teach Information Literacy* (2008), which explored novel uses of emergent technologies by faculty-librarian teams. In this third volume *Collaborative Information Literacy Assessments: Strategies for Evaluating Teaching and Learning* (2009) we continue our principal focus on faculty-librarian partnerships. Through these chapters we argue that collaboration is integral to the design and implementation of assessment efforts for information literacy courses and programs. Each chapter offers a qualitative and/or quantitative approach to assessment and a detailed examination of a course that incorporates information literacy. The author teams discuss some of the challenges they faced in working together and offer suggestions for overcoming institutional barriers to developing collaborative assessment projects. Most importantly, the faculty-librarian teams in this book reflect on what they learned from their assessments to improve student learning in the courses they discuss.

This book demonstrates that when faculty and librarians work together on assessment, a more comprehensive strategy for measuring student learning outcomes is developed than if they work independently. As a result, a more complete picture of student learning emerges than if separate instruments are developed in isolation. The work of these author teams reinforces the importance of taking an integrated approach to assessment that considers the relationship between the evaluation of learning outcomes and improved course design and teaching. Faculty-librarian involvement is critical to the planning and implementation of a pedagogical approach to information literacy assessment, especially if mandated efforts are designed to impact entire programs or influence multiple institutions. The purpose of this book is to promote varied and innovative methods for collaborative information literacy assessment within a context of critical inquiry to guide emerging or established programs.

INSTITUTIONAL SUPPORT FOR ASSESSMENT

A significant change has taken place in higher education from envisioning the classroom as a place where the teacher is at the center, and concentrating on what he or she does to achieve goals, to what the student learns, and how to measure the outcomes. According to Gilchrist and Zald, "the emphasis has now shifted to focus on student learning outcomes, and the real value of assessment in this context is the clarity it provides for students, librarians, and faculty" (2008: 165). Assessment of learning outcomes supports a student-centered dynamic that informs ongoing pedagogical development and course improvement. This process has been recognized by many institutions as crucial to understanding what and how students are learning. For example, in a member survey from the Association of American Colleges and Universities (AAC&U) "more than seven in 10 (72%) AAC&U member institutions assess learning outcomes across the curriculum, and an additional one in four (24%) say they are planning for this assessment" (2009: 2). The same survey indicates that 59 percent of the AAC&U member institutions address information literacy as a common learning outcome (2009: 4).

Accrediting agencies such as the Middle States Commission on Higher Education (MSCHE) promote information literacy in the standards for accreditation (*Characteristics of Excellence in Higher Education*, 2002). This emphasis on learning outcomes as part of the accreditation process has contributed to the strong institutional response from many colleges and universities to develop and assess information literacy initiatives. Middle States emphasizes the importance of developing partnerships at institutions that develop assessment efforts: "implemented effectively, the assessment of student learning will involve the shared commitment of students, administrators and academic professionals" (p. 50). These partnerships necessarily involve faculty and librarians working together on information literacy initiatives. The importance of faculty-librarian collaboration is explicitly mentioned as a "fundamental element" in *Standard 11: Educational Offerings* which promotes: "collaboration between professional library staff and faculty in teaching and fostering information literacy skills relevant to the curriculum" (p. 34).

Assessment was addressed in the American Library Association's (ALA) *Presidential Committee on Information Literacy: Final Report* (1989), which discussed evaluation as part of the "information age school." ALA argued that "evaluation would be based upon a broad range of literacy indicators, including some that assess the quality and appropriateness of information sources or the quality and efficiency of the information searches themselves." Over time, this approach was realized in many ways as colleges and universities assessed information literacy in the curriculum. ALA developed this idea further by suggesting that: "assessments would attend to ways in which students are using their minds and achieving success as information consumers, analyzers, interpreters, evaluators, and communicators of ideas." This approach emphasizes the ways students apply information literacy skills in the real world. It is consistent with Patricia Senn Breivik's vision for information literacy assessment as fundamental to student success and lifelong learning. She wrote, "once faculty accept the importance of information literacy to ensure the academic and career success of their students, and once they seriously plan for and assess achievement of that goal, then students will graduate as lifelong learners and productive citizens for an Information Age" (Breivik, 1998: 55).

In 2000, the Association of College and Research Libraries published the *Information Literacy Competency Standards for Higher Education* (2000). According to ACRL (2000), "the five standards and twenty two performance indicators . . . list a range of outcomes for assessing student progress toward information literacy" (p. 6). These guidelines promote the adaptation of the standards at the local level to consider the unique mission and goals of that particular institution (ACRL, 2000). This approach offers specific information literacy competencies while encouraging innovation in the way the standards are applied in varied courses and programs. At the same time, in its discussion of assessment, ACRL reinforced the importance of developing faculty-librarian partnerships for these endeavors:

In addition to assessing all students' basic information literacy skills, faculty and librarians should also work together to develop assessment instruments and strategies in the context of particular disciplines, as information literacy manifests itself in the specific understanding of the knowledge creation, scholarly activity, and publication processes found in those disciplines. (ACRL, 2000: 6)

ACRL provides a critical framework for faculty, librarians, and administrators to integrate information literacy into the curriculum and to include assessment in the initial planning of these initiatives. It also promotes a collaborative vision for these efforts to include faculty and librarians as equal and active participants in this process. Gilchrist and Zald argue that "the standards now serve as an excellent starting point for campus-based discussions between librarians and faculty members about what information literacy means when viewed through the lens of an institution's unique curriculum, philosophies, and values" (2008: 167). Through these conversations, faculty and librarians have the means to advance collaborative information literacy assessments in a manner that is process oriented and adaptable to change.

Assessment may be met with some resistance from faculty and librarians who are concerned that it means an appraisal of them rather than as a way to measure and analyze learning outcomes. But they may be more willing to participate in a process that is shared and reinforces the learning objectives of the curriculum than one that resembles an individual course evaluation or disconnected in some way from the larger community. This book, which advances collaborative assessments by modeling informed best practices from faculty and librarian teams, promotes the development of innovative information literacy programs that include a necessary focus on student learning. As you will see in the chapters that follow, faculty and librarians develop innovative and effective strategies for assessing information literacy through closely aligned partnerships.

BOOK ORGANIZATION

The book is organized by discipline into three main sections: Part I: Business, Part II: Social Science and Education, and Part III: Humanities. Although this disciplinary emphasis divides the book into three parts, each author team presents an assessment model that could be applied in different fields. In our own review of the chapters we were impressed with the diverse and flexible methodologies taken by each author team. All of the chapters follow a standardized format, with a literature review, case study model, discussion of partnership, examination of assessment data, as well as an assessment of the assessment. Most important, our author teams provide successful models for faculty and librarians who want to design or redesign their own information literacy assessment efforts. We also wrote section introductions with summaries of each chapter and recommendations for applying the assessments in different arenas.

Part I: Business

In the first part of the book, we present two chapters that focus on information literacy assessment within the field of business and finance. The chapter authors explore a methodology based on citation analysis and an embedded model for information literacy assessment. We start the book with a chapter by Casey M. Long and Milind M. Shrikhande from Georgia State University who explore assessment in an elective finance course. Through this case study, the authors examine the use of citation analysis to develop an effective teaching model for information literacy instruction. In the second chapter, Douglas G. Carrie and Lynne M. Mitchell from The University of Auckland Business School in New Zealand describe a holistic approach to information literacy assessment in an undergraduate degree program that prepares students for careers in business.

Part II: Social Science and Education

The second part of this book includes three chapters from the perspectives of social science and education. The faculty-librarian teams in this section examine an integrated library component, collaborative curriculum interventions, and online assessment strategies. Julie K. Gilbert and Christopher P. Gilbert from Gustavus Adolphus College explore the assessment of information literacy in an undergraduate political science curriculum. This data-driven approach provides a big picture analysis that finds a positive link between multiple instruction sessions and the development of information literacy skills. The second chapter in this section is by Amanda A. Harrison and Angela Newton from the University of Leeds. The authors describe the collaborative design of an assessment instrument to measure the information literacy learning outcomes of psychology and nursing students. This section closes with a chapter by Julie Bostock, Susan Graves, and Ruth Wilson from Edge Hill University in the United Kingdom. This author team presents a case study about the collaborative design of an online assessment strategy for adult learners.

Part III: Humanities

The third part of the book introduces three chapters that examine assessment endeavors in the humanities. The author teams in this section describe a self-assessment approach for writing courses, a holistic assessment in a writing program, and an assessment model in the core curriculum. We begin this part of the book with a chapter by Leslie Bussert and Norm Pouliot from Cascadia Community College and the University of Washington Bothell. This team developed a self-assessment model to enhance learning outcomes in writing courses by requiring students to play an active role in the documentation of their own learning. In the next chapter, Deborah B. Gaspar and Pamela S. Presser from The George Washington University describe a holistic assessment project designed for an undergraduate writing program. This author team shares the rubrics they created as part of their collaborative work on an assessment committee for *The Big Read*. The closing chapter is by Becky Canovan, Anne Marie Gruber, Mary Anne Knefel, and Michele McKinlay from University of Dubuque. The authors write about their assessment of an interdisciplinary course on research and writing in the core curriculum.

ASSESSING YOUR COURSES AND PROGRAMS

We encourage faculty and librarians from a range of disciplines to explore these chapters and to consider how a particular technique could be similarly applied at different institutions. Based on the work of the author teams in this book, assessment is a dynamic process that influences effective teaching practices and improves student learning. When carefully designed, it allows instructors to think about teaching and learning in new ways. Although some of the techniques covered here may not fit your particular college or university setting, many of instruments could be easily adapted to different courses, programs, and fields of study. When considering the varied approaches taken in this book, assessment offers a toolkit of possibilities for the design of new instruments, using quantitative and qualitative methods, summative and formative approaches, peer and self-assessments, rubrics and surveys, as well as in-class and online options. These approaches are expanded considerably and applied to disciplinary environments when librarians and faculty work together. Now that the assessment of learning outcomes has become such a major trend in higher education, with wide institutional support, it is time to hear from the faculty and librarians who are at the vanguard of this practice.

The e-mail address of every author is available toward the end of the book in case you have specific questions or comments about any of the chapters.

REFERENCES

American Library Association. 1989. "Presidential Committee on Information Literacy: Final Report." Available: www.ala.org/ala/mgrps/divs/acrl/publications/whitepapers/presidential.cfm (accessed September 30, 2009).

Association of American Colleges and Universities. 2009. "Learning and Assessment: Trends in Undergraduate Education." Available: www.aacu.org/membership/documents/ 2009MemberSurvey_Part1.pdf (accessed September 30, 2009).

Association of College and Research Libraries (ACRL). 2000. "Information Literacy Competency Standards for Higher Education." Available: www.ala.org/ala/mgrps/divs/ acrl/standards/standards.pdf (accessed September 30, 2009).

Breivik, Patricia 1998. *Student Learning in the Information Age*. Phoenix, AZ: The Oryx Press.

Gilchrist, Debra, and Anne Zald. 2008. "Instruction & Program Design through Assessment." In *Information Literacy Instruction Handbook* (pp. 164–192), edited by Christopher N. Cox and Elizabeth Blakesley Lindsay. Chicago: Association of College and Research Libraries.

Middle States Commission on Higher Education (MSCHE). 2002. *Characteristics of Excellence in Higher Education: Eligibility Requirements and Standards for Accreditation*. Philadelphia: Middle States Commission on Higher Education.

Acknowledgments

We acknowledge our faculty and librarian author teams who share their innovative models for information literacy assessment in this book. We appreciated the opportunity to work with you on this project and gained many new insights about assessment from editing your chapters.

We thank Debra Gilchrist for writing the excellent Foreword to our book. Debra brought her own expertise about assessment to this important part of the project and took the time to carefully review all of the chapters in advance.

Further, we appreciate the outstanding support we always receive from the team at Neal-Schuman Publishers, including Charles Harmon, Vice President and Director of Publishing, Amy Knauer, Production Editor, and Sandy Wood, Development Editor.

Part I

Business

SECTION INTRODUCTION

In this first part of the book we introduce two chapters that explore information literacy assessment in business and finance at the undergraduate and graduate levels. The author teams in this section provide assessment models from universities in the United States and New Zealand. They discuss several quantitative and qualitative tools for assessing information literacy including a marking rubric, an online research log, reflective tasks, pre- and posttests, and citation analysis. Both chapters reinforce the value of assessment to better understand student learning and to influence the perception of information literacy instruction within colleges and universities.

We start this first section with "Using Citation Analysis to Evaluate and Improve Information Literacy Instruction" by Casey M. Long and Milind M. Shrikhande from Georgia State University. This case study examines the use of citation analysis to better understand teaching and learning in several sections of undergraduate and graduate courses about international finance. This assessment was also designed to overcome the many challenges of integrating information literacy into the curriculum and to inform the development of an entire program with a focus on information skills at the same institution. This author team presents a comprehensive literature review about citation analysis that offers a convincing rationale for the use of this technique in assessment initiatives. They also describe an initial pre- and postassessment strategy using multiple-choice questions that did not meet their original expectations. Their critical appraisal of this first attempt led to their decision to adopt a citation analysis approach. According to the findings of this faculty-librarian team, citation analysis provided strong statistical evidence that the information literacy instruction in the undergraduate and graduate finance courses made a difference in student learning. The success of this initiative led to a greater level of support for information literacy instruction at Georgia State University. This chapter demonstrates the potential impact of assessment efforts on teaching and learning in discipline-specific courses and the importance of these findings within the wider institutional context. It may be especially valuable to faculty and librarians interested in using quantitative assessment data to garner support for nascent initiatives at institutions in transition or to expand upon the success of existing programs in any academic environment.

In the second chapter, Douglas G. Carrie and Lynne M. Mitchell from The University of Auckland Business School, New Zealand, present "A Holistic Approach to Embedding Information Literacy in the Design, Delivery, and Assessment of an Undergraduate Business Program." This is the first of three chapters in the book that provides an international perspective on information literacy instruction and assessment. The author team describes an information literacy program in business that prepares students with a comprehensive set of information skills for success in the real world. This chapter examines an embedded approach to information literacy based on standards defined by the Australian and New Zealand Institute for Information Literacy (ANZIIL). In their literature review, the authors identify important links between information literacy and the workplace. This perspective reinforces an integrated approach to information literacy in the business curriculum and supports a highly visible role for librarians in teaching and assessing courses in class and online. Writing and critical thinking are both key aspects of information literacy instruction in this program. Some of the innovative assignments discussed in this case study include an analytical report about a New Zealand industry, digital media projects, and collaborative virtual businesses. This chapter reveals a complex scaffolding of information literacy assessment that unfolds over time in multiple classes, from introductory to capstone experiences. The authors describe some of the challenges in assessing a holistic information literacy program, while demonstrating the success of their innovative eight-year partnership between faculty and librarians. This reflective chapter illustrates the value of an assessment model that fully integrates a dedicated librarian in the instructional design and assessment process.

The emphasis of this section on business and finance defines important links between higher education and the real world. It also shows how key competencies such as information seeking, evaluating and synthesizing information, writing, and critical thinking are relevant concerns in different academic settings and the workplace. To apply some of these assessment techniques in your course or program, take into account the following:

- Develop an assessment strategy that scaffolds with the teaching and learning and encompasses multiple courses over time.

- Extend undergraduate information literacy programs and assessment to the graduate level, when appropriate.
- Draw upon the differing expertise and background of librarians and faculty members when considering assessment methods.
- Review the data being collected from assessment efforts, and revise or replace methods that do not provide the type of information being sought.
- Use multiple channels to report upon information literacy successes, as proved by assessment, in order to enhance the need for information literacy instruction in other programs at the institution.
- For some disciplines, highlighting the link between specific information literacy skills and the world beyond academia will provide persuasive evidence of the need for information literacy programs and the assessment of student learning.

As with all the chapters in this book, the assessment strategies and rationales are not confined to the disciplines in whose context they are described. The scaffolding approach, the extension to graduate courses, and the connections between knowledge gained from courses and the wider world, to take just three themes from these two chapters, are all pertinent to many other disciplines as well. Additional elements found in this section are sure to resonate as well.

Chapter 1

Using Citation Analysis to Evaluate and Improve Information Literacy Instruction

Casey M. Long and Milind M. Shrikhande

INTRODUCTION

Information literacy is a complex skill set that is often overly simplified. As many academic librarians know, it cannot be acquired in one in-class session. Students must gradually be introduced and encouraged to apply the concepts through multiple class sessions and assignments. The route to effective information literacy instruction is to understand the student experience, identify the skills needed, and strategically integrate information literacy into core courses. Each information literacy session should build upon another and challenge students to further their skills.

The citation analysis assessment method offers one of the best ways to understand how students locate information, the types of sources they use, and if previous information literacy sessions have effectively altered student research strategies. With this type of data in hand instructors and librarians are able to demonstrate the impact of information literacy instruction, make necessary changes to the original instruction method, and build a foundation for a broader information literacy program. In this chapter we provide a case study on how citation analysis was utilized at Georgia State University to evaluate, revise, and develop a teaching approach that best meets the needs of students in an elective finance class. In addition, we discuss how the evidence gathered through citation analysis is creating opportunities to promote the need for a strategically designed information literacy program.

BRIEF HISTORY OF CITATION ANALYSIS

Citation analysis is essentially a subfield of bibliometrics and is utilized in libraries in several distinctly different ways. There are a number of excellent literature reviews that provide a history of citation analysis (Smith, 1981; Osareh, 1996; Fescemyer, 2000). Although most citation analysis histories and literature reviews date the emergence of citation analysis to the 1960s when citation indices began to appear, they all agree that citation analysis probably originated much earlier. Farideh Osareh indicates there is evidence of bibilo-metric studies as far back as 1890 (Osareh, 1996: 149). Linda C. Smith describes research published in 1929 by Gross and Gross that utilized citation analysis as a collection development tool (Smith, 1981: 97).

There are many branches of citation analysis. Some evaluate the impact a work has on future publications. Others assess the citations in student and faculty work to measure the quality of the library's collection and identify resources that should be added. The branches of citation analysis that are most pertinent to the development and assessment of information literacy are the ones that focus on understanding students' information-seeking skills and measure the impact or quality of information literacy instruction.

An early attempt at using citation analysis to evaluate information literacy instruction appears in a seminal instruction-focused report published in 1966 called the Monteith College Library Experiment. The project actually began in 1960 at Wayne State University as a way to strengthen the connection between the library and college teaching. Through a series of ten library assignments over the course of the degree program, librarians aimed to teach students how to find their way in the library. To assess student's library competency at the end of this program the researchers felt the "products of the assignments themselves could be one source of evidence on student learning" (Knapp, 1966: 108). Unfortu-nately, several events prevented the researchers from gathering the information necessary to complete the analysis. One obstacle Knapp notes is the librarians' dependence on instructors for the implementation of the assignments (Knapp, 1966: 138), illustrating the need for collaborative instruction and assessment.

Another early adopter of this methodology is Thomas Kirk. In an article published in *College & Research Libraries* in 1971 he used this method to compare two library instruction methods. It is possible that Kirk was the first to success-fully execute instruction assessment based on citation analysis. The authors of this chapter were unable to locate earlier studies and the only relevant reference in Kirk's bibliography is to the Monteith College Library Experiment conducted by Knapp. Nonetheless, this work together with other contributions (e.g., Kirk, 1973) on the evaluation of library instruction established Kirk as one of the forefathers of this assessment technique.

A few significant studies on the use of citation analysis emerged in the 1980s and 1990s. Some of these articles showed how citation analysis was used to obtain quantitative data on the effectiveness of an instructional technique (Kohl and Wilson, 1986; Dykeman and King, 1983). Others provided a critique of citation analysis as a library instruction evaluation tool and recommended some standards for conducting such assessments (Gratch, 1985; Young and Ackerson, 1995). All of these studies pioneered the use of citation analysis and variations of these recommended methods continue to be used.

Starting in the late 1990s, the use of citation analysis began to surge and the focus of research published based on this evaluation method changed dramatically in just a few years. A large part of this increase was due to the rapidly expanding role of electronic sources and the Internet in student research. Initially, these studies focused on determining if students took advantage of the electronic and Internet sources available. In their 1997 article published in *Research Strategies*, Malone and Videon state that they wanted, "to discover the extent to which undergraduate students are finding electronic resources for their course-related research" (Malone and Videon, 1997: 152). Their concern was whether students knew how to access electronic resources through the library and the Internet. Interestingly, no less than 84 percent of the 291 bibliographies they examined utilized no electronic resources. Although many studies including the study by Malone and Videon do not use citation analysis to evaluate instruction, these studies provide valuable insights into the information-seeking behavior of students, helping librarians and course instructors to design future instruction sessions.

Shortly after the turn of the millennium, citation analysis studies moved away from determining *if* students were using the Internet to understanding *how* students were using the Internet for research. A major conclusion reached was that librarians would need to provide better guidance to students on citing electronic sources and on evaluating the quality of websites that they chose for their research (Fescemyer, 2000; Davis and Cohen, 2001; Davis, 2002).

It was not long before the Internet became a popular research tool. As a result, the citation analysis studies began looking at the extent to which students used the library and the quality of the research sources being selected. These works compared the ratio of electronic sources to print sources and Internet sources to library sources (Hovde, 2000; Kraus, 2002). An emphasis on evaluating the impact of the instruction on student information-seeking skills was also revived (Emmons and Martin, 2002; Davis, 2003; Ursin, Lindsay, and Johnson, 2004; Robinson and Schlegl, 2004).

Citation analysis is now firmly rooted in the cannon of instruction assessment techniques. Works produced by Kirk, Gratch, Ackerson and Young, and Davis provide the foundation for all citation analysis studies and new research produced each year identifies new uses and techniques for this assessment method. The unique ability of citation analysis assessment to identify student information-seeking behavior ensures it will play an important role in the crafting of information literacy instruction as technologies and tools evolve.

INFORMATION LITERACY AT GEORGIA STATE UNIVERSITY

Like many academic institutions, Georgia State University faces difficulties in promoting information literacy across campus. The first and greatest obstacle is the lack of a formal information literacy program that is supported by the institution and integrated into the core curriculum. Though information literacy is listed as a strategic goal in the University Action Plan (Georgia State University, 2008: 1), information literacy is neither a required component within the core curriculum nor is it integrated formally into any degree program curricula offered at Georgia State University. Information literacy sessions are conducted by librarians at the request of individual instructors.

As it is up to individual professors to integrate information literacy into a course, students' information literacy skills vary depending on the courses they select. Some students sit through two or three information literacy sessions in one semester. Others only receive information literacy instruction in an introductory writing course. An extreme example of poor information literacy coordination involves a group of 25 students in a single cohort participating in the Freshman Learning Community, taking a series of five classes together. In three of the five cohort classes they received information literacy instruction from three different librarians. Neither the librarians, nor the course-instructors were aware that the students were receiving a basic introduction to library resources and research techniques in other classes. This is not an infrequent occurrence, as business librarians at Georgia State University often encounter the same MBA students in multiple information literacy sessions taught throughout the semester. One can argue that the repetitive nature of these sessions helps reinforce the concepts taught by the librarian, but there is an equal probability that the students simply tune out the additional instruction sessions and develop the impression that they are fully skilled in the art of research. Inability to understand students' information literacy needs and lack of coordination between course instructors results in a missed opportunity to expose students to advanced skills.

Another issue Georgia State University faces in promoting information literacy is the diversity of needs among its students. Georgia State University is widely noted for its ethnic and racial diversity, but is also very diverse in the types of students it attracts. For years Georgia State was known as a commuter school. Originally founded as a business night school, Georgia State University continued to serve the needs of professionals pursuing a part-time education as it grew and expanded its degree offerings. The introduction of student housing in 1996, however, initiated a gradual transformation of Georgia State from a commuter school into a traditional college campus. Now the student body at Georgia State consists of students who started their college career at Georgia State, transfer students from local two-year colleges, older students restarting their education, full-time students, and part-time students.

The ability of librarians to plan appropriately for an information literacy session is challenged by the differences in the educational trajectory of students within a class. For instance, librarians can neither assume a third-year student received a basic orientation to the services and tools available through the university library, nor can they assume that the orientation had occurred within the past three years. As an experiment, a professor who teaches two sections of a junior-level business communications course asked her students to raise their hands if they had been at Georgia State since their first year of college. The differences between the two sections of the same course were dramatic. In the first course section only 15 percent of the students raised their hands and in the second course section 75 percent of the students raised their hands. This anecdotal evidence suggests that information literacy sessions must be tailored to these diverse audiences if they are to succeed.

To conduct an effective information literacy session librarians need to develop a course module that identifies and fulfills the learning needs of the students in the classroom. The size of the institution also presents a challenge. Currently there are more than 27,000 students pursuing degrees in more than 250 areas of studies. Though the library has librarians who focus on meeting the needs of first- and second-year students and another group of librarians who address the discipline-specific needs of students, many students graduate without any information literacy skill instruction. Students attending an information literacy session in their final semester at Georgia State University frequently wish they had received this type of instruction earlier in their degree program. To ensure students build strong information literacy skills, librarians must be able to work collaboratively with departments and designers of the core curriculum to maximize effectiveness of the offered information literacy instruction.

In summary, librarians at Georgia State University face several challenges. Building stronger relationships with faculty, improving coordination of information literacy efforts, and understanding the student experience are some examples. Citation analysis assessment has the potential to address these challenges. Our initial collaborative efforts in this direction have led to improved organization of information literacy instruction in the College of Business at Georgia State University. This case study demonstrates how citation analysis assessment improves the efficacy of information literacy instruction and contributes to the development of an institutionalized information literacy program.

A PARTNERSHIP TO IMPROVE STUDENT INFORMATION-SEEKING SKILLS

Teaching innovations are often triggered by observations and through strongly felt needs for improvement by classroom instructors. After several years of assigning term projects in an international finance class, one of our professors began to explore ways to improve this course assignment. Satisfied that students were learning core course concepts from this independent team assignment, he felt there was need to strengthen the students' research skills so they could complete this assignment at a higher level. During the national Financial Education Association Meetings (2003), he attended a presentation on information literacy and was inspired to begin building such skills among students working on the independent team assignments. Coincidentally, upon his return from the conference, the finance professor received an e-mail message from a business librarian offering information literacy instructional services and a partnership to develop an information literacy instruction method began. The focus of this collaboration was to encourage appropriate information-seeking behavior among graduate and undergraduate students.

The business librarian prepared an hour-long research session that highlighted key resources, introduced search techniques, explained how to use the library, and discussed plagiarism. This was the basic approach the business librarian took with each of her classes. Confident in this approach, the business librarian believed the assessment result would demonstrate how the information literacy session improved students' skills. She did not expect the assessment would prompt her to question her approach to teaching.

To measure the results of this instructional effort, the business librarian developed a pretest/posttest assessment tool that utilized a series of multiple choice questions. This tool began with basic questions designed to gather demographic information and develop an understanding of students' prior information literacy experience. Then the tool delved into some questions aimed at understanding students' familiarity with business resources. The results of the pretest, however, proved unreliable and did not gather the type of data needed to understand students' knowledge levels. It was difficult to tell from the results whether students were actually able to correctly identify which databases provided access to specific types of business information. This was partially the result of poor design. On questions in which the test design-ers intended students to select the best database for a particular type of infor-mation, student responses indicated dissonance. Students selected tools that did contain the type of data requested by the question but not necessarily the best database for the purpose. In addition, the multiple choice nature of the test enabled some students to successfully guess the correct answer. It became clear that even if the pretest assessment tool was properly designed, this method would not provide the data needed to understand how students were applying the concepts taught in class. This method only measured whether the students remembered the names of databases and basic procedures for accessing these resources. It did not provide insight into whether students utilized these tools and how effective they were at finding the information they needed for assignments.

After carefully researching other methods for assessing the information liter-acy instruction the team selected citation analysis as their assessment tool and developed an instrument to measure their effectiveness vis-à-vis the intended goals of the instruction session. This tool was then utilized throughout three semesters in undergraduate and graduate international finance classes in which students worked on an independent team assignment. The tool prompted changes over the course of three semesters, including the following:

- shifting the instruction session from the regular classroom into a com-puter lab to facilitate greater hands-on research instruction;
- creating a research template to streamline students' thinking regarding issues faced by their chosen organization and help students avoid infor-mation overload;
- designing a Web-based research guide to provide further assistance; and
- altering the instruction session to help students build a greater under-standing of the research process.

In addition to these instructional components, the data gathered from the citation analysis assessment combined with observations from interactions with students seeking assistance led to the realization that the in-class library research sessions needed to be complemented by consultations for the students, individually or in teams. Thus, both the faculty member as well as the business librarian began setting up regular consultations with the students to answer their questions, to provide guidance and perspective, and to consolidate their information literacy skills.

These research instruction sessions provided students, especially the unini-tiated ones, with a framework for analysis and the generation of ideas that would grow into fully thought-out term papers. Consequently, the librarian-faculty team started observing a marked improvement in the submitted projects along the dimensions of variety and quality of resources being used. After using the citation analysis assessment method for three semesters the assessment data indicated the combination of instruction techniques was effective in improving students' information-seeking skills. The team discontinued assessing the information literacy sessions each semester. They still plan to use this assessment to ensure the instruction approach continued to be effective, but they felt that the development of an information literacy instruction package was complete.

Although most librarians are familiar with many of the techniques used by this team to teach information literacy, it is the combination of the different techniques that fulfilled the specific needs of students in this course. The citation analysis assessment method guided the redesign; however, a key component for the success of this endeavor is the faculty-librarian collaboration. Without a joint commitment to information literacy, the time required to tailor the instruction to this course may not have been available. To develop lifelong information literacy skills among students it is essential that sustained faculty-librarian collaboration combines different methods and inputs that can be refined over time. Working in coordination with each other, the faculty member and librarian have to complement each other's role by providing opportunities for multiple interactions with student teams during the course of the semester.

DESIGNING OUR CITATION ANALYSIS ASSESSMENT TOOL

We selected citation analysis as the method to assess our information literacy efforts because it enabled us to see how students were finding, evaluating, utilizing, and citing information sources. Using this method required that we create a citation analysis tool to measure students' abilities. In this section we describe the steps we took to develop our citation analysis assessment instrument.

Developing Clear Objectives

Thomas Kirk advocates that all instructional design should begin with the setting of instruction goals and objectives. He states that "the objectives are going to be there whether or not we consciously decide what they are going to be" (Kirk, 1973: 5). When we conducted our first assessment using the pre/posttest method we found Kirk's statement to be true. We knew in general what we wanted to accomplish, but did not develop an outline of these goals. As a result we were uncertain how to measure the effectiveness of the session and in retrospect the instruction approach lacked focus. We quickly realized we needed to articulate what we actually aimed to achieve. Our goals were simple and based broadly on the information literacy standards established by the Association of College and Research Libraries (ACRL, 2000). Through our sessions we aimed to:

- introduce students to key sources respected and used by financial professionals;
- encourage students to use a variety of sources that express different viewpoints;
- teach students to cite their sources; and
- ensure that students understand how to paraphrase and synthesize information properly.

Identifying Criteria for Assessment

Once the instructional goals were set we established criteria to measure students' success within that goal. The criteria we identified included an assessment of:

- *Quality of Sources:* Are the sources appropriate for the topic and scope of the paper? Are the sources well-respected sources in the discipline?
- *Variety of Sources:* Are there enough sources to sufficiently develop a well-rounded argument/perspective? Do the sources provide diverse perspectives?
- *Citation Format:* Is a consistent citation format utilized? Is enough information provided in the citation to enable the reader to locate the source referenced?
- *Information Use:* Is there evidence of plagiarism? Are information sources properly paraphrased or quoted?

Establishing a System to Grade Information Literacy Achievement

After establishing our criteria for assessment, our next step involved creating a scoring system. We refer to our system as an information literacy grading scale. To create this scale, we used a zero to five-point scale for each item with one being the lowest score and five being the highest. If a student team did not integrate one of the lessons learned during the information literacy instruction into their paper, the team was assigned a one for that criterion. If the team consistently applied all the lessons learned into their paper, the team was assigned a five. Zeros were occasionally assigned when no evidence was available upon which to evaluate the paper. For instance, when a paper was discovered to be plagiarized it received a zero. If no sources were used or listed the team was assigned a zero for that category.

Learning goals are not always created equal. In the goals we set for ourselves we felt that some of the learning objectives were more important than others. As a result we weighted each of the categories according to the overall importance for information literacy achievement. Our primary goals were to ensure use of a variety of appropriate sources, to reduce plagiarism, to introduce students to key sources in the discipline, and to ensure students learned to utilize them appropriately. For us, citation format was considered less important than all of the other criteria. To adjust for these differences, we assigned the following weights to each characteristic:

- Quality of Sources = 40 percent
- Variety of Sources = 20 percent
- Citation Format = 10 percent
- Information Use = 30 percent

The weighted scores were then added together to create what we termed "an information literacy score" for the team project. This score measured how well students demonstrated these information literacy skills. All the scores for each semester were then averaged together to provide an overall information literacy score for that semester. These scores were separately ascertained for undergraduate students and graduate students as we wanted to measure each of these groups independently.

Outlining Grading Guidelines to Ensure Rating Consistency

Because our project spanned multiple semesters it was important to develop a set of standards that could be used every semester to measure achievement in each category. This helped our grading to be consistent from semester to semester. Creating guidelines also helps in limiting the subjectivity of the evaluation process, especially if multiple individuals are scoring the papers. Appendix 1.1 provides a detailed overview of the guidelines we established.

Analyzing the Citations in Context

Citation analysis, as the name implies, places a heavy emphasis on evaluating the resources listed in the bibliography of a paper, but to obtain a full understanding of how students use and cite information we found it necessary to review the content of each paper. Our evaluation of information use within the paper included assessing:

- the appropriateness of the information for the topic and scope of the paper;
- the extent to which the sources cited in the bibliography were actually used within the paper; and
- whether the student teams synthesized the information into their own arguments.

Through this additional level of assessment we found several instances of plagiarism that may have previously gone unnoticed. Minor examples involved students citing sources in their bibliography that were not actually used as sources within the paper. One blatant instance involved a bibliography in which all of the sources cited were published years prior to the data that was actually reported in the paper. Further analysis of this paper led to the surprising revelation that the bibliography itself was actually taken from a completely different report published by a professor in Denver. Several other extreme examples of plagiarism were found, but most instances of plagiarism appeared to be examples of unintentional plagiarism. This level of analysis provided great insight into how and why students may plagiarize. As a result we were able to alter our instruction session to address plagiarism more extensively. We discussed the university guidelines on academic honesty and the finance professor made a point of referencing these guidelines throughout the course. This analysis also gave us examples of plagiarism that we could convey to the students so they had a better understanding of what was expected.

WHAT WE LEARNED THROUGH THE ASSESSMENT TOOL

The tangible results provided by the citation analysis assessment were encouraging. The tool provided us with data that indicated both undergraduate and graduate students benefited from the information literacy instruction at statistically significant levels. As shown in Figure 1.1, each of the three semesters in which an information literacy instruction session was integrated into the course, the information literacy scores of both undergraduate and graduate students consistently improved. By the end of the third semester, graduate student skills improved from 66.6 percent to a very high 95.2 percent of the maximum score attainable of 5.0, and undergraduate student skills improved from 46.8 percent to a significantly higher level of 96.3 percent of the maximum score attainable of 5.0. The undergraduate students benefited more compared to the graduate students. This difference was attributed to the higher maturity and awareness levels of graduate students due to earlier exposure to information literacy at the workplace and in their prior academic training. Graduate students started at a high threshold; therefore the marginal improvements were not as striking as those for undergraduate students. However, in absolute terms, both groups seemed to have gained significantly in their learning and skills for lifelong information literacy applications.

The qualitative outcomes of the citation analysis assessment are difficult to demonstrate. In scoring the papers using the citation analysis instrument, we were able to note specific trends in the ways in which students completed their papers. For instance, after reviewing papers in the control group and in

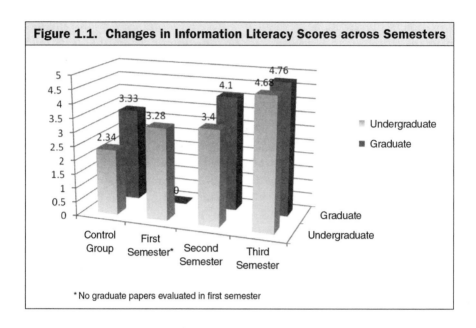

Figure 1.1. Changes in Information Literacy Scores across Semesters

* No graduate papers evaluated in first semester

the first two semesters of instruction, it was clear from the content analysis that students were simply regurgitating information from the sources they selected. The information was properly summarized or quoted. However, the papers consistently lacked an element of critical thinking by students that is essential for supporting mere opinions. To remedy this problem, an in-class activity was designed that helped students understand better what we expected to see in their assignments. Students were given a packet of documents that were found in the library databases on a specific company. They were asked to work in teams for 15 minutes to identify a paper topic on that company and outline their strategy. At the end of the 15 minutes, the student teams presented their outlines and described the types of information sources they would need. After each student team completed their summary, we jointly evaluated their approach and provided constructive feedback. This approach clarified expectations for the students. As a result, not only did the information literacy scores improve dramatically, fewer student teams sought additional assistance from the librarian. If we had not reviewed the contents of the paper to determine how students were utilizing these sources, we may not have identified this issue.

ACHIEVING OUR GOALS

As noted in the previous section, our quantitative results showed a dramatic improvement in student information literacy skills. Because the information literacy scores were high we felt we achieved our goals and created an instructional approach that could be used for future classes. We discontinued conducting a citation analysis after each semester and decided to utilize this technique periodically to ensure the information literacy session continues to be successful.

After the final semester of using this tool, however, we conducted a small survey of students who had completed their studies at Georgia State University to see if the information was retained and useful to the students after graduation. We received only 17 responses, but these responses were pretty well balanced in terms of representation for the different semesters. In the survey:

- 82 percent indicated that they developed more effective information searching skills;
- 76 percent indicated that they learned about relevant information sources; and
- 59 percent of the respondents indicated that they used the skills gained in the library research workshop in other settings such as the workplace, in other classes, or in another degree program.

In the free text comments of the survey, at least seven respondents clearly stated that they had not known about these resources previously and wish they had been introduced earlier. One student wrote:

> i [*sic*] was never aware of the tremendous amount of resources available to us until this class which happened to be one of my last semesters. i use some of those resources at work now. i think every student should be given a course by Ms. Long as one of the first courses.

USING CITATION ANALYSIS TO INSTITUTIONALIZE INFORMATION LITERACY

The data gathered in the single elective finance course proved to be a launchpad for greater efforts. Pleased with our results, we applied for two awards to share our experience with others. We received both awards. One was given by the College of Business for innovative instruction. The other was given by the University Center for Teaching and Learning for instructional effectiveness. The key reason noted for our achievement of these honors was our ability to provide quantitative evidence of improvement in student learning.

These awards quickly raised the profile of information literacy within the College of Business. The faculty members were more receptive to the integration of information literacy instruction into their courses. The librarian took advantage of this new interest in information literacy to begin establishing a comprehensive, well-coordinated undergraduate information literacy program in the College of Business. At this point in the process, she is close to full integration into two business courses that all undergraduates are required to take and is working on identifying a third. By working with a set of three required courses, the business librarian is able to introduce students to basic information literacy skills in one course and address additional information literacy concepts in subsequent courses. She is hopeful this will ensure all students are not only introduced to information literacy skills, but are able to achieve more advanced skills that are normally not addressed in information literacy sessions due to the lack of time available.

Outside of a collaborative effort, librarians and information literacy do not usually receive this level of attention. Simply the fact that the integration of information literacy instruction into a single course was highlighted as innovative instruction illustrates the lack of visibility librarians and information literacy can have in an organization. By collaborating with a faculty member and providing clear evidence of impact, information literacy finally received the level of attention it deserved within this organization.

ENSURING RESULTS ARE VALID MEASURES OF INFORMATION LITERACY

In the previous section we indicated the achievement of our intended goals and how we succeeded in improving visibility of information literacy instruction at the College of Business. The achievement of intended goals needs to be confirmed by ensuring that the results of our case study provide valid measures of information literacy. These quantitative robustness checks for reliability and validity of our results are discussed in this section.

Use of a Control Group as a Benchmark

An important principle of field study research is to compare the assessment of the sample of students in the experiment with a control group that has not benefited from information literacy instruction. We used a control group from a semester prior to the multisemester field study on information literacy instruction. Students' information literacy skills by the end of the third semester were benchmarked against the control group.

Use of Multiple Evaluators

Researchers using this assessment technique emphasize the need to use more than one person in evaluating student papers, especially while discussing the development of appropriate citation analysis tools. Some advise that those rating the citations should be individuals without a strong connection to the subject matter or course (Gratch, 1985; Hovde, 2000; Scharf et al., 2007). Others argue that only librarians should rate the bibliographies.

Because we evaluated all the student papers and not just a sample from the course, we decided it was too much work to enlist the assistance of outside graders. Instead, the librarian conducted an initial review of all the papers. Then without revealing the librarian's assessments, 20 percent of the papers were randomly selected for the professor to cross-validate the librarian's assessments. The scores were then compared with the scores assigned by the librarian. The correlations between the scores of the two graders compared well on each attribute, ranging between 0.81 and 0.95. The overall correlation between the two graders' scores was about 0.91. The dual grading approach also helps validate the rubric detailed in Appendix 1.1 for citation analysis and information literacy assessment.

Test the Reliability of Results

To establish that the student teams sampled across the different semesters were from the same population as far as the means and variances of their academic proficiency were concerned, we used two statistical tests, a t-test for equality of means, and Levene's test for equality of variances (using SPSS [Statistical Package for the Social Sciences]). Academic proficiency was measured by using average GPA (grade point average) within student teams and comparing such average GPA scores across different semesters. These tests were conducted for undergraduate and graduate student teams separately to compare proficiency across a pair of semesters at a time.

We also conducted a statistical analysis of the performance by student teams across semesters. Although the scores indicated continuous improvement in the quality of resources used, variety of resources used, citations, and proper use of information, it is again imperative that such findings be validated statistically. A multivariate analysis of variance (MANOVA) test was conducted to indicate statistically significant improvement in student team performance across different stages of the field study across the different semesters. This test was implemented on a large enough sample of student teams to ensure that the number of student teams exceeded the number of dependent variables, as required for MANOVA.

CONCLUSION

Using citation analysis for instruction assessment is not appropriate for all instructional efforts. Time and human resource demands are potential limitations of this approach compared to the time normally spent on such instruction in the classroom. The evaluators need a sufficient time to review the student work. This requires the course instructor to allow enough time for evaluation between the submission of the student papers and the return of these works to the students. In addition, students must be taught how to cite sources in such a manner that will enable the instructor to determine the source and the quality of the information. If, however, adequate time and resources are available, citation analysis provides a powerful tool to improve information literacy skills among students.

In this chapter, we presented a case study on how citation analysis was utilized at Georgia State University to evaluate, revise, and develop a teaching approach to best meet the needs of students in an elective finance class. Sustained efforts and a committed partnership between the finance professor teaching this international finance course and the business librarian resulted in outstanding information literacy skills developed by undergraduate and graduate business majors. The citation analysis assessment provided unexpected insight into the research methods students employed. It also highlighted weaknesses in the approach students used. In addition, citation analysis allowed us to evaluate our own teaching methods. Being able to recognize areas in which students failed to achieve the desired results enabled us to identify areas for potential change in our instruction methods. Once the change was implemented, we were able to use citation analysis to evaluate the effectiveness of the new teaching approach.

Overall, citation analysis assessment enabled us to perfect our instructional approach. In addition, the quantitative data measuring the success of our effort allowed us to demonstrate to the other instructors at the College of Business the need for greater opportunities to develop students' information literacy skills. These are just a few of the benefits we discovered in using citation analysis. Appendix 1.2 provides additional ways in which citation analysis may be used to improve information literacy instruction. We hope others will be inspired to utilize this assessment technique in one of its many diverse applications.

REFERENCES

Association of College and Research Libraries (ACRL). 2000. "Information Literacy Competency Standards for Higher Education." American Library Association. Available: www.ala.org/ala/mgrps/divs/acrl/standards/informationliteracycompetency.cfm (accessed September 30, 2009).

Davis, Philip M. 2002. "The Effect of the Web on Undergraduate Citation Behavior: A 2000 Update." *College & Research Libraries* 6, no. 1 (January): 53–60. Google Scholar (accessed January 5, 2009).

Davis, Philip M. 2003. "Effect of the Web on Undergraduate Citation Behavior: Guiding Student Scholarship in a Networked Age." *portal: Libraries and the Academy* 3, no. 1 (January): 41–51. Project Muse, John Hopkins University Press (accessed January 5, 2009).

Davis, Philip M., and Suzanne A. Cohen. 2001. "The Effect of the Web on Undergraduate Citation Behavior 1996–1999." *Journal of the American Society for Information Science and Technology* 52, no. 4: 309–314. ERIC, EBSCOhost (accessed January 5, 2009).

Dykeman, Amy, and Barbara King. 1983. "Term Paper Analysis: A Proposal for Evaluating Bibliographic Instruction." *Research Strategies* 1, no. 1: 14–21.

Emmons, Mark, and Wanda Martin. 2002. "Engaging Conversation: Evaluating the Contribution of Library Instruction to the Quality of Student Research." *College & Research Libraries* 63, no. 6 (November): 545–560.

Fescemyer, Kathy. 2000. "Information-Seeking Behavior of Undergraduate Geography Students." *Research Strategies* 17, no. 4: 307–317. ScienceDirect, Elsevier (accessed January 6, 2009).

Georgia State University. 2008. "2008 Action Plan." Atlanta: Georgia State University. Available: www.gsu.edu/str_and_act_plans.html (accessed September 30, 2009).

Gratch, Bonnie. 1985. "Towards a Methodology for Evaluating Research Paper Bibliographies." *Research Strategies* 3, no. 4: 170–177.

Heller-Ross, Holly. 2002. "Assessing Outcomes with Nursing Research Assignments and Citation Analysis of Student Bibliographies." *Reference Librarian* 37, no. 77: 121. Library, Information Science & Technology Abstracts, EBSCOhost (accessed January 5, 2009).

Hovde, Karen. 2000. "Check the Citation: Library Instruction and Student Paper Bibliographies." *Research Strategies* 17, no. 1: 3–9. ERIC, EBSCOhost (accessed January 5, 2009).

Kirk, Thomas. 1971. "A Comparison of Two Methods of Library Instruction for Students in Introductory Biology." *College & Research Libraries* 32, no. 6 (November): 465–474.

Kirk, Thomas. 1973. "Bibliographic Instruction—A Review of Research." In *Evaluating Library Use Instruction* (pp. 1–29), edited by Richard J. Beeler. New York: Pierian Press.

Knapp, Patricia. 1966. *Monteith College Library Experiment.* New York: Scarecrow Press, Inc.

Kohl, David F., and Lizabeth A. Wilson. 1986. "Effectiveness of Bibliographic Instruction in Improving Coursework." *RQ* 27, no. 2 (Winter): 206–211.

Kraus, Joseph R. 2002. "Citation Patterns of Advanced Undergraduate Students in Biology, 2000–2002." *Science & Technology Libraries* 22, no. 3/4: 161–179.

Malone, Debbie, and Carol Videon. 1997. "Assessing Undergraduate Use of Electronic Resources: A Quantitative Analysis of Works Cited." *Research Strategies* 15, no. 3: 151–158. ScienceDirect. Elesevier (accessed January 6, 2009).

Osareh, Farideh. 1996. "Bibliometrics, Citation Analysis and Co-citation Analysis: A Review of Literature I." *Libri: International Journal of Libraries & Information Services* 46, no. 3: 149–158. Library, Information Science & Technology Abstracts, EBSCOhost (accessed January 5, 2009).

Robinson, Andrew M., and Karen Schlegl. 2004. "Student Bibliographies Improve When Professors Provides Enforceable Guidelines for Citations." *portal: Libraries & the Academy* 4, no. 2 (April): 275–290. Business Source Complete, EBSCOhost (accessed January 5, 2009).

Scharf, Davida, Norbert Elliot, Heather A. Huey, Vladimir Briller, and Kamal Joshi. 2007. "Direct Assessment of Information Literacy Using Writing Portfolios." *Journal of Academic Librarianship* 33, no. 4: 462–477. Academic Search Complete, EBSCOhost (accessed September 10, 2009).

Smith, Linda C. 1981. "Citation Analysis." *Library Trends* 30, no. 1: 83–106. Google Scholar (accessed January 10, 2009).

Ursin, Lara, Elisabeth Blakesley Lindsay, and Corey M. Johnson. 2004. "Assessing Library Instruction in the Freshman Seminar: A Citation Analysis Study." *Reference Services Review* 34, no. 3: 284–292. Library, Information Science & Technology Abstracts, EBSCOhost (accessed January 5, 2009).

Young, Virginia E., and Linda G. Ackerson. 1995. "Evaluation of Student Research Paper Bibliographies: Refining Evaluation Criteria." *Research Strategies* 13, no. 2 (Spring): 80–91.

Appendix 1.1. Guidelines Used in Evaluating Citations within the Paper

Quality of Sources

Using a five-point scale, the use of recommended sources or those available through the library should rank higher than those that were not included in the instruction session. This indicates that the students retained knowledge of the tools discussed in the information literacy session or utilized the learning aids that were distributed in class. The information literacy session does, however, emphasize the evaluation of Web-based resources. If a resource was not recommended or available through the library Web site, such a resource should be examined to determine level of authority and appropriateness for the paper. If that resource proves to be reliable and appropriate to the content of the paper it should be ranked at the same level as any recommended resource and other tools available through the library.

Variety of Sources

A sufficient number of sources for the length of the paper should be listed in order to receive a five. Broadly, the number of sources listed should exceed five unless there is evidence that the paper topic required few sources to make a strong case for the thesis of the paper. These sources should present different perspectives. To illustrate, the company's annual report should be complemented with information from independent analyst reports, market research reports, substantial news articles that are not based on press releases, or other sources not published by the company itself. Within the paper, evidence should indicate that each of these sources was used. If one source dominates the bulk of the paper, the paper should receive a lower score.

Citation Format

A consistent use of a citation style (either an established style or a homegrown style) throughout the paper will result in a score of five. Homegrown styles should provide enough information for the reader to evaluate the quality of that resource and enable the readers to easily locate the resource. Papers with minor inconsistencies should receive a three or four depending on the severity of the inconsistencies. Limited attempts to document sources should result in a one or a two. No citations should receive a zero.

Utilization of Information

If it is evident the entire paper is plagiarized, the score is listed as zero as the student has not presented any work that can be evaluated. Clear and blatant forms of plagiarism used consistently throughout the paper result in a one. Smaller and potentially accidental forms of plagiarism are given scores of two, three, or four depending on the frequency. These may include poor paraphrasing in which the student simply reversed the order of a sentence. For example, if instead of "the bear went over the mountain" the student wrote, "over the mountain the bear went" the evaluators would note this as a minor plagiaristic incident. No evidence of plagiarism will result in a score of five.

Appendix 1.2. Citation Analysis Assessment

- **Evaluate Instructional Tools:** Ursin, Lindsay, and Johnson used citation analysis to determine how frequently freshmen used the resource guides provided by librarians. This team reviewed papers from 21 sections of a freshman class and identified citations to resources recommended by the research guides. From this research the team learned that the resources listed in the guides were not being used even when the guides provided students with easy access to the resources (Ursin, Lindsay, and Johnson, 2004). The ability to confirm anecdotal evidence based on observations with quantifiable data enabled the research team to recognize a need to try new approaches and build new partnerships on campus.

- **Evaluate the Effectiveness of an Instruction Method:** In institutions that have extensive information literacy programs, Hovde asserts that it is possible to use citation analysis to observe what students are not doing and from there make assumptions regarding the quality of information literacy training collectively (2000: 5). This can create a control group that may serve as a baseline for future evaluative efforts. It can also alert the instruction team to weaknesses in the current model of instruction.

- **Compare Instruction Methods:** The studies conducted by Kirk (1971) and by Kohl and Wilson (1986) both used citation analysis to compare two instruction methods. Kirk compared a lecture-demonstration method to a guided exercise approach. Kohl and Wilson compared tool-focused versus cognitive strategy approaches to instruction. By teaching the same material in different ways to at least two groups of students, these researchers were able to determine which instructional method was more effective. In Kirk's study a significant difference in the impact of the instruction was not discovered. Kohl and Wilson, however, did find a difference. These types of conclusions, especially when conducted over time and with different sets of students, help provide guidance not only to librarians and course instructors at one institution, but to all instructors of information literacy.

- **Measure Impact of Changes to an Instruction Package:** Young and Ackerson measured (1995) the impact of adding three hours of instruction and access to a computer laboratory staffed by a librarian to the traditional 50-minute lecture style instruction at University of Alabama. The case study described in this chapter uses citation analysis to build a teaching package that best met the learning styles and needs of students completing a specific assignment.

- **Assess Library Collection and Services:** A study by Holly Heller-Ross (2002) used citation analysis to identify differences in the types of resources used by on-campus and distance learners. This enabled the library to measure the quality of the services and tools available to each group.

- **Understand Student Information-Seeking Behavior:** Several studies use citation analysis to understand how students are gathering information. These types of studies create awareness of student behavior and help librarians and teaching faculty alter instruction to influence this behavior in a more favorable direction.

Chapter 2

A Holistic Approach to Embedding Information Literacy in the Design, Delivery, and Assessment of an Undergraduate Business Program

Douglas G. Carrie and Lynne M. Mitchell

INTRODUCTION

This chapter describes the way that information literacy assessment is being holistically embedded within an undergraduate business degree program at the University of Auckland in New Zealand. The Bachelor of Business and Information Management (BBIM) was first launched in 2001. The aim of the program is to prepare graduates for business careers in which they will benefit from a strong set of technical and personal skills in managing information. The assessment of information literacy plays an important role in BBIM teaching and learning because the degree's focus is on how business people locate, manage, and use information for problem solving, decision making, and business growth. Throughout the program, faculty and the BBIM librarian work in close collaboration to develop the business information literacy capabilities our students will need to succeed in the workplace.

RELATED LITERATURE

Three key areas in the literature on teaching and learning have influenced our approach to collaboratively embedding information literacy into course design, delivery, and assessment throughout the BBIM program. The first of these areas is a body of literature related to the specific needs of business students and the importance of employability and lifelong learning skills in business curricula. The second area is the literature on information literacy, specifically in relation to the importance of embedding and infusing information literacy within courses and programs. The third area is a growing body of knowledge emphasising collaborative librarian-teacher partnerships.

The Needs of Business Students

Our approach to embedding information literacy is grounded in developing the information management skills that our students will need for careers in fast-changing workplaces. The sheer amount of business information readily accessible from employee desktops continues to increase rapidly. The tools and technologies needed to access and make sense of all of this information are also constantly evolving. Added to this is a trend toward the disintermediation of information, where information searching and environmental scanning are spread evermore widely across different employee roles. According to the latest LexisNexis Workplace Productivity Survey, white collar professionals now spend an average of 2.3 hours daily conducting online research, with one in ten spending four hours or more on an average day (LexisNexis, 2008).

The importance of information literacy to the business workplace is well documented. Drucker (1995) has stated that wealth creation in business enterprises requires information so that executives can make informed judgments. His concern though is that few executives seem to ask themselves questions such as: "What information do I need to know to do my job? When do I need it? In what form? And from whom should I be getting it?" (Drucker, 1992: 8) Beyond skills in finding information, and in line with the University of Auckland's Information Literacy Policy, we view critical thinking and enquiry as core cognitive elements of business information literacy. "Employers can't afford people who come to work and are asked to research a topic and then believe everything they read online" (Bland, 2007). According to Eisenberg (2008: 39), "information and technical literacy is clearly the basic skills set of the 21st century."

Our business students tend to be confident technology users and, as Cunningham (2003) has described, business students are also one of the most overconfident groups of library users. The challenge is that students can equate being competent with information technology to being information literate (Brown, Murphy, and Nanny, 2003). Students must recognize that they also need the skills to judge and evaluate the information they find, and they need to be aware of other business information sources beyond the Internet.

Business students have been characterized as preferring Web based resources over print, being overconfident in relying on search engines, and being more concerned with saving time when researching than with the quality of information found (Leigh and Gibbon, 2008). Our challenge is how to encourage the critical thinking and problem-solving skills necessary for true business information literacy.

Employers and business school accreditation agencies are increasingly requiring that students show competency in information literacy (Gilinsky and Robison, 2008). For business schools worldwide, there is still much to be done. A recent survey of AACSB-accredited business schools reported that only one-third were incorporating information literacy standards into instructional efforts with business students and only 27 percent were assessing information literacy within the business curriculum (Cooney, 2005: 16).

Preparing our BBIM students to be information literate has some unique aspects. In a New Zealand context, it is particularly important that our students learn to access and evaluate the electronic business sources they are most likely to use in their future work environments. For example, students may overlook useful business data on various government Web sites. Statistics New Zealand has a useful data tool that allows Web based access to government statistics and census data. The data is presented in tables from which variables can be selected to create a customized table or graph. New Zealand commercial Web-based directories are freely available, such as the UBD Business Directory, which can provide competitive business intelligence. A challenge is that New Zealand business information sources are not as comprehensive and sophisticated as the large specialized North American and European business databases, and so our students need to learn to access a range of sources rather than to rely on a few major databases. For this reason, as will be described when we outline some of our coursework assessments, our business information literacy assessment needs to incorporate skills for locating and using New Zealand information.

When they undertake research using international databases, our students face different information literacy challenges. For example, not only are U.S. spellings different in major international business databases such as Business Source Premier and ABI/Inform—e.g., *organizational behavior* in the United States versus *organisational behaviour* in New Zealand—but there are also often regional differences in commonly used business terms or expressions. Whereas this presents challenges, it also presents opportunities for developing the critical thinking skills of our students. For example, regional differences can be used positively to highlight the necessity of thinking carefully about database search terms and using multiple synonyms to overcome variations in English usage, e.g., searching for both "renting" and "leasing" of equipment, or for both "return on investment" and "rate of return," or for both "personnel management" and "human resources."

Embedding Information Literacy in Coursework

Research strongly indicates that embedding information literacy in curriculum design is the most effective way to develop information literacy capabilities (Fiegen, Cherry, and Watson, 2002). The aim with the BBIM is to embed information literacy and its assessment so deeply within the curriculum that in many instances, as described by Nerz and Weiner (2001), students are not even aware that the instruction is happening. We believe that this perception can also extend to those involved in teaching and that once information literacy is truly deeply embedded, opportunities to reinforce can then continue to occur and evolve almost spontaneously and instinctively.

Our approach to embedding information literacy is holistic in a number of ways. It is not completely anchored to any particular course and instead permeates the entire degree program. It is also holistic in that that teaching and support staff play shared roles in supporting information literacy. Finally, it is holistic in that we take a broad approach that aims to merge both the technical and cognitive aspects of information literacy. In this, we share Bruce's (1997) holistic representation of the concept of information literacy as going beyond digital competencies and information-seeking skills to applying a critical approach to information use and knowledge construction.

Faculty-Library Partnerships

Our rationale for collaborative information literacy assessment is reflective of a body of research that emphasises faculty-librarian shared responsibilities as a key to successful information literacy (Mackey and Jacobson, 2005; Leigh and Gibbon, 2008). According to Van Cleave (2007: 178):

> Truly integrated teaching of information literacy and disciplinary knowledge can only take place in a context of collaborative partnerships between librarians and faculty, academic programs, and campus support services. This makes it possible for librarians and teaching faculty to blur the boundaries between teaching and learning of content and process in a way that draws on the expertise of an entire institution.

A librarian role such as this, however, has not yet been widely accepted in business schools and overall librarian-faculty collaboration has been described in a recent survey of AACSB accredited business schools as "overwhelmingly moderate" (Cooney, 2005: 3).

INFORMATION LITERACY AT
THE UNIVERSITY OF AUCKLAND

Established in 1883, The University of Auckland has a current enrollment of about 38,000 students. It has recently been ranked sixty-fifth in the world's top universities and therefore within the top 1 percent of all universities internationally (Times Higher Education, 2008). The University of Auckland Business School is one of eight faculties at the university. The Business School is internationally recognized, holding all three of the leading international accreditations for higher education in business: AACSB International (Association to Advance Collegiate Schools of Business), EQUIS (the European Quality Improvement System), and AMBA (the Association of MBAs). The Business School's undergraduate degree programs are three years in length. Three-year undergraduate degree programs are the norm in New Zealand, partly due to a high school system that includes a 13th year of study.

In 2006, the University of Auckland Senate approved an information literacy policy. This policy adopts the definition and standards of the Australian and New Zealand Information Literacy Framework as developed by the Australian and New Zealand Institute for Information Literacy (ANZIIL). Figure 2.1 outlines the six ANZIIL standards, linking each with an example of how that standard is assessed within a particular first-year course assignment to be discussed following in greater detail. The concept of information literacy is defined for our university teaching and support staff as "a way of thinking and being that encompasses identifying, accessing, evaluating, organising and communicating information relevant in all learning environments and fields of endeavour" (University of Auckland Library, 2006). Thus our institutional view of information literacy is a wide definition that has critical thinking at the core.

Information literacy is recognized in the University of Auckland graduate profiles and in the university's teaching and learning policy. The university's graduate profiles indicate that a graduate from any faculty should have "an ability to recognize when information is needed and a capacity to locate, evaluate, and use this information effectively" and "a capacity for critical, conceptual, and reflective thinking" (University of Auckland, 2003). Furthermore, the university's Annual Plan requires that graduate profiles are integrated into faculty and teaching and learning plans (University of Auckland Library, 2006).

THE BACHELOR OF BUSINESS AND INFORMATION
MANAGEMENT DEGREE PROGRAM

The Bachelor of Business and Information Management (BBIM) degree program complements and coexists alongside the business school's long-standing but more traditional Bachelor of Commerce (BCom) program. Whereas the BCom

Figure 2.1. Standards of the Australian and New Zealand Institute for Information Literacy (ANZIIL) Framework	
An important assessment in the BBIM's first semester is a management consulting report assignment for the BUSINESS 191 "Introduction to Business" course. The ANZIIL standards are listed below with an example of how each of these standards is assessed within this BUSINESS 191 assignment.	
THE ANZIIL STANDARDS	**EXAMPLE OF HOW THIS IS ASSESSED WITHIN THE BUSINESS 191 ASSIGNMENT**
Standard One *The information-literate person recognizes the need for information and determines the nature and extent of the information needed.*	Management consulting report requires students to investigate, discuss, and summarize a business situation in order to be able to provide strategic recommendations.
Standard Two *The information-literate person finds needed information effectively and efficiently.*	Management consulting report requires secondary research from library resources including business databases and the Internet.
Standard Three *The information literate person critically evaluates information and the information seeking process.*	Management consulting report requires a range of sources to be considered and at least six relevant high-quality sources to be drawn on for the report.
Standard Four *The information-literate person manages information collected or generated.*	Management consulting report includes a reference list. Students use Endnote or other database tools to save, store, or manage articles found.
Standard Five *The information-literate person applies prior and new information to construct new concepts or create new understandings.*	Management consulting report requires students to integrate a range of business models and frameworks to analyze the given business situation.
Standard Six *The information-literate person uses information with understanding and acknowledges cultural, ethical, economic, legal, and social issues surrounding the use of information.*	Management consulting report requires correct in-text citing and acknowledging of sources, as well as knowledge of copyright and fair use in accessing electronic sources.
Source: Bundy, A. (2004). *Australia & New Zealand Information Literacy Framework: Principles, Standards and Practice*, 2nd ed. Adelaide: Australian and New Zealand Institute for Information Literacy.	

offers a wide range of choice in course and major combinations, the BBIM instead offers a cohort-based learning experience in which students flow together from class to class and year to year as they complete a structured program of study. In their final semester, BBIM students complete a capstone project course with a large research component that integrates and assesses their overall learning across the degree. The design of the BBIM enables information literacy and its assessment to be embedded sequentially in an almost seamless manner.

Each year realizes an intake of about 120 new BBIM students. As Figure 2.2 outlines, these students will complete a total of 24 courses over their three years in this double-major degree program. Students complete eight core BBIM courses, eight courses of a first major in information management, and six courses of a second major chosen from either accounting or marketing. Once students have made their choice of their second major, the set of 22 BBIM-specific courses within the degree is completely prescribed and most students will complete these courses in a recommended order. The two remaining courses students will need to complete are electives that can be chosen from a wide selection of General Education courses offered by other faculties.

The package of eight core BBIM courses is designed to support the other majors and to provide a well-rounded general background in business. In addition to foundation courses in accounting, commercial law, economics, and statistics, there is a set of four sequential courses with a business label, i.e., Business 191, 192, 291, and 292. Two of these courses are taken in the first year and two in the second year. As will be outlined, these four business courses provide a central support structure for the embedding of business information literacy within the degree.

The Information Management (Infomgmt) major in the BBIM is not a traditional computer science or information systems major as the emphasis is on how information is managed and organized for business purposes. Students gain a wide range of information technology skills, from programming to Web site development, database design and management, data mining and decision support, and digital media production. The difference, however, is that the BBIM's aim is to develop broad and general proficiencies rather than specialist depth and expertise in specific areas of computing. Also, the focus is on how information technology tools can best be used in a business context to manage business information. BBIM graduates may not be the people who actually develop company Web sites or design corporate database systems, for example, but they will be managers who can understand and work closely with information technology specialists. BBIM graduates will also have an inherent appreciation of the value of information literacy in the workplace.

Overall, the uniqueness of the BBIM program lies in its focus on information management capabilities and in the packaged and sequential delivery of courses to students who will move through the degree in a close cohort. This design ensures that there are tremendous opportunities for teaching faculty to learn what is being taught in other courses, both within and across the different subject areas. This also allows the teaching team great flexibility to

Figure 2.2. Bachelor of Business and Information Management Degree Structure

BBIM students take a total of 24 courses over three years of study. Students will complete eight core courses, plus eight courses of an Information Management major, plus six courses of a Business major chosen from either Accounting or Marketing. The final two courses are General Education electives offered by other faculties at the university.

	YEAR 1		YEAR 2		YEAR 3	
	Semester 1	Semester 2	Semester 3	Semester 2	Semester 1	Semester 2
Core Courses and General Education	BUSINESS 191	BUSINESS 192	BUSINESS 291	BUSINESS 292	ELECTIVE	ELECTIVE
	ACCTG 191	ECON 191		COMLAW 191		
	STATS 191					
Information Management Major	INFOMGMT 191	INFOMGMT 192	INFOMGMT 291	INFOMGMT 292	INFOMGMT 393	INFOMGMT 391
				INFOMGMT 293		INFOMGMT 392
PLUS						
Accounting Major		ACCTG 192	ACCTG 292		ACCTG 391	PROJECT
			ACCTG 293		ACCTG 392	
OR						
Marketing Major		MKTG 291	MKTG 292		MKTG 391	PROJECT
			MKTG 293		MKTG 392	

BUSINESS 191 = Introduction to Business
BUSINESS 192 = Business Management
BUSINESS 291 = Communication Processes
BUSINESS 292 = Project-Based Management

ACCTG 191 = Accounting Information for Decision Making
STATS 191 = Quantitative Methods for Business
ECON 191 = Business Economics
COMLAW 191 = Law in Business and Information Management

INFOMGMT 191 = Business Productivity Tools
INFOMGMT 192 = Business Analysis and Applications
INFOMGMT 291 = Web Applications for Business
INFOMGMT 292 = Database Applications
INFOMGMT 391 = Information Systems Management
INFOMGMT 392 = Digital Media Production
INFOMGMT 393 = Data Mining and Decision Support

ACCTG 192 = Accounting Information Support
ACCTG 291 = Cost Accounting Systems
ACCTG 292 = Financial Reporting
ACCTG 391 = Financial Decision Support
ACCTG 392 = Financial Reporting and Analysis

MKTG 291 = Marketing Perspectives
MKTG 292 = Creating Marketing Knowledge
MKTG 293 = Understanding Consumers
MKTG 391 = Strategic Services Marketing
MKTG 392 = Advertising and Communications

PROJECT = Capstone Project Support

collaborate in designing appropriate linkages and integration throughout the program.

THE BBIM PROGRAM LIBRARIAN

Because of the BBIM's focus on information, a decision was made at the inception of the program to have a dedicated librarian. The BBIM program librarian is truly embedded within the program in the sense that she or he is tasked with supporting the degree and is located in the business school building (not in the university's central library). The librarian's office is in close proximity to the offices of academic staff and next door to the BBIM director. From this highly visible location, the librarian also offers open-door support to BBIM students.

A collaborative working environment has been further encouraged through the establishment of a core BBIM teaching and learning team that includes the BBIM librarian. Reflecting the BBIM's packaged and multidisciplinary approach to learning, this core team has been explicitly tagged to support the BBIM and works closely together to encourage integration across majors and courses in the degree. Individual members of the core BBIM teaching and learning team remain as members of their respective disciplinary departments within the business school but they also have dual reporting to the BBIM Director. All members of the core teaching team have significant BBIM teaching duties; however, they also teach across other business school programs. Also, to prevent potential over exposure of students to individual instructors, a wider group of teaching staff also have teaching responsibilities on the BBIM.

A key feature of the BBIM learning environment is that some of the information literacy assessments incorporated into course work are administered and graded by the librarian. Collaborative responsibility for credit-bearing tasks requires a level of collegial trust as the librarian has direct input and access to student marks. Although having librarian involvement in the grading process for information literacy tasks is proving to be a successful innovation in the BBIM, this is not yet widely accepted or practiced elsewhere. According to Cooney's (2005: 18) research of AACSB-accredited business schools, "only a small percentage of librarians report jointly grading information literacy assignments with business faculty."

The librarian has access to all BBIM courses via Cecil (short for CSL or Computer Supported Learning), the University's Web-based enterprise learning management system. Depending on the librarian's level of collaborative involvement with a course, the librarian can use Cecil to communicate directly with students through class announcements or individual e-mails, participate in class discussion forums, monitor student participation in information literacy assessed components, and manage certain aspects of online assessments and grading.

The librarian is also visible in the online learning environment through BBIM course library Web pages. Here, faculty and the librarian collaborate online to create information literacy content and to provide targeted learning support specific to particular courses. These course library pages are accessed by students either via Cecil or the library's Web site. Reflecting their collaborative partnership, contact details for both the teacher and the librarian are displayed on these pages. In addition to providing academic course content (e.g., durable links to digitized readings), BBIM course library page resources are also organized under assignment and task headings to direct students to appropriate business information literacy support resources. These might include links to library guides, information literacy tutorials, or specifically tailored resources relating to a current course task or assessment. In this way, online information literacy resources are available to students at the point of need every time they access their course online.

Close collaboration ensures that the librarian is aware of the BBIM program schedule and familiar with class activities and assignments. Indeed, the librarian often works with faculty to research potential assignment topics or to co-create course assessments. This means that the librarian has a clear understanding of students' information needs if they request further support and advice. Also, the librarian is able to use this knowledge to tailor supplementary information literacy sessions and to timetable these at appropriate points in the semester when they will be most relevant and useful to students.

DEVELOPING THE INFORMATION LITERACY CAPABILITIES OF BBIM STUDENTS

Figure 2.3 shows the information literacy capabilities we are working to instill in our students over the three-year BBIM program. These capabilities scaffold on each other, with reinforcement occurring at each level as students move through the degree. In year one, the focus is on developing basic information literacy capabilities. Year two then concentrates on subject depth, while year three consolidates and focuses on business information literacy for lifelong learning. Overall, these capabilities represent our practice to date on the degree, and reflect what the core teaching and learning team has come to believe are the cognitive information literacy abilities we can expect from students at each year of the program.

ASSESSMENT IN YEAR ONE

In the first year of the program, two courses provide a broad introduction to the study of business while also playing a pivotal role in introducing the basic

Figure 2.3. Business Information Literacy Capabilities for BBIM Students

FIRST-YEAR INFORMATION LITERACY (BASIC)

- Understand the higher-level thinking skills required for academic work, e.g., Bloom's taxonomy
- Understand learning techniques such as brainstorming and concept mapping
- Library skills including basic search strategies, keywords, synonyms used in business databases
- Knowledge of key New Zealand business periodicals
- Understand the difference between primary and secondary sources of information
- Understand the difference between scholarly and popular journals
- Basic Internet search skills
- Apply criteria to evaluate information sources
- Correct APA referencing
- Introduction to sources of NZ company, product, and industry information

SECOND-YEAR INFORMATION LITERACY (SUBJECT DEPTH)

- Access a range of business databases to obtain global perspectives on a business topic
- Synthesize information for business research from both popular business press articles (for examples of business practice) and academic articles (for research)
- Locate print and electronic information on a given New Zealand industry or product
- Locate New Zealand statistical data and use StatisticsNZ data tools
- Access a wide variety of library material, such as reports, government documents, and e-books
- Apply evaluation criteria to a range of sources of information, both print and electronic
- Sophisticated use of the Internet and Google Scholar
- Undertake research for future careers and employability
- Reflections on learning

THIRD-YEAR INFORMATION LITERACY (LIFELONG LEARNING)

- Appreciate the role of information in business growth and decision support
- Integrate New Zealand business information together with global trends and data to analyze and provide recommendations for business decision making
- Use high level of critical and creative thinking skills to present information in different ways, including presentations, poster sessions, and as a formal business plan
- Locate seminal literature from high-level academic databases, such as Science Direct or Emerald and use the sophisticated functionality of academic databases
- Locate financial data and New Zealand company intelligence using financial databases
- Knowledge of business information sources used for career development and employability
- Familiarity with freely available Web resources that can be used in the workplace
- Use Endnote and WEB 2 tools for information management

information literacy capabilities that are outlined in Figure 2.3. Business 191 "Introduction to Business" is taken in a BBIM student's first semester and Business 192 "Business Management" follows directly in the second semester. In the discussion to follow, specific information literacy assessments within each of these courses are outlined and explained. Our belief is that a core information literacy skill is the ability to integrate research into written work through correct referencing. Therefore, much of our effort in these two first-year courses is anchored around the applied development of academic writing skills. The basic information literacy capabilities introduced in Business 191 and 192 can then be further developed through appropriate linkages to other first-year courses, as well as through reinforcement in the reminder of the degree.

Management Consulting Report and Related Support Modules

The major coursework assessment in Business 191 "Introduction to Business" is a written report that is worth 30 percent of a student's grade in the course. Our information literacy initiatives in Business 191 are built around supporting this assessment so that students can appreciate the immediate relevance of what they are learning. Whereas specific topics and contexts for the assignment change from semester to semester, the central task always involves students researching a New Zealand industry and preparing a management consulting report. In this report, students are required to analyze a current business situation and then provide some broad strategic recommendations for a given New Zealand enterprise.

For a number of years, two online instructional tutorials were integrated into the course to prepare students for this assignment. One was an academic honesty tutorial and the other was an information literacy tutorial. Both tutorials included four modules and students had a total of eight modules to complete at their own pace over the first four weeks of the course. Each module was assessed through a short multiple-choice quiz delivered through Cecil and managed and marked online by the librarian. At 1 percent per quiz, these credit-bearing assessments had a combined course credit of 8 percent of a student's grade in Business 191. The four modules in the Academic Honesty Assistance tutorial were:

1. the academic environment,
2. strategies to avoid plagiarism including paraphrasing,
3. disciplinary policies of the University of Auckland, and
4. APA referencing format.

The four modules in the Information Literacy tutorial were:

1. research and critical thinking skills,
2. business databases,
3. New Zealand Web sources for business data, and
4. locating New Zealand industry and product information.

In 2009, the online tutorials and quizzes that previously supported the management consulting report assignment have been restructured and replaced. This is due to the university's redevelopment and launch of Referencite (www.cite.auckland.ac.nz) as a centralized academic honesty and referencing portal for the entire university. This is an interesting example of where faculty-librarian collaboration in the BBIM program has had an impact on the wider institution. The BBIM librarian and the BBIM Director both serve on the central Teaching and Learning Quality working groups responsible for the development of Referencite. This has enabled us to contribute knowledge gained through experiences with online information literacy tutorials and related resources in the BBIM. This also means that we have been able to ensure that Referencite will now continue to serve the needs of BBIM students in this area.

Figure 2.4 provides a sample information literacy schedule showing the latest faculty-librarian collaboration process within the 12-week sequence of Business 191. In the early weeks of the semester, students are told that this process is about developing an "Academic and Business Skills Portfolio" that will directly support the subsequent development of their major management consulting report assignment. The modules in this portfolio include:

1. succeeding in the academic environment,
2. locating and using business information,
3. business research and report writing, and
4. referencing business sources.

The "succeeding in the academic environment" module in Week 2 provides a broad introduction to the academic environment in a one-hour class session that is delivered jointly by the BBIM librarian and course instructors. The session stresses the importance of research and critical thinking skills and explains the scholarly writing process. Students are also directed to engage with the university's Referencite portal for introductory content on referencing and academic honesty. They are then advised of a single question half-hour writing assessment to take place in class the following week. The reflective short-essay question requires students to display an understanding of the reasons behind acknowledging sources both in academic writing and for ethical societal purposes. Worth 5 percent of a student's grade in the course, this first assessment serves a dual purpose in providing instructors with an early sample of students' academic

Figure 2.4. A Sample Information Literacy Collaboration Schedule for BUSINESS 191			
Week	Instructor	Information Literacy Teaching or Reinforcement	Formal Assessment
1	Faculty	Introduction to management consulting report assignment and its grading rubric	
	Faculty and Librarian	Introduction to Librarian and to online course page with assignment-related information resources	
2	Faculty and Librarian	In-Class module on academic honesty and succeeding in the academic environment	Short Essay in-class quiz in Week 2 (5%)
3	Faculty and Librarian	In-Class module on business report writing	
	Librarian (Outside Class)	Manages online tutorial tailored to guide students through the process of preparing their management consulting report assignment	
4	Librarian	Workshop on locating and using business information, especially New Zealand information	
5	Librarian	Workshop on referencing business sources with direct relevance to the course assignment	Short Essay in-class quiz (5%)
	Faculty and Librarian	Extended office hours outside class to provide support for the approaching assignment due date	Secure online test (10%) completed outside class time
		MID-SEMESTER TWO WEEK BREAK	
6	Faculty (Outside Class)	Grading and feedback of first assignment submission. Grading rubric stresses information literacy criteria such as "quality of research," "referencing," "communicating," and "citing/quoting."	First "checkpoint" submission of Management Consulting Report (10%)
	Librarian (Outside Class)	Librarian directly contributes to marking of assignments through additional comments on referencing and information sources	
8	Faculty and Librarian	Assignment Feedback session	
9	Faculty and Librarian	Extended office hours outside class to provide support for the coming Assignment due date	
10	Faculty (Outside Class)	Grading and feedback of final assignment submission. Grading rubric again stresses information literacy criteria.	Second and Final submission of Management Consulting Report (20%)
	Faculty (Outside Class)	Librarian again contributes to marking of assignments through additional comments on referencing and information sources	
12	Faculty and Librarian	Course conclusion, including assignment feedback	

writing capabilities. If necessary, feedback can be provided and language support offered to those who might benefit.

For the "locating and using business information" module in Week 3, the BBIM librarian is back in class for another one-hour session. The first half of this session focuses on *locating* business information through databases and business e-books. Specific emphasis is placed on the New Zealand databases, topic guides, online directories, and government Web sites that students will need to access for their management consulting report assignment. This learning is ultimately assessed through the marking rubric for the assignment.

The second half of the "locating and using business information" module then focuses on *using* business information. Students will never be successful in academic writing unless they can integrate sources into their work. Therefore, we stress the importance of paraphrasing and correct referencing. Students are reminded of appropriate content within Referencite and they are also directed to additional online library tutorials in order to prepare for an assessment the following week. This 30-minute assessment, again worth 5 percent, asks student to identify key information in a short article from the business press, to rewrite this into their own words as a paraphrase of at least two sentences, and to incorporate this into a complete paragraph with the paraphrase correctly cited. Students are told that their paragraph should incorporate some of their own ideas as if they were writing a paragraph in a report where they had selected and paraphrased this particular information to make a point. The librarian manages the delivery, marking, and feedback process for this particular assessment. There is growing literature for such librarian involvement in writing instruction, specifically with paraphrasing, as students with little confidence in the ability to paraphrase will find citing resources difficult (Bronshteyn and Baladad, 2006).

The "business research and report writing" module in Week 4 is built around a new interactive Business Information Skills Online tutorial that has been developed by the business librarian team. Although this tutorial is intended for use by students across all of the business school's programs, it includes a specific module which steps students through the process involved in researching and writing a business report. This module content was developed by the BBIM librarian and the Business 191 course coordinator and so it correlates closely with the Business 191 management consulting report assessment. The online tutorial is introduced and explained in a class session and the report writing module is then available for students to repeatedly engage with as they move through the process of preparing their report. The module contains interactive questions relating to the research process and best practice for report writing. While this does not include any credit bearing assessment, students have every incentive to engage as it is directly related to their major coursework assignment.

The final module in Week 5 focuses on referencing business sources. This is delivered by the BBIM librarian as an assignment workshop that aims to reinforce referencing-related content from the previous weeks. In addition to this in-class session, the librarian also offers supplementary workshops at this important stage of the assignment and continues to promote the online information literacy support. To further encourage participation and active engagement across all four of these Academic and Business Skills Portfolio modules, students are told that their mid-semester test worth 10 percent will include questions on this content.

It is through the grading of the management consulting report assignment that students ultimately receive the most comprehensive information literacy feedback and reinforcement. A marking rubric is provided to students at the start of the course. This marking rubric explicitly embeds criteria such as "quality of research," "referencing," and "citing/quoting." To further reinforce the importance of these marking criteria, students hand in their management consulting reports twice. An early "checkpoint" version, worth 10 percent of a student's grade in the course, is submitted in Week 6 of this 12-week course. Students are graded firmly but fairly on this checkpoint version. Comprehensive feedback is provided to help students to improve their reports and to ensure that they realize just how essential correct referencing and quality of information sources are to obtaining a good grade with their final submission. If students are having referencing or research problems with their checkpoint submission, they will also be advised to visit the librarian for further help. The full and final version of the management consulting report, worth 20 percent, is then submitted in Week 11 of the course. Whereas teaching faculty do the formal marking and assigning of grades for both submissions, the BBIM librarian plays a collaborative support role in re-checking the referencing and research components of these assignments and in providing any related feedback to students.

Annotated Bibliography and Research Essay

In Business 192, the BBIM's second semester course, student teams run a virtual business. The business information literacy component embedded in this course is research on the effective management of work teams. Assessments are designed to support this learning and to holistically reinforce the information literacy basics that were first introduced in Business 191.

Students are first required to present an annotated bibliography on the management of work teams. Instructions for this task are very precise on the type of information sources to use (see Figure 2.5). This ensures that students access the recommended business electronic sources they have learned about previously, and that they understand the differences between popular and

---

Figure 2.5. Library Course Page Information Search Instructions in BUSINESS 192

This is an example from the BUSINESS 192 library course page of instructions to students who are carrying out research on the effectiveness of teams. We deliberately provide more precise information/assistance like this to first-year students to make them aware and enthusiastic about available library resources.

Research on work teams

YOU MAY NOT USE THE INTERNET AS A SOURCE OF INFORMATION

IMPORTANT HINT—The subject heading used to search in both Voyager and the databases for teams is **Teams in the Workplace**.

Chapters from electronic books

Voyager, the Library catalogue, accesses the records to both print and electronic books. Electronic books can be accessed in Voyager by using the subject heading given above, or by searching netLibrary and Ebrary electronic book databases directly. In the subject search box in netLibrary or Ebrary enter *teams* as a keyword or *teams in the workplace* as a subject to get a list of books.

Articles

Locate articles on teams in the workplace by searching the recommended LEARN business databases.

Retrieve relevant articles by using the Advanced search feature of the databases. In ABI/Inform use the terms *teamwork* and *teams* as **subject** terms. In Business Source Premier, the subject term used is **teams in the workplace**. Combine these subject terms in an advanced search with other keywords such as *best practice*, *successful*, *optimal*, *organizational effectiveness*, *advantages*, etc., in the **abstract** or **article text** search fields.

---

scholarly journal articles. Importantly, students are required to evaluate their information sources and select those most relevant for application to their own team experience.

The annotated bibliography task requires that articles from the business databases and chapters from business e-books are cited correctly in APA format. For their annotated bibliography, students are required to select their three best sources for the bibliography and write an informative and evaluative annotation explaining why that particular source was selected. The librarian participates in a class session that explains the process of creating annotated bibliographies. This annotated bibliography task is marked by the instructor; however, the librarian checks APA referencing and information sources on the submitted bibliographies.

As part of their annotated bibliography assessment, Business 192 students are also required to submit an online research log documenting their information search processes. Again, correct APA referencing is required as well as a detailed description of search strategies and sources used to find the selected articles or chapters. This assessment is managed by the BBIM librarian. Students access a research log outline form from the course library Web page. They fill this form in online and submit it to the librarian who marks the research logs before returning the logs electronically to students. The librarian then enters the grades into the Cecil learning management system. Through being able to directly evaluate the quality of students' information search strategies in Business 192, the librarian is also able to implicitly evaluate the effectiveness of prior learning that was undertaken in Business 191.

The annotated bibliography task provides students with information resources they will need to succeed in the next component of the course where they work in teams to run a virtual business. Their next course assessment is to write a 1,500 word research essay in which they reflect on their individual contribution toward their team's performance. Within this essay, students must analyze a management issue or theory selected from the research they carried out in order to complete their annotated bibliography. They must then discuss this issue or theory in relation to how this is affecting their team's ability to achieve its goals. In addition to reinforcement within the course from annotated bibliography and research log through to the research essay, this Business 192 assessment package further reinforces the academic writing, paraphrasing, and referencing skills that were introduced in Business 191.

Faculty-librarian collaboration in Business 192 and other courses also often extends to collaboration with other university student support services. For example, embedded in Business 192 is a class session on "careers in a knowledge society," delivered in conjunction with the university's Careers Centre. Students are asked to think about their future careers in business while also engaging with the BBIM Graduate Profile. This activity helps to further reinforce the value of information literacy as an employability and lifelong learning skill. There is also an opportunity here for the librarian to reinforce information skills required to locate New Zealand company and industry information when preparing for future job interviews.

Other First-Year Information Literacy Assessments

Other first-year courses also include collaborative assessments to reinforce information literacy. For example, the core first semester information management course includes an essay on an information technology topic that requires research, writing competencies, and correct referencing. In managing the Infomgmt 191 course library page, the librarian is able to highlight appropriate information technology information sources, including computer databases and journals. The emphasis on how information is managed and organized for business purposes can also be illustrated by librarian involvement in two class sessions in Infomgmt 191. One session is on advanced Google search engine functionality and search strategies. The second session is on using Web 2.0 tools for managing information. This includes tools such referencing software, bookmarking, blogs, and RSS (Really Simple Syndication) feeds. This learning is assessed in a course test and will be relevant to further learning in the degree. It is also intended that students will see these information management tools and techniques as immediately transferable to the workplace.

In 2008 and 2009, a particularly interesting first semester assessment pathway was synchronized across Business 191 and Infomgmt 191. In Infomgmt 191, students were using Microsoft PowerPoint to make professional standalone electronic presentations. An Infomgmt 191 course assignment was designed in which students would translate their first "checkpoint" management consulting report submission from Business 191 into a digital media presentation. By timing this assessment carefully into the period between the first and second submissions of the Business 191 report, these students were engaging with the need to rethink how their work could be communicated in a quite different delivery style and format for Infomgmt 191. In later returning to a written report format for the final submission of their management consulting report in Business 191, this inevitably led to a reflective learning process in which many students made significant improvements in the ways that they were structuring and communicating this business information.

The reinforcement of information literacy in the first year of the BBIM also continues once students make their choice of business major in the second semester and take their first course in that major. For example, the second semester Marketing 291 "Marketing Perspectives" course has a marketing intelligence report assessment that links directly back to reinforce and build on the research skills first introduced in Business 191. Once again the librarian plays a significant embedded role in Marketing 291, collaborating in class sessions and on course assessments. In another example, the second semester Accounting 192 "Accounting Information Support" course has incorporated a concept mapping assignment. By encouraging abilities to graphically represent concepts and the links between these concepts, the task serves to foster critical thinking even more widely across the BBIM program.

ASSESSMENT IN YEARS TWO AND THREE

Whereas some information literacy instruction and assessment would not be unusual in first-year courses in many undergraduate degree programs, the packaged nature of the BBIM encourages a holistic approach that allows considerable subsequent reinforcing and linkages throughout the program. The BBIM librarian, although not always as visible in subsequent courses to quite the same extent as with the core first-year courses, nonetheless continues to act as an important central resource for staff and students. For example, every BBIM course has an online course library page, created in collaboration with the instructors, to reinforce information literacy learning. In this way, the librarian also monitors connections across courses and encourages communication among teaching faculty.

In many cases, a spirit of open communication has been the key to the reinforcing of information literacy within the second and third years of the degree, even in cases with no direct faculty-librarian collaboration for assessment in a given course. For example, once teaching faculty are aware of the importance attached to referencing in the first year of the degree, they are then much more likely to expect and demand correct referencing and to design their own course assessments and marking rubrics with this in mind. Our experience is that ideas and synergies for integrating our teaching have often come through weekly casual meetings and coffee breaks rather than through formal planning workshops or retreats. This has also often been the case in developing shared understandings within the BBIM core team for scaffolding and reinforcing core student competencies up through the degree.

In their second year, BBIM students take two further courses that follow directly on from Business 191 and 192. These are Business 291 Communication Processes and Business 292 Project Based Management. Both courses are implicitly about using and communicating business information. For example, Business 291 includes an assessment that requires students to analyze a case study of a communication event and include further research to support this analysis. The marking rubric assesses information literacy for "standard of research and related theory." A second Business 291 assessment then involves a group oral presentation about a particular company scenario. This reinforces and assesses the effectiveness of prior business information literacy knowledge gained in locating relevant information from the popular New Zealand business press. Business 292 also includes a research project management scenario and also requires a group presentation.

Other courses in the second and third years see students concentrating on building a strong foundation in their two disciplinary majors. Here, information literacy assessments tend to concentrate on subject and disciplinary depth, with continuing faculty-librarian collaboration in the development of course resources. For example, specific Web guides have been created for newly introduced information management topics such as business process reengineering. These guides are freely available on the library Web site and so they also become learning resources for students from outside of the degree.

As the expectation is for higher-level critical thinking skills to be displayed in the second and third years of the degree, reflective tasks are increasingly seen as another way to assess information literacy. These can be personal reflections on a learning or teamwork experience (e.g., self or peer assessment), or weekly journals as part of the process of completing a course. Here the librarian often collaborates with teaching faculty in planning such reflective task assessments, and in sourcing appropriate resources to support students as they engage with these tasks.

In their third year, students take Infomgmt 392, a course in digital media production, in which they develop practical skills in photography and videography. In an interesting illustration of faculty-librarian collaboration that reflects the BBIM's integrated approach to information literacy, a prior assignment in this course asked students to create a series of video clips on potential academic honesty scenarios that students might face at university. These clips were later used by the librarian in first-year BBIM academic honesty tutorials. Infomgmt 392 students therefore had information literacy as an interesting and relevant topic around which to base their digital media assignment. Because these video clips were developed by BBIM students, the final products were particularly relevant and meaningful to first-year BBIM students as part of their orientation to academic honesty.

In their final semester of the degree, students work in groups to complete an applied capstone project course that consolidates, reinforces, and assesses their information management knowledge as well as their general and subject-specific business knowledge. With the third-year focus now solidly on information literacy for lifelong learning, efforts are put into polishing the professional skills of our students and into reinforcing and bringing together the various information literacy initiatives that have been embedded throughout the degree. By this stage in their learning, students should display competencies in business information literacy at a workplace level. Librarian support therefore tends to be one-on-one for often specific research.

The capstone project requires a substantial research component in selecting and researching a suitable business idea. This culminates in two major assessment deliverables: a comprehensive written business plan and a professional presentation of this plan to potential investors. Built in and around these two group-work deliverables are other individual assessments. For example, an individual writing task early in the course encourages initial brainstorming by asking students to reflect widely on their learning across the degree and to incorporate this into a discussion of a proposed initial business idea. Once the final written business plans and presentations have been delivered, students are also asked to write individual critiques of another team's business plan. Information literacy assessment is buried deeply within this project. Students are assessed on the quality of their business research, on their critical thinking and analysis of business information, and on their presentation of this analysis in both written and oral formats. Students also often incorporate advanced digital media productions within their final presentations to add value in the presentation of information and to display the skills they have developed through the information management major of the degree.

MEASURING SUCCESS AND IMPACT

The embedding of information literacy within the BBIM remains an ongoing process and there is still much scope for continuing improvement and development. For example, although there is considerable buy-in from core BBIM teaching faculty, many instructors also come and go from the degree from year to year. These can include, for example, visiting lecturers or other teaching faculty assigned to teach a BBIM course for a semester or two. In such cases, it requires effort to instill our culture of communication and collaboration. Also, as with any program that aims to integrate across courses and disciplines, challenges exist with a business school organizational structure that still divides the faculty into traditional disciplinary departments. There are also other tensions between teaching and research. Although collaboration for information literacy assessment can be both efficient and rewarding, some teaching faculty prefer to focus on their own courses in isolation because of the perceived time and effort involved in collaborative approaches.

Overall, trying to assess the effectiveness of our information literacy assessments to date requires a holistic approach to measurement. This is because we are not necessarily aiming to assess the effectiveness of any particular information literacy assessment, but rather we are hoping to take a programwide perspective over time in looking at the cumulative effect of an embedded series of assessments that evolves from year to year. It is possible, for example, to look at performance and course marks for introductory information literacy assessments in Business 191 and 192. However, students' mastery of information literacy builds over time in the degree and is mostly embedded into the overall assessment of broader BBIM coursework assignments and projects.

A growing consensus across the University of Auckland supports the importance of information literacy, but formal assessment of information literacy is not yet compulsory across faculties and programs. However, one universitywide assessment of undergraduate students' information literacy comes through the University of Auckland Final Year Undergraduate Student Survey. This survey asks our BBIM students and all undergraduate students to rate their response to the question, "As a result of this degree, my mastery of information sources and methods of information gathering is improving." Although confidential to our institution, the results of this survey are made available to faculty and librarians and these results for the BBIM have been highly encouraging.

In terms of other formal measures of effectiveness, we can measure and gather statistics on the BBIM program's use of the library's electronic resources. This readily validates our view of BBIM students as enthusiastic users of electronic information formats. For example, BBIM course library page statistics show very high use with the Business 191 course library page alone attracting approximately 10,000 hits from 240 students over its most recent two semesters. Similarly, using the administration features of the library's e-book databases, we can gauge BBIM use of e-books and link this to specific information literacy assessments. For example, records of access to the e-book database titles on teamwork show high usage when BBIM students are undertaking research on team effectiveness. Beyond the use of electronic resources, we also collect data on student participation in voluntary library sessions and on students' additional requests for librarian assistance.

Another way of assessing the effectiveness of our information literacy initiatives is through observation, for example by teaching faculty and the librarian noting patterns of satisfactory student coursework that demonstrates an understanding of correct referencing formats, including in-text citing and paraphrasing. Business 192 students, for example, show competency in their abilities to reference chapters in e-books, database articles, and a range of Web sources through the high marks they receive for the annotated bibliography and research log task. Student peer assessment of information literacy also occurs in Business 192 teamwork and other BBIM courses. As an example, there are group research projects in a number of courses in which the quality and evaluation of sources obtained by an individual will be critiqued by the group. In addition, it has been interesting to observe patterns in which students post questions on their online course discussion forums relating to referencing and business research, and these are often answered correctly by their peers before faculty or librarian can respond. Finally, the librarian's direct teaching involvement in so many BBIM courses allows considerable programwide observation of students' information and critical thinking abilities in the classroom and in computer lab sessions.

Further feedback comes from employers. There is demand for BBIM graduates who can use their information management skills to bridge the gap between information technology and business. Employers show clear patterns of hiring one BBIM graduate and then coming back for more. This seems to occur because the packaged nature of the program means that employers have a good sense of what they are getting when they hire a BBIM graduate. Employers often comment on our graduates' flexible skills in managing a range of information tasks.

There is also anecdotal evidence reported by BBIM colleagues, especially those who teach across both the Bachelor of Commerce and the BBIM, regarding the strong research and referencing skills of BBIM students following their first year of university study. Informal discussion and reflection has occurred regarding the low perceived level of plagiarism in the BBIM.

As another measure of impact, the BBIM is serving as an incubator for information literacy innovation. A number of information literacy components first developed and embedded within the BBIM have since been taken up by other programs within the business school. These include information literacy and academic honesty tutorials, online course library pages, annotated bibliography and research log tasks, and library collaborations to embed information literacy within the curriculum. In various accreditation visits, departmental reviews, and other similar processes in recent years, it has been gratifying to see how often information literacy teaching and assessment examples from the BBIM have been commended as evidence of innovation or best practice within the business school.

Finally, close faculty-librarian collaboration in the BBIM has also led to a number of joint learning initiatives and professional activities. These include academic papers and conference presentations, as well as successful proposals for teaching improvement grants to create and enhance information literacy teaching and learning resources. The collegial environment has extended beyond the program to BBIM faculty and librarian involvement in business school–wide initiatives such as curriculum mapping exercises and international accreditation efforts.

FURTHER REFLECTIONS AND CONCLUSION

The structured and sequential design of the BBIM was an important precursor in encouraging a collaborative "big picture" approach to curriculum development and delivery. However, with hindsight, we now realize there were also other environmental factors at play that helped stimulate and support our holistic approach to the embedding of information literacy across the program. For example, the BBIM was a completely new program with fewer political barriers to change and innovation. Given the integrated vision for the degree, teaching faculty were encouraged to focus at the program level as well as at the course level. Information literacy initiatives also benefited from enthusiastic faculty who were excited about teaching on this new degree and who were keen to collaborate and to embrace new e-learning technologies.

Furthermore, the inception of the degree happened to coincide with a time of change where University of Auckland librarians were being actively challenged to collaborate more directly in teaching and learning and to explore new ways of engaging with staff and students. Finally, these technology-oriented BBIM students were themselves uniquely well suited and open to our emphasis on information literacy. Indeed, a holistic and all-encompassing focus on information was implicit to the degree program they had selected to study.

We now have a sustained eight-year record of faculty-librarian collaboration for information literacy and its assessment. Indeed, promoting and embedding information literacy is now becoming such a fundamental way of doing business on the BBIM that it is often indistinguishable from the wider curriculum. This is not only to students who see information literacy as an integral part of their learning, but also to faculty who see information literacy as an integral part of their courses.

The key challenges in assessing our embedded information literacy program are that so many different information literacy learning activities are dispersed throughout the three years of the degree, and that these are typically buried deeply within coursework. With a focus on reiteration and reinforcement over time, it is not enough to try to evaluate the impact of any single information literacy assessment. Furthermore, the most effective demonstration of students' information literacy capabilities tends to take place within applied coursework assessments such as business reports, presentations, and plans where it is difficult to directly relate this to the specific impact of any particular information literacy tutorial or training intervention. A further challenge lies in the fact that this embedded approach to information literacy is unique within our institution and is not currently part of any overall business school generic learning assessment methods. For example, although information literacy is included as a graduate attribute, the business school's standardized semester teaching and course evaluations do not address information literacy. Information literacy is consistently included in BBIM marking rubrics and so we are in some ways acting out of the mainstream culture of our current business school learning environment.

Although it is not common to see such a high degree of faculty-librarian cooperation in business degree programs, our experience suggests much can be gained through a dedicated program librarian model. This is especially the case when the librarian is seen as a valued member of the teaching and learning team who can contribute where appropriate to coursework design, development, and assessment. The one caveat is that the effectiveness of our model might easily be diluted without an integrated program, and without a high level of motivation on the part of teaching and support staff. This is because it is time consuming, at least initially, to tailor information literacy learning tasks to course assessments.

Meaningful library faculty collaboration for information literacy requires common goals for learning, a shared commitment to students, and mutually agreed philosophies and responses. We believe this is indeed the model in the BBIM program. Individual learning assessments and staff within the BBIM will alter and change over time, yet it is hoped that a spirit of teaching innovation will remain that fosters information-literate graduates who can contribute positively to New Zealand's economic growth.

REFERENCES

Bland, Vicki. 2007. "Students Lack IT Savvy." *New Zealand Herald*, February 21. Available: Newztext database (accessed November 20, 2008).

Bronshteyn, Karen, and Rita Baladad. 2006. "Perspectives on . . . Librarians as Writing Instructors: Using Paraphrasing Exercises to Teach Beginning Information Literacy Students." *Journal of Academic Librarianship* 32, no. 5: 533–536.

Brown, Cecelia, Teri J. Murphy, and Mark Nanny. 2003. "Turning Techno-savvy into Info-savvy: Authentically Integrating Information Literacy into the College Curriculum." *Journal of Academic Librarianship* 29, no 6: 386–398.

Bruce, Christine S. 1997. *The Seven Faces of Information Literacy*. Adelaide: Auslib Press.

Bundy, Alan. 2004. *Australian and New Zealand Information Literacy Framework*, 2nd ed. Adelaide: Australian and New Zealand Institute for Information Literacy. Available: www.anziil.org/resources/Info%20lit%202nd%20edition.pdf (accessed September 30, 2009).

Cooney, Martha. 2005. "Business Information Literacy Instruction: A Survey and Progress Report." *Journal of Business & Finance Librarianship* 11, no. 1: 3–25.

Corrall, Sheila M. 2007. "Benchmarking Strategic Engagement with Information Literacy in Higher Education: Towards a Working Model." *Information Research* 12 , no. 4 (paper 328). Available: http://InformationR.net/ir/12-4/paper328.html (accessed September 30, 2009).

Cunningham, Nancy A. 2003. "Information Competency Skills for Business Students." *Academic BRASS* 1, no 1. Available: www.ftrf.org/ala/mgrps/divs/rusa/sections/brass/brasspubs/academicbrass/acadarchives/volume1number1/ALA_print_layout_1_356821_356821.cfm (accessed September 30, 2009).

Drucker, Peter F. 1992. "Drucker on Be Data Literate—Know What to Know." *Wall Street Journal*, Europe. December 4.

Drucker, Peter F. 1995. "The Information Executives Truly Need." *Harvard Business Review* 73, no. 1: 54–62.

Eisenberg, Michael B. 2008. "Information Literacy: Essential Skills for the Information Age." *DESIDOC Journal of Library & Information Technology* 28, no. 2: 39–47. Available: http://publications.drdo.gov.in/ojs/index.php/djlit/article/viewFile/288/182 (accessed September 30, 2009).

Fiegen, Ann M., Bennett Cherry, and Kathleen Watson. 2002. "Reflections on Collaboration: Learning Outcomes and Information Literacy Assessment in the Business Curriculum." *Reference Services Review* 30, no. 4: 307–318.

Gilinsky, Armand Jr., and Richard Robison. 2008. "A Proposed Design for the Business Capstone Course with Emphasis on Improving Students' Information Competency." *Journal of Management Education* 32, no. 4: 400–419.

Leigh, Jennifer S. A., and Cynthia A. Gibbon. 2008. "Information Literacy and the Introductory Management Classroom." *Journal of Management Education* 32, no. 4: 509–530.

LexisNexis 2008. "National Workplace Survey Reveals American Professionals Over-whelmed, Headed for 'Breaking Point'." LexisNexis Workplace Productivity Survey. Available: www.lexisnexis.com/media/press-release.aspx?id=1041.asp (accessed September 30, 2009).

Mackey, Thomas P., and Trudi E. Jacobson. 2005. "Information Literacy: A Collaborative Endeavour." *College Teaching* 53, no. 4: 140–144.

Nerz, Honora F., and Suzanne T. Weiner. 2001. "Information Competencies: A Strategic Approach." *Proceedings of the 2001 American Society for Engineering Annual Conference & Exposition.* Available: http://eld.lib.ucdavis.edu/fulltext/00510_2001.pdf (accessed September 30, 2009).

Times Higher Education. 2008. "World University Rankings." (Supplement). London. Available: www.timeshighereducation.co.uk/hybrid.asp?typeCode=243&pubCode=1 (accessed September 30, 2009).

University of Auckland. 2003. "Graduate Profile." Auckland. Available: www.auckland.ac.nz/uoa/home/for/current-students/cs-academic-information/cs-regulations-policies-and-guidelines/cs-graduate-profile (accessed September 30, 2009).

University of Auckland Library. 2006. "Information Literacy—Academic Staff." Auckland: University of Auckland. Available: www.library.auckland.ac.nz/instruct/docs/academic.pdf (accessed September 30, 2009).

Van Cleave, Kendra. 2007. "Collaboration." In *Proven Strategies for Building an Information Literacy Program* (pp. 177–192), edited by Susan Carol Curzon and Lynn D. Lampert. New York: Neal-Schuman Publishers.

Part II

Social Science and Education

SECTION INTRODUCTION

In this second part of the book we introduce three chapters that explore information literacy assessment in social science and education. This section includes assessment models developed specifically for undergraduate courses in political science and psychology, as well as a multidisciplinary professional program for adult learners. The pedagogical perspectives in this section extend from the United States to the United Kingdom and cover both in-class and online methodologies. The author teams present outcomes based on student survey data, narrative self-assessments, multiyear student skills analysis, and a multi-layered approach with e-learning evaluation. These chapters describe the benefits and challenges of collaboration and this work is grounded in student reflection and classroom practice.

We begin this second part of the book with "Assessing Integrated Library Components to Enhance Information Literacy in Political Science" by Julie K. Gilbert and Christopher P. Gilbert. This chapter illustrates the value of mutual faculty-librarian interest in improving discipline-specific information literacy skills at different times in a student's academic career. The approach taken by the authors encompasses both lower-level and upper-level skills and is instructive to librarians and faculty members teaching at either end of the spectrum, or at various points in between. It also identifies some of the cognate skills related to information literacy, such as research, writing, critical thinking, and information organization, that are useful for any institution to better understand through assessment. This faculty-librarian team examines the effectiveness of multiple instruction sessions integrated into the political science curriculum.

The methodology for this study included student perceptions of research skills as well as citation analysis. They employed multiple techniques such as end-of-semester surveys, source analysis of student developed annotated bibliographies, and narrative evaluations written by students. Through this comprehensive assessment strategy the authors found that the multiple instruction sessions integrated into the curriculum had a positive impact on student research abilities. This finding is especially valuable to institutions that offer library instruction sessions but have not found a way yet to incorporate this work into specific disciplines, or do not have an assessment plan.

The second chapter in this section, "Assessing Undergraduate Information Literacy Skills: How Collaborative Curriculum Interventions Promote Active and Independent Learning," describes the partnership by authors Amanda A. Harrison and Angela Newton. This chapter explores the design of a formative multiple-choice survey to measure undergraduate information literacy skills based on the Society of College, National, and University Libraries (SCONUL) Seven Pillars model in the United Kingdom. The authors provide a compelling introduction that describes the vast changes in technology at their institution and within the larger information environment. They discuss the impact of this technological transformation on student learning and the challenges it poses to information literacy instruction. Through this partnership, the authors developed a survey instrument that was tested with cohorts of psychology and nursing students at two different institutions and implemented over multiple years. The primary goal of this assessment was to redesign the information literacy curriculum based on data analysis in an effort to better prepare students as independent learners. The authors found that the way students performed on the information literacy assessment is closely aligned with how they performed in their academic program. This provided crucial evidence that valued information literacy education and led to a collaborative redesign of the program that emphasized visible faculty-librarian partnerships in the classroom. This chapter reinforces the importance of information literacy instruction in higher education and presents a convincing case for any instructor who may be unsure about the role of collaboration in this process.

We close this section with "Collaboration in Action: Designing an Online Assessment Strategy for Adult Learners" by Julie Bostock, Susan Graves, and Ruth Wilson. This chapter examines a formative and summative assessment plan to measure the effectiveness of embedded information literacy modules. The students in this cohort are adult learners pursuing professional development credit on a part-time basis. The author team describes a learner-centered online environment that was sensitive to the needs of adult learners who may be less experienced with technology than traditional age students and who may not be fully prepared for advanced-level learning. The approach discussed in this chapter values student experiences and builds on current competencies through online modules that encourage self-directed and independent learning. One of the particularly novel aspects of this case study is that the e-learning modules were delivered in a blended format that combined face-to-face tutoring with online instruction. In an effort to assess this work, the authors developed a multilayered method that included such tools as a skills audit, reflective assignments, questionnaire, online evaluation, and content analysis. The authors found that embedding the information literacy instruction in the curriculum improved student skills and enhanced student confidence in their own abilities. It also helped prepare students for their studies as self-directed and independent learners. This chapter illustrates how instructors can combine different assessment techniques to better understand the relationship between in class and online instruction. It also explores effective teaching strategies for adult learners in e-learning environments.

In this second part of the book, faculty-librarian teams describe various assessment techniques that were designed within specific disciplinary frameworks. To apply these practices at your own institution, within your own fields of study, consider the following:

- Since faculty and librarians have a common interest in advancing student learning, identify the aspects of an information literacy assessment project that are mutually beneficial and promote a shared strategy.
- Assessment initiatives may involve single classes or several courses within programs that span upper and lower-level competencies.
- Consider the design and implementation of multiple instruments for the same assessment effort.
- The use of both quantitative and qualitative methods makes valuable contributions to assessment endeavors.
- Assessment outcomes provide insights into student learning and may reinforce the importance of faculty-librarian collaboration in information literacy instruction.
- Test a survey instrument with different cohorts to determine how well it addresses diverse learning styles and abilities.
- Compare data on individual learning outcomes in specific courses or modules with student performance in their program of study.
- Reflect on the relationship between formative and summative strategies in the design of an assessment initiative.
- Develop assessment strategies that recognize diverse student populations, including adult learners.

The assessment models introduced in these chapters demonstrate that information literacy improves research, writing, and critical thinking skills in multiple disciplines and prepares students for independent lifelong learning. The disciplinary perspectives in this section include both social science and education, yet the practical assessment strategies examined here are not limited to any particular field of study. Collaboration is central to the assessment initiatives described in this second part of the book and enhanced the sophistication of each plan.

Chapter 3

Assessing Integrated Library Components to Enhance Information Literacy in Political Science

Julie K. Gilbert and Christopher P. Gilbert

INTRODUCTION

This chapter examines the development and assessment of an integrated information literacy component designed to enhance student learning in political science. The decision to implement an information literacy program grew out of the overlapping goals of library faculty and political science faculty. Political science faculty sought ways to enhance student research skills at an introductory level and to enhance students' critical thinking skills and ability to organize sophisticated information at an advanced level. Library faculty sought to expand efforts to partner with academic departments in teaching and assessing information literacy skills among undergraduate students. Both library and political science faculty also wished to understand more precisely the impact of new teaching strategies on student learning.

Our study measures the impact of multiple instruction sessions on student information literacy skills at various points in the political science curriculum at our institution. Gathering assessment data is central to our approach. The data provide valuable insight into the development of student research behaviors, and we will use our findings to advocate for further support of information literacy programs in this and other departments at our institution. This chapter highlights our collaborative approach in designing course modules and assignments to meet the goals of political science and library faculty. We also present important findings from our assessment plan that demonstrate the positive impact of this approach on student learning.

LITERATURE REVIEW

Assessing Integrated Library Components

The library science literature provides models for assessing student learning outcomes in integrated library components. Several of these studies involve assessment of multisession library instruction models. Smiti Gandhi (2004) assessed learning outcomes for a five-session library instruction sequence by using a pretest, a posttest, and a teaching evaluation survey. As a result of the five-session model, students in the experimental group demonstrated higher levels of learning than students who had the traditional one-shot session. Rui Wang (2006) assessed the long-term effects of a library credit-bearing course on student information literacy skills, with an assessment model utilizing a citation analysis of final papers. One of the most comprehensive approaches to information literacy assessment is the Augustana Model employed at the University of Alberta. The Augustana Model includes assessment of discipline-specific information literacy courses using pretests, posttests, course assignments, and exams (Goebel, Neff, and Mandeville, 2007).

Other studies assess the impact of one or two library instruction sessions on student learning outcomes. Teresa S. Bowden and Angela DiBenedetto (2001) incorporated an information literacy component into a general biology course. Bowden and DiBenedetto used student feedback questionnaires and evaluation of final projects to develop further integration of information literacy skills into the course. Mark Emmons and Wanda Martin (2002) assessed an inquiry-based information literacy program through a comparison of citations in research papers collected before and after program implementation. Although results indicated little change in student research behavior, the authors planned to use assessment data to modify the instruction program. Kate Zoellner, Sue Samson, and Samantha Hines (2008) used an assessment project to test the effectiveness of a research component embedded into a public-speaking course; pretest and posttest data confirmed that students expressed higher levels of research confidence as a result of the research component. Similar to our study, these studies used multiple means for gathering assessment data and used the data to chart the impact of these new methods on student learning outcomes in information literacy.

Assessing Information Literacy in Political Science

The instruction literature within political science reveals emerging trends in both teaching and, to an extent, assessing information literacy skills. In 2008, the Association of College and Research Libraries (ACRL) approved the *Political Science Research Competency Guidelines,* which were developed by the Law & Political Science Section (LPSS) of ACRL (2008) and based on ACRL's *Information Literacy Competency Standards for Higher Education* (2000). The guidelines recognize the unique nature of political science research and urge setting information literacy goals within the context of the discipline. The guidelines also promote collaboration between faculty and librarians by assigning specific outcomes to be addressed by either the faculty member, the librarian, or both.

The literature examining information literacy in political science confirms Ann Grafstein's (2002) advocacy for a discipline-based approach to information literacy and centers on ways of connecting the discipline to the library. Through an analysis of pretest and posttest data of students completing a political science research paper, Michelle Hale Williams and Jocelyn Jones Evans (2008) determined that information literacy was indeed discipline specific and should be integrated into political science curricula. Barbara P. Norelli (2006) outlined explicit classroom methods to tie the LPSS *Political Science Research Competencies Guidelines* to instruction, including an assessment measure involving a citation analysis. Christy R. Stevens and Patricia J. Campbell (2008) provide an impressive argument for more collaboration between political science faculty and librarians; their approach highlighted benefits for moving beyond one-shot bibliographic instruction sessions and included assessment data supporting collaboration.

Other studies rely even more heavily on assessment data to support information literacy efforts within political science. B. Gregory Marfleet and Brian Dille (2005) incorporated information literacy into two sections of a methods course, assessed learning outcomes through a standardized information literacy test, and compared results to students in two sections of a nonmethods course. Students in the methods course improved, as well as students in the nonmethods course who had no dedicated information literacy exposure. Marfleet and Dille (2005) argue that information literacy can be developed throughout the curriculum instead of remaining solely in the jurisdiction of a research methods course. Stephen Thornton (2008) utilized diagnostic questionnaires and found that incorporating an information literacy module in a politics curriculum led to increased information literacy skills among students.

Two additional studies discuss assessment of information literacy components within the context of collaboration between political science faculty and librarians. Elizabeth O. Hutchins (2003) outlined a rubric she developed to assess student learning outcomes related to information literacy instruction in two political science classes. The rubric helped determine students' information-seeking behavior and also promoted extensive conversations between classroom and library faculty. In 2007, Christy R. Stevens and Patricia J. Campbell outlined a collaborative approach to incorporate information literacy into a lower-level American Government course, a mid-level Comparative Politics course, and an upper-level African Politics course. Their assessment plan included a pretest, posttest, course assignments, and student feedback. Whereas students in the mid-level and upper-level classes demonstrated a sizeable increase in information literacy skills, first-year students improved only slightly. Results from their study confirmed a need for information literacy to be built into the political science curriculum at their institution and provided a road map for further collaboration (Stevens and Campbell, 2007).

INSTITUTIONAL CONTEXT AT GUSTAVUS ADOLPHUS COLLEGE

Gustavus Adolphus College is a private liberal arts college located in St. Peter, Minnesota. The college educates 2,600 undergraduates, representing 38 states and 17 countries. Most students graduate within four years with a bachelor of arts degree. The college is known for its academic and service-learning programs.[1]

The Folke Bernadotte Memorial Library (FBML) at Gustavus houses more than 300,000 monographs and provides access to dozens of electronic databases. FBML is a teaching library and the six library faculty members are responsible for delivering library instruction to the campus. The instruction program mainly consists of traditional one-shot sessions arranged by classroom faculty in collaboration with library faculty to teach library and research skills to students. Students typically experience the library instruction program in their first semester as part of the required First Term Seminar program. Repeat visits for students frequently occur in research methodology courses, other major courses, senior seminars, and some general education courses. The library instruction program is self-selecting: upon graduation, some students have had several instruction sessions whereas others have had only one or two, depending on whether their course professors arranged for library sessions.

Current assessment practices of the FBML instruction program consist of solicited student evaluations and a questionnaire for course faculty. The evaluation asks students to describe what they learned, indicate what is still confusing about the library, and rate the effectiveness of the librarian leading the session. The questionnaire asks faculty to assess how well they felt the library session helped students to complete coursework and solicits ideas for improving the sessions. Evaluations and questionnaires are returned to the librarian leading the session to provide feedback and assist with shaping future library sessions.

The political science department at Gustavus consists of six tenure-track and two visiting faculty members. The department serves 125 majors and enrolls approximately 900 students annually in courses covering all major subfields in political science. As with all academic programs at Gustavus, political science has developed its own assessment plan, which was substantially revised in 2007. The assessment plan identifies six learning objectives that address outcomes for majors as well as other students who take department courses; development of research, writing, and analytical skills constitutes one of these six objectives. These skills are developed primarily in two required courses for political science majors: Analyzing Politics, a research methods course typically taken in the sophomore year, enrolling students who have completed at least two of the three required introductory courses and thus serving as a bridge between introductory and advanced coursework; and the capstone senior seminar, in which the primary course requirement is a substantial research-based senior thesis paper. We provide a more detailed review of key course components in the assessment section.

As noted in the LPSS *Political Science Research Competency Guidelines*, research in political science parallels most disciplines in the use of traditional academic sources such as scholarly journals and books, yet it also utilizes unique sources that are often unfamiliar to undergraduates: "Notably among them are government documents produced by local, state, federal, or international bodies and data sets that can be analyzed with statistical software" (2008: 1). To best meet the needs of undergraduate political science students at Gustavus, the department and the library have been collaborating to introduce a comprehensive, systematic information literacy program into the department curriculum. The instructional practices we undertake in this study form the base for the new program. In the future, additional departmental information literacy goals will be identified and incorporated into the curriculum with the assistance of the library.

INTEGRATING INFORMATION LITERACY INTO THE POLITICAL SCIENCE MAJOR

Our collaborative efforts began during fall semester 2006 after discussions of the challenges we both encountered while working with undergraduates in our respective roles. In the classroom, C. Gilbert found that his political science students increasingly exhibited weak research skills and a lack of familiarity with the library. These concerns arose in both the research methods course (which C. Gilbert teaches each semester) and in senior seminars (taught by numerous department faculty). We began collaborating on information literacy efforts after determining that C. Gilbert's desire to reinforce research skills in political science students dovetailed with J. Gilbert's interest in providing the most efficient and comprehensive approach to teaching library and research skills to students. Political science department colleagues shared these concerns about student research abilities and endorsed the idea of implementing an information literacy program to improve student abilities. We wanted to find ways to encourage students to think critically about information within a disciplinary perspective. We also sought to enhance these aspects of student learning across the political science major, not just in the research methods course. Throughout this collaborative study, our guiding hypothesis has been that students exposed to more library instruction sessions would demonstrate stronger research skills, have more positive perceptions of their own research skills, and use better sources in their research assignments.

The research methods course, Analyzing Politics, seeks to ground students in the literature and research methods of the discipline. Hence it proved to be the most logical place in the political science curriculum to begin incorporating information literacy principles. Fall 2006 Analyzing Politics students served as the control group for our study. They received no library instruction sessions; their exposure to library research skills was limited to discussion of one chapter in the course textbook during one class period. Students in spring 2007, fall 2007, and spring 2008 received a three- or four-session instruction arc. We will refer to this set of students as experimental group one. Initial assessment results among experimental group one students indicated stronger research skills and broader use of high-quality research materials, leading us to then develop a weekly lab component taught by J. Gilbert to fall 2008 Analyzing Politics students (experimental group two). Students in this lab section met once per week with the librarian (12 total sessions) and completed graded library assignments.

This project also grew to incorporate library instruction efforts in political science senior seminar courses. The spring 2008 and fall 2008 sections of the U.S. Interest Groups seminar (taught by a different political science faculty member) each received a five-session library instruction module. As we explain in more detail in this section, research behaviors and perceptions of this set of seminar students can be compared with students in three other senior seminars that did not have a multisession library instruction component.

We designed our assessment efforts to connect with learning objectives developed for both experimental groups of Analyzing Politics and the U.S. Interest Groups seminar. Learning objectives for experimental group one intended to enhance students' use of high-quality information sources and make students more efficient in their research. We also attempted to assess the impact of multiple library sessions on students' confidence in their own research abilities. We hypothesized that greater exposure to a broad array of research sources and methods in Political Science would increase student confidence levels.

We expanded and further defined our initial goals for experimental group two, the Analyzing Politics lab students, to incorporate the following learning objectives:

- Think critically about information sources in political science, including where they come from, how to locate them, and how to use them.
- Explore research tools and collections appropriate to the study of political science.
- Develop information literacy skills to conduct effective research in the discipline.
- Discuss ethical and practical questions related to information.
- Acquire research and information literacy skills necessary to write a political science thesis or some other major research paper.

Weekly lab topics centered on the diverse formats of information available to political science students, including government documents and statistical sources. Students also discussed methods for evaluating and incorporating sources into their own work.

The spring and fall 2008 U.S. Interest Groups seminar included a mix of students from the Analyzing Politics control, experimental, and lab component groups, bringing a diverse range of library experience to the seminar. Working with the seminar instructor, J. Gilbert developed learning objectives for the five-session library instruction module, which were focused on equipping students with the resources to conduct thorough research for their senior theses:

- Identify a broad range of sources appropriate for the topic.
- Achieve fluency with advance search techniques in library databases and catalogs.
- Gain familiarity with cited references searching.
- Establish criteria for evaluating sources.
- Use every source appropriately and ethically, including proper citation.

These learning objectives sought to expand on the information literacy skills students brought to the seminar. Assessing outcomes from the senior seminar sections complements the Analyzing Politics assessment of information literacy skills and will help shape the library's and department's ongoing response to students' library and research needs.

ASSESSMENT MODEL

We developed our assessment model based on methods highlighted by studies that include measures of both student perceptions' of their own research skills and source analysis of student research (Gandhi, 2004; Bowden and DiBenedetto, 2001); we also drew on newer studies to further refine our citation analysis measure (Knight-Davis and Sung, 2008; Mill, 2008). These studies led us to develop a multifaceted set of assessment tools. First, for Analyzing Politics students, we administered surveys on the research process at the end of each semester included in the study. These surveys centered on a common assignment—preparation of an annotated bibliography on a research question of the student's choosing—and inquired about multiple aspects of student research behavior and attitudes. We asked students what sources of assistance they utilized in preparing papers for the course, how much time they spent searching for sources, and whether they perceived that the research process for the annotated bibliography was easier or harder compared to other Analyzing Politics papers and to research assignments in other courses. We also asked students about their level of confidence in their own research skills. This combination of objective and subjective questions yields considerable insight into student behavior and into student perceptions of their own research abilities. (All assessment instruments can be found in Appendix 3.1.)

Second, we collected annotated bibliographies from each Analyzing Politics student and analyzed the sources used in these papers. This method provides an independent analysis of the quality of student work. For each paper we counted the total number of sources utilized as well as types of source—books, academic journal articles, newspapers and periodicals, and Internet sources. To address whether multiple library sessions influenced student choices of sources, we used a citation analysis with a measure of high quality sources: peer-reviewed academic journal articles, books from university presses, articles from leading newspapers such as the *New York Times* and elite periodicals such as *The Economist*; and Internet sites sponsored by leading political organizations or government agencies.[2]

Finally, Analyzing Politics students in the lab section semester wrote a narrative assessment of their research skills at the end of the semester. This form of assessment is rarely used in addressing student research skills. It gives students much more of an opportunity to reflect on their work than closed-ended survey questions. The assignment prompt asked students to provide concrete examples of changes in their research behavior, to discuss any changes in research skills, to explain how lab assignments have impacted their work for other courses, and to discuss what aspects of the library remain confusing or unclear. This assignment offers a rich array of insights into how student learning has been affected by the activities designed by the librarian and course instructor.

Assessment of student learning and attitudes in the senior seminar courses is more straightforward. Students in each seminar section filled out a common assessment survey at the end of the semester, developed by political science department faculty. This survey instrument was modeled on the one used for Analyzing Politics, but modified to reflect the more advanced research conducted by seminar students. Students rated their confidence levels in their research skills, compared the quality of their thesis paper to other papers written during their college careers, and assessed (where applicable) the library sessions conducted for their seminars.

These assessment tools allow detailed analysis of student learning outcomes and student attitudes in both courses. The quasi-experimental research design also allows us to assess differences in student learning and attitudes between sections with no library sessions and sections with one or more such sessions. Our central question is whether research behaviors and perceptions differ among students who participated in multiple library instruction sessions, compared with students who received zero or one such session. We hypothesize in all cases that additional library instruction sessions should enhance student information literacy skills and student perceptions of their own research abilities.

ASSESSMENT OF STUDENT LEARNING AND PERCEPTIONS

Analyzing Politics

As noted earlier, for purposes of analysis, Analyzing Politics students are divided into three groups: the control group (fall 2006) that received no library instruction sessions; experimental group one (spring 2007, fall 2007, spring 2008) that had three or four instruction sessions during the semester; and experimental group two (fall 2008 lab section) that participated in the weekly lab component (12 total sessions). These groups total 127 students across the five semesters.[3] Hence, modest differences across the groups are unlikely to be statistically significant. Where applicable, we have indicated intergroup differences that approach or exceed statistical significance at the 0.1 level (90 percent confidence).

Behavioral questions on our end-of-semester assessment instrument focus on the annotated bibliography paper completed by students in all sections. Table 3.1 shows student self-reports about their sources of assistance for multiple research assignments, starting points in their research process for the annotated bibliography, utilization of specific types of resources on the annotated bibliography, and time spent finding sources for this paper.

Table 3.1 presents important differences across groups in terms of sources of assistance used in completing papers for the course. The most striking finding is that students in both experimental groups were nearly three times more likely than control group students to ask a reference librarian for assistance in completing research papers ($p < .028$); experimental group two students were slightly more likely than experimental one students to do so. Overall, both experimental groups used more sources of assistance on average ($p < .150$), and

Table 3.1. Research Behavior, Analyzing Politics Students	Control Group	Experimental Group 1	Experimental Group 2 (lab section)
Sources of assistance used in completing papers for course			
Professor	55.9	68.5	70.6
Reference librarian	17.7	42.5	47.1
Another student in class	47.1	58.9	58.8
None	17.6	6.8	5.9
Mean sources of assistance used	1.44	1.97	1.94
Resources used at any point in completing papers for course			
Search engine	67.6	65.8	82.4
Folke Bernadotte Memorial Library Web site	97.1	89.0	100.0
Online database	97.1	97.3	100.0
Course Web site	29.4	32.9	56.3
Discussion with professor	20.6	19.2	17.6
Discussion with reference librarian	8.8	26.0	31.3
Used 4 or more resources	38.2	38.3	82.3
Mean number of resources used	3.23	3.36	3.82
Starting point in search for annotated bibliography sources			
Search engine (e.g., Google)	11.8	11.0	5.9
Folke Bernadotte Memorial Library Web site	38.2	27.4	35.3
Online database	44.1	52.1	52.9
Course Web site	0.0	2.7	5.9
Mean hours spent finding annotated bibliography sources	3.03	2.73	3.28
Number of students	34	73	17

Note: Values are in percentages unless otherwise indicated. Control group students received zero library instruction sessions; experimental group one students received three or four sessions; experimental group two (lab section) students received weekly sessions (12 total).

showed higher rates of assistance from the course professor and other students in the course. On the other end, although the vast majority of students in all groups did request some form of assistance, control group students were three times as likely not to ask for any assistance in completing their papers ($p < .089$). As one of the goals of multiple library instruction sessions is to expose students to more forms of library assistance, the Table 3.1 results confirm that students appear more likely to use these sources of assistance the more they are exposed to such sources. The fact that experimental students taught multiple times by the same reference librarian were then far more likely to seek out a reference librarian outside of class is a very strong indicator that an active library instruction program will have the residual payoff of greater traffic to the reference desk.

Table 3.1 also shows how often students report using specific types of resources in completing research papers for the course. Once again, both experimental groups used reference librarians far more often—three times more often among experimental group one students and almost four times more often among lab section students ($p < .085$). Lab section students also used the class Web site much more often than control group or experimental one students ($p < .150$) and were somewhat more likely to use a search engine such as Google as well. As all groups were about equally likely to ask the course professor for assistance, we are confident that the reference librarian visits are expanding upon and not displacing student conversations with the course professor. Overall, lab section students utilized more forms of assistance on average (3.82, versus 3.23 for control group and 3.36 for experimental group one) and the percentage of students using four or more resources jumps from under 40 percent among the first two groups to more than 80 percent among lab students ($p < .01$). Thus Table 3.1 shows that having multiple instruction sessions (experimental group one) only slightly shifts the forms of resources used by students (specifically, reference librarian assistance frequency), but usage frequency rises across a wider range of resources and the volume of resource usage rises significantly when the instruction sessions become a weekly course component.

Another important goal of multiple library instruction sessions is to enhance students' ability to find appropriate resources efficiently. Lab student behavior in this regard deviated in modest ways from the control group and experimental group one. Lab students were half as likely to start their search for annotated bibliography sources by using a search engine such as Google or Google Scholar. As we will detail later with the narrative evaluations of lab section students, search engines became less promising as an efficient search tool once students became more comfortable with searching online databases and the variety of resources linked from the college library Web site. Indeed,

Table 3.1 demonstrates that students in both experimental groups were more likely to commence their search for sources with an online database or the class and library Web sites (which have links to specific research resources) and less likely to use some other starting point.

Efficiency in time spent conducting research is much harder to judge through student self-reports. Students bring different levels of motivation to the task along with differing research abilities. Table 3.1 presents an interesting pattern regarding the time spent finding sources for the annotated bibliography. Control group students reported an average of 3.03 hours spent finding sources. The mean for experimental group one drops to 2.73 hours. Considering that control group and experimental one group students use essentially the same total amount of resources in their source searches, we can posit that multiple instruction sessions did make experimental one students somewhat more efficient. The truly compelling deviation is among lab section students, whose average time spent rose to 3.28 hours. This is not a statistically significant difference from the other two groups combined ($p < .310$); however, the rest of Table 3.1 clearly indicates that lab section students spent more time in pursuit of more forms of research assistance—time well spent, in other words, a finding confirmed by lab section narrative comments as well.

The final behavioral component to compare across Analyzing Politics sections concerns the actual sources students used in their annotated bibliography papers. As noted previously, we used two basic measures to analyze these papers: the total number of sources students cited in their bibliographies, and the percentage of those sources that could be considered high quality. The assignment prompt across all semesters indicated that "[t]he annotated bibliography should have roughly between six and ten source[s] (six is a minimum)." In addition, all students had access to a set of sample outstanding annotated bibliographies from previous course sections; these example papers averaged nine sources. Thus we would expect the total number of sources used to vary across papers, although we hypothesize that students in both experimental groups would include more sources (and lab students likely would include the highest number of sources). We also expect students in both experimental groups to have a higher percentage of high quality sources compared to the control group. Table 3.2 presents the results of the annotated bibliography source analysis.

Table 3.2 shows a sharp jump in high quality source usage and total source usage with each expansion in library instruction. Three-quarters of the sources used by control group students were high quality. This figure jumped to 82 percent among experimental group one students and to more than 96 percent among experimental group two students; both increases are statistically significant ($p < .01$). We found a similar, statistically significant increase ($p < .01$) in

Table 3.2. Annotated Bibliography Source Usage, Analyzing Politics Students			
	Control Group	Experimental Group 1	Experimental Group 2 (lab section)
High-quality source usage			
Mean number of HQ sources	5.18	7.06	9.72
Percent of all sources that were HQ	74.2	82.3	96.6
Mean number of total sources	7.00	8.48	10.11
Number of students	34	71	18

Note: Control group students received zero library instruction sessions; experimental group one students received three or four sessions; experimental group two (lab section) students received weekly sessions (12 total).

the number of high quality sources used. Total source usage also rose substantially across the groups—the greater time spent by lab students thus translated into both more research resources used and more sources included in the annotated bibliography paper ($p < .001$).

These differences cannot be solely attributed to the quality of students across the sections. In fact, the highest mean grades on annotated bibliography papers occurred in the control group semester. Taken as a whole, the evidence presented in Tables 3.1 and 3.2 strongly suggests that expanding the number of library instruction sessions has measurable, positive effects on student research behaviors.

Student perceptions of their own research abilities offer a different form of insight into the effects of introducing multiple library instruction sessions into a course. These perceptual data are presented in Table 3.3. We asked two sets of questions to address student perceptions. First, we asked students to compare the ease or difficulty finding annotated bibliography sources compared to another research paper in Analyzing Politics and compared to research assignments for other courses. The intra-class comparison question was asked to both experimental groups. Forty-eight percent of students in experimental group one felt that finding sources for the annotated bibliography was easier ("somewhat easier" and "much easier" combined) than finding sources for the other Analyzing Politics paper (which had been completed earlier in the semester). This figure jumped to 82 percent among lab section students, who had experienced seven more library instruction sessions than their experimental group one peers by the time their annotated bibliographies were due.

Table 3.3. Perceptions of Research Skills, Analyzing Politics Students

	Control Group Posttest	Exper. Group 1 Pretest*	Exper. Group 1 Posttest	Exper. Group 2 Initial**	Exper. Group 2 Posttest
Finding sources for annotated bibliography compared to another paper for course					
Much easier	—		15.1		17.6
Somewhat easier	—		32.9		64.7
About the same	—		28.8		11.8
Somewhat more difficult	—		17.8		5.9
Much more difficult	—		5.5		0.0
Finding sources in this course compared to research for other courses					
Much easier	8.8		11.0		5.9
Somewhat easier	32.4		16.4		35.3
About the same	50.0		35.6		35.3
Somewhat more difficult	8.8		31.5		17.6
Much more difficult	0.0		5.5		5.9
Confidence in research skills					
Very confident	**44.1**	17.9	**46.6**	5.9	**70.6**
Confident	**52.9**	67.9	**50.7**	58.8	**29.4**
Not very confident	**2.9**	14.3	**2.7**	35.3	**0.0**
Not at all confident	**0.0**	0.0	**0.0**	0.0	**0.0**
Number of students	34	28	73	17	17

Note: Values are percentages unless otherwise indicated. Control group students received zero library instruction sessions; experimental group one students received three or four sessions; experimental group two (lab section) students received weekly sessions (12 total). On the first comparison question above, control group students were asked to compare to a course assignment not used in other semesters, hence results are not comparable to question asked to both experimental groups.

* Experimental Group 1 pretest administered in Spring 2007 only.
** Experimental Group 2 students were asked to recall their initial confidence levels on the posttest survey.

Comparing their work with research for other courses, a less consistent pattern emerges. Control group and lab section students were equally likely (41.2 percent) to find their Analyzing Politics research easier than their research work for other courses. But only 27.4 percent of experimental group one students found the Analyzing Politics research to have been easier, and 37 percent reported it was more difficult than research for other courses (compared to just 8.8 percent of control group students and 23.5 percent of lab section students reporting greater difficulty with Analyzing Politics research; $p < .05$). Thus having one or more library instruction sessions does not consistently lead experimental group students to perceive class research as easier than their work for other courses.

Student confidence levels show a more consistent pattern across our three groups of students. Table 3.3 presents responses to questions about confidence levels at the end of each semester, with some data about initial confidence levels as well. We used a pretest for the first semester of experimental group one students only, and the lab section's end-of-semester survey asked students to recall their initial confidence levels. Hence some caution is warranted in interpreting these results due to shifts in when questions were asked and to whom. Still, the final confidence levels are directly comparable across groups, and Table 3.3 presents trends consistent with the data analyzed earlier.

The first result to note is the high degree of confidence exhibited by all students at the end of each semester. Virtually every student was at least confident in his or her research skills in the control group and experimental group one, and all students in the lab section were confident or very confident. Interestingly, confidence levels were virtually identical among control group and experimental group one students. By contrast, 70 percent of lab section students were very confident in their research abilities, a statistically significant increase ($p < .087$). When we began this assessment project, we hypothesized that students in the first experimental group might have lower levels of confidence at the end of the semester—we hoped in some ways that they would recognize how much more they had to learn about library resources. But this was not the case; students uniformly exited the course confident in their research skills, whether they received library instruction or not. Clearly the lab section students experienced a greater boost in their confidence levels.

The pretest data from experimental groups one and two shows that these students did not enter the class with high confidence in their research skills. Experimental group one students reported higher initial confidence than the lab section students. We suspect that the lower initial confidence levels recalled by lab section students indicate their retrospective recognition of how much they could gain through the additional library instruction sessions, rather than some idiosyncratic lack of initial confidence among this particular set of students.

Narrative Assessment

Student response to the narrative assessment tool assigned at the conclusion of the lab component was overwhelmingly positive. Students were asked to comment on the extent to which they felt their research skills had changed over the course of the semester, ways in which lab content helped them complete research in other courses, and what they still found confusing about the library. Unlike our other assessment tools, this assignment was not anonymous and thus results may be skewed; however, anonymous responses on the course evaluation were similarly positive and raise confidence in the validity of the narrative assessment tool.

By and large, lab section students indicated that, although they had felt somewhat confident in their research skills at the beginning of the semester, the lab component helped them become more skilled at conducting research:

- "I do research more efficiently."
- "[M]y research skills have been refined."
- "This past semester my research abilities and skills have grown substantially."
- "I find research a lot more fun now because I am more familiar with the many paths I can take to attain necessary information."
- "I felt as if I continually learned how to better navigate search engines and databases in order to find articles."
- "I am able to cite sources more easily and accurately."

Students also discussed very specific ways the lab component helped them complete research in other courses. Several students commented that they employed cited reference searches to find related materials, even though conducting a cited reference search was not required for the other course. One student reported that he used some of the advanced features of a database to see how often a certain article had been cited in order to determine if the article was significant to the field. Students also indicated that they felt better equipped to evaluate sources. One student said she now felt much more comfortable approaching a reference librarian for help. None of the students said the lab was not useful for research they conducted in other courses.

Students also offered many candid comments on aspects of the library and research that they still found confusing after taking the lab credit. Perhaps unsurprising to us, given their tricky shelving and classification system, students listed government documents as the aspect that confused them the most.

Some students commented that the layout of the library itself still confused them, and a few students mentioned that interlibrary loan procedures still posed some challenges. We will use these findings to adjust lab component activities in order to provide better exposure to and reinforcement of some of these topics.

We also asked students to identify what they felt was the most useful part of the lab. The cited reference search appeared in a number of narratives, as did the information about where to find statistical data. Several students mentioned that they valued how the lab helped them become more familiar with the library. One student mentioned specifically that the lab component has prepared her to do research in advanced political science classes. Others appreciated exposure to the variety of tools to help them conduct research. One student also singled out the out-of-class assignments: "As much as they sometimes felt like a burden, I believe that the most useful aspects of the lab to me were the out-of-class assignments. These assignments forced me to practice using the different research tools that we had discussed in class on my own."

Analysis of the narrative assessment tool reveals student feedback that is entirely consistent with the other data collected from lab section students. Behavioral and perceptual data all indicate that the weekly lab component enhanced student research skills, altered research behaviors in a positive direction, and gave students more confidence in their ability to conduct research in political science and, significantly, in other courses as well.

Senior Seminar

In the course of developing our assessment model for Analyzing Politics over several semesters, we came to recognize the advantages of expanding our quasi-experimental research design beyond one course and one faculty member/librarian team. The political science department's senior seminar courses afforded an additional opportunity to examine whether the presence of one or more library instruction sessions altered student research behaviors and perceptions. Taught by multiple faculty members in the department, these seminars cover different topics with a common central assignment: preparation of a 25- to 30-page research paper (the senior thesis) on a topic of the student's choice. Individual faculty members are responsible for determining how they work with students toward successful completion of senior theses. One consequence is that the number of scheduled library instruction sessions differs across the seminars—one faculty member in the study scheduled zero sessions, two faculty scheduled one session each, and as noted previously one faculty member scheduled five sessions for both of her U.S. Interest Groups seminar sections taught during the time period we studied. We took advantage of this additional natural experiment opportunity by adding questions about student research behaviors and perceptions to the department's senior seminar assessment survey, which was introduced in fall 2007 and administered each semester thereafter through the time frame of our study. This research design allows us to conduct a preliminary examination of the difference a single library instruction session makes versus no session, and what difference more than one session makes versus just one session.

Senior seminar students come to this capstone course with more experience than their Analyzing Politics counterparts: generally senior students have accumulated twice the number of credits, have likely sat through many more library instruction sessions in these courses, and are likely to have more experience conducting college-level research and writing longer, more in-depth research papers. In addition, the set of senior seminars examined here (three seminars from the 2007–2008 academic year and two seminars from fall 2008) includes a majority of the students from the control group section of Analyzing Politics two years prior, plus many students who were part of experimental group one (these students were not clustered in one seminar). We did not ask students to identify whether they had participated in previous library instruction sessions for Analyzing Politics or other courses; however, we knew that overall, this set of senior seminar students would have received far more prior exposure to library instruction than seminar students in previous years (although some students would have received no exposure in Analyzing Politics).

As a consequence, we hypothesized that we would find less variation across the three student groups assessed: the seminar control group (no library sessions), seminar experimental group one (one session), and seminar experimental group two (five sessions). Based on analysis of the Analyzing Politics data, however, we also hypothesized that seminar experimental group two would utilize a greater variety of library resources and would interact more with reference librarians. We also expected seminar experimental group two to exhibit higher levels of confidence in their research skills.

Tables 3.4 and 3.5 present data collected from senior seminar students, divided into our three groups for analysis. Most of these seminars are quite small and due to different methods of distributing the seminar assessment survey, not all seminar students responded; thus a total of 54 students completed surveys. Significance tests are unlikely to reveal statistically significant differences for this sample size, but again we note significant (and close to significant) findings where applicable.

As expected, Tables 3.4 and 3.5 show less variation across seminar groups on most indicators of behavior and perception, but what variations we do find both fit with expectations about enhancing student research skills through

Table 3.4. Research Behavior, Senior Seminar Students			
	Control Group	Experimental Group 1	Experimental Group 2
Resources used for thesis research			
Reference books	60.0	37.5	56.5
Library catalog	93.3	81.3	87.0
Interlibrary loan: books	53.3	50.0	65.2
Interlibrary loan: articles	13.3	25.0	39.1
Online databases	100.0	93.8	95.7
Course resource page on library Web site	26.7	75.0	43.5
Reference librarian (outside class time)	60.0	62.5	47.8
Other library resources (gov. docs)	13.3	6.3	26.1
Borrowed resources from professor	0.0	31.3	26.1
Mean total library resources used	4.20	4.31	4.61
Mean total resources used	4.20	4.63	4.87
Used 4 or more library resources	66.7	86.7	87.0
Used 6 or more library resources	13.3	31.3	30.4
Number of students	15	16	23

Note: Values are percentages unless otherwise indicated. Control group students received zero library instruction sessions; experimental group one students received one session; experimental group two students received five sessions.

library instruction, and reveal a pattern that reinforces what we observed among Analyzing Politics students.

Examining research behavior, we asked if students used any of nine different resources in conducting their thesis research. Eight of these nine were library-based resources (the ninth was resources borrowed from the seminar professor). On several indicators, students with one or more library sessions were more likely to utilize a particular resource. The course resource pages prepared by library faculty were utilized far more often by the two experimental groups ($p < .022$) compared to the no-library-session control group students. Use of interlibrary loan (ILL) to obtain articles was also much more common among the experimental groups ($p < .212$), with experimental group two students the most likely to request articles via ILL (39.1 percent), far more than experimental group one (25 percent) and the control group (13.3 percent). By contrast, experimental group two students were only slightly more likely to request books via ILL compared to the control and first experimental groups.

Table 3.4 also shows modest differences in likelihood of consulting a reference librarian. Sixty percent of control group students did so, but so did 62.5 percent of students in experimental group one, whereas the lowest percentage is actually found among experimental group two (47.8 percent). Although not close to statistical significance, this result is interesting: having access to a reference librarian in class more often seems to lead students to seek out reference librarians less often outside of class, the opposite of what we found among Analyzing Politics students.

In terms of total library resources used, with Analyzing Politics students we found the key differences between the control group and both experimental groups—experiencing multiple library instruction sessions (whether a few or many) boosted students' use of library resources. Control group students used an average of 4.2 library resources for their research. In comparison, experimental group one students (one library session) were marginally higher at 4.31 but experimental group two students were notably higher in mean total resources used (4.61). This would appear to indict the single-session model as ineffective, but even a single session can make a difference: two-thirds of control group students used four or more library resources, whereas 87 percent of students in both experimental groups used four or more resources. The pattern was replicated for students using six or more resources: 13 percent in the control group and just over 30 percent for both experimental groups. Experimental group two included a few more heavy consumers of library resources (using seven or all eight resources included on the assessment), which drove the mean value up, but clearly having even one library instruction session led to broader use of library resources. Among control group students, the four most common resources used are the most obvious ones any senior student would know about: books found via the library catalog, reference books, online databases such as JSTOR, and ILL book requests. Senior seminar students exposed to one or more library sessions utilized more and a greater variety of resources.

Table 3.5 examines student perceptions of their own research skills and confidence levels. We found no statistically significant differences across the groups, but some variations were nonetheless present. Across all three groups, about 87 percent believed their research skills improved after completing the seminar, despite some modest differences about how strong research skills were to begin with (experimental group two students recalled their starting points as more positive overall). Similarly, start-of-semester recalled confidence levels differed slightly across the groups, but the differences faded over time. End-of-semester confidence levels were marginally higher among both experimental

Table 3.5. Perceptions of Research Skills, Senior Seminar Students			
	Control Group	Experimental Group 1	Experimental Group 2
Rating of research skills, beginning of semester (recalled)			
Very strong	13.3	6.3	13.0
Strong, more than adequate to complete thesis	46.7	37.5	47.8
Good enough, adequate	26.7	37.5	30.4
Fair, not quite adequate	13.3	18.8	8.7
Poor, not adequate	0.0	0.0	0.0
Perceived change in research skills			
Greatly improved	26.7	12.5	26.1
Improved	60.0	75.0	60.9
Remained the same	13.3	12.5	13.0
Worse or much worse	0.0	0.0	0.0
Confidence in research skills, beginning of semester (recalled)			
Very confident	6.7	12.5	8.7
Confident	53.3	56.3	65.2
Hard to say	33.3	6.3	13.0
Not very confident	6.7	18.8	13.0
Not at all confident	0.0	6.3	0.0
Confidence in research skills, end of semester			
Very confident	26.7	56.3	43.5
Confident	60.0	37.5	52.2
Hard to say	6.7	6.3	0.0
Not very confident	6.7	0.0	4.3
Not at all confident	0.0	0.0	0.0
Evaluation of library sessions			
Very helpful	—	13.3	26.1
Helpful	—	46.7	43.5
Okay	—	33.3	26.1
Not very helpful	—	0.0	4.3
Not at all helpful	—	6.7	0.0
Number of students	15	16	23

Note: Values are percentages unless otherwise indicated. Control group students received zero library instruction sessions; experimental group one students received one session; experimental group two students received five sessions.

groups (about 95 percent confident or very confident) compared to the control group (86.7 percent confident or very confident), although experimental group two students were 13 percentage points less likely than experimental one students to be very confident.

Finally, Table 3.5 reports on perceptions of the library session(s) by the experimental group students. Experimental group two students were somewhat more positive: twice as likely to find their multiple sessions very helpful and somewhat more likely to rate the sessions at least helpful. Only one student in each experimental group found the session to be not very helpful or not at all helpful (and one of these students wrote on the survey "I have had so many library sessions already").

EVALUATING AND REFINING ASSESSMENT STRATEGIES

Throughout the two-year time frame we have been examining, our assessment tools have continued to evolve along with our implementation of new pedagogical approaches and our ongoing analysis of data. Indeed, all of the key differences between the Analyzing Politics control group and experimental group one appeared after the first semester of the experiment, an important validation of our general approach that served to propel us forward on multiple fronts. Thus our core research interests shifted from the basic question all assessment projects ask—is there a measurable change in student learning?—to a broader and richer set of queries: can we replicate the measurable change in student learning, in this course and in other courses taught by other faculty and/or other librarians? Are we gathering the best data with which to assess student learning (and if not, what else should we do)? How can we expand on demonstrably effective pedagogical strategies in ways that continue to meet the needs of both the political science department and the library faculty?

For the Analyzing Politics course, our assessment of the assessment has clearly been (and will remain) a continuous process. The basic posttest survey instrument has changed incrementally, and the creation of the weekly lab component allowed us to collect a greater quantity of detailed data from students. Having reviewed our work to date in preparing this chapter, we know that one aspect of the assessment process to strengthen centers on the collection of data at the start of each semester. The limited pretest data and recalled attitudes we have presented here strongly suggest that we could and should do more to understand precisely what skills, experiences, and attitudes students bring into the course. We would then reexamine and redesign end-of-semester assessment tools as necessary, in order to track students from start to finish. This redesign would likely include an identification system for individual students, so that source usage in papers, pretest and posttest responses can be analyzed at the individual level.

We will also investigate how the content of specific library instruction sessions impact information literacy outcomes. To date, our assessment plan has not examined the connection between individual class sessions and student learning. For example, do classroom exercises centered on government documents enhance students' abilities to find and use government documents? Such assessment outcomes would also help us further refine student learning objectives in the course.

One additional aspect to investigate is the role of the political science faculty member. A different instructor now alternates with C. Gilbert in teaching Analyzing Politics. Thus we can assess how different faculty-librarian collaborative teams affect student learning outcomes.

One obvious way to extend analysis of senior seminar students' research skills is to examine the sources used in the finished products (the department maintains a complete archive of senior theses) to see how student reports of their research behaviors translate into the actual work they submitted. At the time of this writing, we have not yet conducted citation analysis of senior seminar papers. But we would expect to find, consistent with the data analyzed in this section, that all seminar students would utilize a high percentage of high quality sources, and that students in the two experimental groups would have a marginally higher percentage of high quality sources, as well as using more sources overall. Paralleling anticipated additions to the Analyzing Politics assessment tools, we also see advantages to adding a pretest instrument, asking seminar students about their Analyzing Politics experience and their exposure to library instruction in other courses. For at least the next two academic years, such pretest data would allow us to compare the end-of-semester student responses and completed theses of students who had the lab component experience and students who did not, thus adding a longitudinal component to our assessment of student learning across the political science major.

Finally, based on the success to date in enhancing student learning in these two courses, library and political science faculty continue to discuss ways of incorporating information literacy skills into introductory political science courses (the vast majority of Gustavus students take only one such course) and the advanced courses taken (primarily by majors) between the sophomore and senior years. A comprehensive approach to information literacy across the department curriculum would of course necessitate the use of assessment tools within courses (the department's research-oriented learning objectives address all students, not just majors) and an effective means of longitudinal analysis to track major students.

CONCLUSION

Our assessment findings to date confirm that providing students with an increase in formal library interactions, such as multiple instruction sessions, positively impacts their information literacy skills. We see this most dramatically in the Analyzing Politics course; students in the 12-week lab section exhibited much higher confidence levels, used more sources and a much higher percentage of high quality sources in their papers, and were far more likely to seek out assistance from reference librarians. Although there is less variation across senior seminar groups, having at least one library instruction session led to a broader use of library resources and slightly higher confidence levels. Our findings clearly indicate that exposing students to the library—especially doing so early in their college careers and in sessions that are deeply embedded within the overall goals of a course—makes a positive difference with respect to student learning. We will continue to share assessment data with library faculty and the political science department to continue to shape and expand the information literacy component. We will also use the data to advocate for similar programs in other departments.

Throughout our work, we have learned several lessons that will be useful to faculty considering collaboration between librarians and academic departments, and faculty seeking to understand how to integrate information literacy into academic programs. First, integrating library sessions with course content is essential. Students respond more positively and learn more when the collaborating faculty mutually reinforce course goals, and when information literacy course material is tangibly connected to other course material and graded assignments. Analyzing Politics students in both experimental groups were told repeatedly that library sessions were designed specifically to help them complete research projects for the course, an approach that was reinforced even more with experimental group two (lab section). Results from the narrative assessment demonstrate that students were aware of and valued the connections.

Second, partnerships between library and academic department faculty must go beyond separate development of course objectives and assignments. Students respond and learn more when all course materials and activities interrelate. In practice this means the faculty involved should prepare syllabi and plan class sessions and assessment instruments jointly. Achieving this integration probably took more time than any of the assessment strategies we implemented here but it was time well spent, as the assessment data demonstrate. We made sure that key sets of resources (e.g., online databases) and particular skills (e.g., conducting a cited reference search) were discussed in lab, with graded assignments to reinforce and extend student learning, before such resources and skills were to be used to complete course assignments. We sought to maximize the situations in which course topics and lab topics overlapped with one another, and we adopted the same pedagogical strategies in both types of classes—both instructors used active learning techniques and kept formal presentations to a minimum (and never lectured for a full class period).[4]

Finally, assessment of information literacy skills among undergraduate college students must be as varied as the skills themselves. Instructors will receive valuable information through indicators of student perceptions about their research skills, student-reported measures of time spent on assignments and types of information resources accessed, and analysis of student papers. This last component is a critical "reality check" on perceptual data and self-reported research practices—although students throughout our study period report high levels of confidence in their own research skills, our data also show that the quality of sources used in student papers has improved with the addition of more sustained classroom and library activities centered on information literacy.

NOTES

1. General information about the college was adapted from the following: http://gustavus .edu/news/GAfacts.cfm (accessed January 15, 2009).
2. Our definition of "high quality" is necessarily broad because the types of research questions posed by students cover a broad range of topics. Focusing only on peer-reviewed journals as high quality would underreport the success of a student who used leading newspapers or periodicals to examine a contemporary topic. We also took context into account when assessing whether a source was high quality; for example, an annotated bibliography on the 1992 U.S. presidential election could include *Washington Post* articles published the day after the election, but such "instant analysis" pieces would be far less useful (and thus not deemed high quality) compared to the large number of academic journal articles and books that have been published about the 1992 electoral outcome and its causes.
3. We analyzed assessment survey data separately from annotated bibliography source usage data. Some students completed surveys but did not submit completed annotated bibliography papers; a small number turned in papers but were not present to complete the survey. Thus the survey data (Tables 3.1 and 3.3) include 124 students and Table 3.2 figures are based on 123 students.
4. The existence of the weekly lab in fact helped solve an ongoing issue with the course. Previously students frequently told C. Gilbert they had no ideas about what topic to pursue for their annotated bibliography; in contrast, the lab students were asked virtually every week by J. Gilbert to think of a topic as they worked on specific library resources and skills, and when the annotated bibliography came around no student found himself/herself bereft of a topic.

REFERENCES

Association of College and Research Libraries (ACRL). 2000. "Information Literacy Competency Standards for Higher Education." American Library Association. Available: www.ala.org/ala/mgrps/divs/acrl/standards/informationliteracycompetency.cfm (accessed September 30, 2009).

Bowden, Teresa S., and Angela DiBenedetto. 2001. "Information Literacy in a Biology Laboratory Session: An Example of Librarian-Faculty Collaboration." *Research Strategies* 18, no. 2 (April): 143–149.

Emmons, Mark, and Wanda Martin. 2002. "Engaging Conversation: Evaluating the Contribution of Library Instruction to the Quality of Student Research." *College & Research Libraries* 63, no. 6 (November): 545–560.

Gandhi, Smiti. 2004. "Faculty-Librarian Collaboration to Assess the Effectiveness of a Five-Session Library Instruction Model." *Community + Junior College Libraries* 12, no. 4: 15–45.

Goebel, Nancy, Paul Neff, and Angie Mandeville. 2007. "Assessment within the Augustana Model of Undergraduate Discipline-Specific Information Literacy Credit Courses." *Public Services Quarterly* 3, no. 1/2: 165–189.

Grafstein, Ann. 2002. "A Discipline-Based Approach to Information Literacy." *The Journal of Academic Librarianship* 28, no. 4: 197–204.

Hutchins, Elizabeth O. 2003. "Assessing Student Learning Outcomes in Political Science Classes." In *Assessing Student Learning Outcomes for Information Literacy Instruction in Academic Institutions* (pp. 172–184), edited by Elizabeth Fuseler Avery. Chicago: Association for College and Research Libraries.

Knight-Davis, Stacey, and Jan S. Sung. 2008. "Analysis of Citations in Undergraduate Papers." *College & Research Libraries* 69, no. 5 (September): 447–458.

Law and Political Science Section (LPSS). 2008. *Political Science Research Competency Guidelines*. Association of College and Research Libraries. American Library Association. Available: www.ala.org/ala/mgrps/divs/acrl/standards/PoliSciGuide.pdf (accessed September 30, 2009).

Marfleet, B. Gregory, and Brian Dille. 2005. "Information Literacy and the Undergraduate Research Methods Curriculum." *Journal of Political Science Education* 2, no. 1: 175–190.

Mill, David H. 2008. "Undergraduate Information Resource Choices." *College & Research Libraries* 69, no. 4 (July): 342–355.

Norelli, Barbara P. 2006. "Basic Training: Putting Undergraduate Government Students through the Paces." In *Teaching Information Literacy Skills to Social Sciences Students and Practitioners: A Casebook of Applications* (pp. 198–209), edited by Douglas Cook and Natasha Cooper. Chicago: Association of College and Research Libraries.

Stevens, Christy R., and Patricia J. Campbell. 2007. "The Politics of Information Literacy: Integrating Information Literacy into the Political Science Curriculum." In *Information Literacy Collaborations That Work* (pp. 123–146), edited by Trudi E. Jacobson and Thomas P. Mackey. New York: Neal-Shuman Publishers.

Stevens, Christy R., and Patricia J. Campbell. 2008. "Collaborating with Librarians to Develop Lower Division Political Science Students' Information Literacy Competencies." *Journal of Political Science Education* 4, no. 2: 225–252.

Thornton, Stephen. 2008. "Pedagogy, Politics and Information Literacy." *Politics* 28, no. 1: 50–56.

Wang, Rui. 2006. "The Lasting Impact of a Library Credit Course." *portal: Libraries and the Academy* 6, no. 1 (January): 79–92.

Williams, Michelle Hale, and Jocelyn Jones Evans. "Factors in Information Literacy Education." *Journal of Political Science Education* 4, no.1: 116–130.

Zoellner, Kate, Sue Samson, and Samantha Hines. 2008. "Continuing Assessment of Library Instruction to Undergraduates: A General Education Course Survey Research Project." *College & Research Libraries* 69, no.4 (July): 370–383.

Appendix 3.1. Assessment Instruments

Analyzing Politics End-of-Semester Student Survey

1. In completing the literature review and annotated bibliography paper I asked questions and/or received assistance from (*check all that apply*): [course professor; reference librarian; another faculty member; another student in this class; another student not in this class; other (specify)]

2. Where did you *begin* your search for sources on your annotated bibliography paper? (select one) [search engine (e.g., Google); Gustavus library Web site; online database (e.g., JSTOR); course Web site; discussion/e-mail with course professor; discussion with a reference librarian; other (specify)]

3. Which of these resources did you use *at any point* in completing your literature review or annotated bibliography papers? (*check all that apply*) [search engine (e.g., Google); Gustavus library Web site; online database (e.g., JSTOR); course Web site; discussion/e-mail with course professor; discussion with a reference librarian; other (specify)]

4. How much time (approximate number of hours) did you spend searching for sources for your annotated bibliography paper?

5. Compared to the literature review paper, for my annotated bibliography paper I [spent much more time finding sources; a little more time; about the same amount of time; a little less time; much less time].

6. Compared to the literature review paper, finding sources for my annotated bibliography paper was [much easier; somewhat easier; about the same; somewhat more difficult; much more difficult].

7A. Compared to research assignments I have done *for other courses*, finding sources for my lit reviews and annotated bibliography paper was [much easier; somewhat easier; about the same; somewhat more difficult; much more difficult].

7B. Are there any specific reasons why you answered this way?

8. Which of these comes closest to your own rating of your research skills at the *beginning* of this semester? [very strong; strong; good; fair; poor]

9. After completing this course, how have your research skills changed? [greatly improved; improved; remained the same; become worse; much worse]

10. Rate your confidence in your ability to find appropriate sources for research papers and projects at the *start of the semester* and *today*. [*for both ratings*: very confident; confident; hard to say/don't know; not very confident; not at all confident]

11. Is there anything else that stands out in your mind as you think about the process of writing papers for this class?

Senior Seminar End-of-Semester Student Survey

Only questions related to information literacy project are included here (questions 1–5 and 19).

1. Rate your research skills at the beginning of the semester, in terms of whether they were adequate (or better, or less than adequate) to complete the thesis assignment. [very strong; strong, more than adequate; good enough, adequate; fair, not quite adequate; poor, not adequate to complete thesis]

(Continued)

Appendix 3.1. Assessment Instruments *(Continued)*

Senior Seminar End-of-Semester Student Survey *(Continued)*

2. After completing this seminar, how have your research skills changed? [greatly improved; improved; remained the same; worse; much worse]

3. At the beginning of the seminar, in general how confident were you in your ability to find appropriate sources for research papers and projects? [very confident; confident; hard to say; not very confident; not at all confident]

4. Today, in general how confident are you in your ability to find appropriate sources for research papers and projects? [very confident; confident; hard to say; not very confident; not at all confident]

5. How helpful were the library session(s) in this seminar for doing your thesis research? [very helpful; helpful; ok; not very helpful; not at all helpful]

19. Which of these library and other resources did you use during your thesis research? Check *ALL that apply.* [reference books; MnPALS (library catalog to search for books); interlibrary loan for books; interlibrary loan for articles; online databases (e.g., JSTOR) for articles, and specify databases you remember using; course resource page on the library Web site; reference librarian (not including time spent in class); borrowed resource(s) from the professor; other (specify)]

Chapter 4

Assessing Undergraduate Information Literacy Skills:

How Collaborative Curriculum Interventions Promote Active and Independent Learning

Amanda A. Harrison and Angela Newton

INTRODUCTION

It has been 50 years since The University of Leeds received its first computer, Pegasus. In 1958, Pegasus was to be used to teach a select group of research students the principles and practice of programming, and although this machine had brothers and sisters at five other UK universities, they could not in any contemporary sense be "networked." The past ten years have seen an unprecedented expansion in personal computing power, which has heralded major changes in the way we all publish and access information.

In 2009, The University of Leeds, like so many others, is awash with personal computers and handheld devices joined together by remarkable connectivity. A new wave of portable technology for the twenty-first century, so brilliant in its complexity, and astonishing in its usability is making access to information more flexible and instantaneous than ever before. "Finding out" has never been easier since Google, launched in 1998, made Web searching efficient, fast, and simple with its revolutionary PageRank algorithm. The implications for student learning in this tumultuous information environment have been huge. Once fettered to the reference shelf in search of elusive facts and figures, it is believed that contemporary undergraduates do not try their patience flicking through tables of contents and index lists, but rather reach for the small white box in their Google toolbar. In a matter of microseconds they are confident that the fact will be found, the query satisfied, another question answered.

LITERATURE REVIEW

Given the immense quantities of information now available online, it is unsurprising that Internet users have turned en masse to Google, which has become a trusted brand to help users negotiate this virtual hypermarket of information (Superbrands, 2008). A recent research project examining human information behavior (HIB), described the almost infinite choices now available to digital information consumers:

> The Web is really all about choice and the excitement of making choices within information seeking, and therefore, the information behaviors must surely reflect that. The problem has moved from having to put up with something that was not quite perfect or relevant, to having to choose from an Aladdin's cave of shifting information sources. (Nicholas et al., 2006: 206)

Patricia Senn Breivik highlights a commonly voiced concern that the vast quantities of information available online may not provide the optimum environment for learning, and that information literacy is crucial in making sense of this in an age of multimedia:

> Information literacy is a survival skill in the information age. Instead of drowning in the abundance of information that floods their lives, information-literate individuals know how to find, evaluate, and use information effectively to solve a particular problem or make a decision, whether the information they select comes from a computer, a book, a government agency, a video, or any of a number of other possible resources. (Breivik and Gee, 2006: 29)

Information professionals and academic staff have found themselves discussing several questions in parallel with this information technology (IT) revolution, including whether this picture of the Googling student is really true. What impact might this have on student learning? Does being IT literate equate to information literacy? How information literate are our undergraduates? And are those skills adequate for students' academic work?

Information literacy has become such an important concept to information professionals and academics around the world that multiple models have been developed in an attempt to pin down our collective understanding of the concept. A close inspection of the predominant United Kingdom (UK) and United States of America models reveals a special relationship between the two, with a significant shared vocabulary and set of values. In the UK, the prevalent model used across higher education is the Society of College, National and University Libraries (SCONUL) Seven Pillars, launched in 1999. The position paper in which the model was introduced went further than simply proposing a set of standards, and recommended a more rigorous and proactive approach to information literacy in UK higher education: "It is proposed that the development of the idea of 'information literacy' requires a collaborative and integrated approach to curriculum design and delivery based on close co-operation between academic, library and staff development colleagues" (Society of College, National and University Libraries, 2007).

This call to arms was followed by the launch in 2001 of the highly influential Big Blue project, surveying the current state of information skills teaching in higher and post-16 education in the UK. An early report from this project revealed that 69 percent of respondents to their survey on the state of information skills teaching in higher education and post-16 institutions in the UK, had no form of assessment of these skills in place (Mackenzie, 2001). Consequently, one of the outcomes of the Big Blue project was a series of recommendations including: "That assessments be carried out to examine the baseline skills of students and how these improve over time, following information skills training and the application of these skills to their academic work" (Mackenzie et al., 2002).

Although information literacy initiatives the UK are very often instigated by librarians, the concept as represented by the SCONUL Seven Pillars model does not stand apart from the standards governing curriculum design and development. The Quality Assurance Agency for Higher Education sets out Subject Benchmark Statements against which UK universities are periodically audited. Although these statements do not directly refer to information literacy, the principles as set out in the SCONUL Seven Pillars model are definitely in evidence throughout. The importance of developing skills in information handling, retrieval, and synthesis for example, are all included in a typical Subject Benchmark Statement (Quality Assurance Agency, 2007).

The need for information literacy skills among undergraduate students is therefore in no doubt. Taking forward the recommendations of the Big Blue project, this chapter demonstrates the significant benefits of gaining a detailed understanding of undergraduate skills through a formative multiple-choice-based assessment. It also emphasizes the power of collaborative academic practice informed by both library and academic staff.

INFORMATION LITERACY STRATEGY AT THE UNIVERSITY OF LEEDS

The University of Leeds is a member of the Russell Group of Universities, and is one of the UK's top 20 research intensive universities. Leeds is the UK's second largest university with 30,500 students from more than 130 countries, offering 700 undergraduate and 470 postgraduate courses. The university has a reputation for excellent teaching, as evidenced by the fact that it has more National Teaching Fellows than any other university in England or Northern Ireland. The research-led teaching provided at the university integrates contemporary research findings with learning and teaching activities, and requires students to engage with research literature, thus promoting active and independent learning among undergraduates.

Information literacy has been promoted at the university over a number of years, and an institution-wide Information Literacy Strategy was formally discussed and accepted through the Learning and Teaching Board in the academic year 2003–2004. Based on the SCONUL Seven Pillars model, the strategy provided a firm basis on which information literacy could be discussed by librarians with academic departments, with particular reference to undergraduate students (Leeds University Library, 2003).

As a research intensive university, Leeds integrates current research and scholarship into undergraduate degree programs, creating a distinctive and unique study experience. Undergraduate students are actively encouraged to work autonomously, taking the initiative for aspects of their learning, for example, by undertaking an independent research project in their final year of study. Problem solving, applying research methods and the questioning of received wisdom are all attributes that are fostered by the research-led teaching environment. Information literacy skills are integral to the armory of skills required by undergraduates to complete their academic work effectively, and the acceptance of the Information Literacy Strategy at The University of Leeds was a reflection of this fact.

Since its implementation, the strategy has facilitated wide-ranging and ongoing discussions between librarians and academic staff, and it now forms the basis for current and future developments in information literacy teaching at the university.

Psychology: A Multidisciplinary Science

The Institute of Psychological Sciences (IPS) is a member of the Faculty of Medicine and Health in The University of Leeds. It offers a three-year, British Psychological Society accredited, bachelor of science degree program which has, at its core, extensive training in research methodology and data analysis. The undergraduate degree program aims to develop active and independent learners, prepared to enter the workforce in a diverse range of careers.

Psychology as an academic discipline does not easily fit into traditional faculty systems due to its multidisciplinary approach to studying the mind and behavior. It offers explanations from many different perspectives, bridging the gaps between the biological sciences, health sciences, and social sciences. Students are constantly faced with the nature/nurture debate in their endeavors to understand both normal and abnormal behavior. They constantly need to evaluate theories, and in doing so they must find and assess an extensive array of information from a diverse variety of sources. This is highlighted by the need for students to provide wide-ranging and appropriate evidential support for claims made, and to show extensive and critical knowledge of relevant theory in order to achieve high grades at Leeds. It is not surprising, therefore, that the Quality Assurance Agency's Subject Benchmark Statement for academic standards in psychology includes aspects of information literacy (Quality Assurance Agency, 2007).

In response to both the national and local agenda, Leeds University Library and the IPS devised and introduced a new program of information literacy teaching for psychology undergraduate students, in an attempt to enhance independent student engagement with knowledge and research. The program consisted of three compulsory sessions and one optional session, integrated into the existing undergraduate curriculum, and aimed to provide timely and progressive teaching (see Table 4.1).

Table 4.1. The Institute of Psychological Sciences Information Literacy Undergraduate Teaching Program

Teaching Session	Time	Topic
1 (compulsory)	Year 1, semester 1, week 1	• recognizing an information need • identifying ways to fill an information need (library catalog) • locating and accessing information (books)
2 (compulsory)	Year 1, semester 2, week 1	• identifying ways to fill an information need (online resources) • locating and accessing information (online resources) • organizing and applying information (referencing and plagiarism) • (referencing and plagiarism) • comparing and evaluating information from different sources (peer review)
3 (compulsory)	Year 2, semester 1, week 2	• constructing a search strategy • locating and accessing information • bibliographic databases • comparing and evaluating information from different sources
4 (optional)	Year 3, semester 1, week 4	• literature searching refresher

STRENGTH THROUGH DIVERSITY:
AN ACADEMIC-LIBRARIAN PARTNERSHIP

Higher education values collaboration and communication extremely highly, and the collaborative relationships that librarians seek to propagate above all others are those with academic staff. Making and maintaining meaningful and mutually useful relationships between these two groups of university staff is of considerable importance, but it has in the past been described by librarians in fairly difficult terms. Librarians have typically bemoaned their difficulties in contacting academics, or the perceived scepticism of academic staff for information literacy and their need to "seduce" them into allowing information literacy related activities to be included in the curriculum (Julien and Given, 2002; Watts, 2002). Academic staff, however, have remained rather quiet on this topic, and joint publications with librarians have remained a relative rarity.

So much has been written by librarians on the "problems" that they have in their relationships with academic staff, that one might reasonably assume that there are so few examples of good practice as to be negligible. The reality between these unhelpful stereotypes, however, is that positive working relationships between the two parties exist throughout universities, and where they exist, good academic practice blooms.

At The University of Leeds, the acceptance of the Information Literacy Strategy provided an excellent platform for librarians and academic staff to discuss shared areas of interest and concern in learning and teaching. Providing a context for these discussions helped to encourage a collective reflection about the information literacy skills that academic staff expected students to use to successfully complete their academic work. The logical conclusion of these discussions was to consider what practical support students needed to develop these skills effectively. The level of detail involved in these discussions matched the good practice recommended by Secker, Boden, and Price (2007), who stressed the importance of a number of factors when incorporating information literacy into the undergraduate curriculum: engaging with students at a time when they will use the skills; putting information literacy activities into the context of their subject; encouraging student support sessions to be compulsory; and getting feedback and evaluating support sessions (Secker, Boden, and Price, 2007).

When the discussions described previously took place between Leeds University Library and the IPS, a number of issues arose. Although the academic staff in the institute recognized the importance of information literacy skills to the performance of their undergraduate students, the support for the development of these skills was minimal and possibly inconsistently provided. Students were expected to write essays in their first year of study and provide bibliographies at the end of this piece of coursework. However, feedback about the essays was provided by the student's tutor, one of approximately 30 staff members, who focused on the important issues as they perceived them individually. Thus the different priorities of individual tutors contributed to the lack of consistency in the development of student information literacy skills. In the second- and third-year curricula a great deal of emphasis was placed on developing student research skills with extensive timetabled support for research methodology, statistics, and report writing. In contrast, the equally important information literacy skills needed to access and use the research literature were not explicitly present in the curriculum.

In 2003 it was recognized that in order for students to meet the academic demands of their course, the IPS needed to provide explicit and consistent information literacy teaching integrated into the curriculum in a timely manner. This was the start of a long-term collaboration between the university library and the IPS. Given the complexities of the issues involved in developing information literacy provision for these students, the expertise of both parties was invaluable.

The staff of the IPS provided an indispensable context for information literacy as it relates to the field of psychology, as well as knowledge of the academic demands faced by students during this degree program. Library staff provided an in-depth knowledge and understanding of the academic information environment, and information literacy in numerous contexts, across the campus, nationally, and internationally. Together, academic and library staff therefore provided a complementary knowledge base from which to design the new information literacy teaching (see Table 4.1). Although curriculum interventions were designed, both parties recognized that without an understanding of the existing information literacy skills of their undergraduates, the introduction of additional teaching was at best a well-meaning guessing game.

In the academic year 2004–2005, a collaboratively designed, context-sensitive, multiple-choice-based assessment was developed to assess the information literacy skills of psychology students. By working together on the design of the assessment tool, and using the results to create new information literacy support for the students, the library and the IPS have developed a valuable working relationship that has provided further opportunities for collaborations with other universities and invitations to share this good practice with colleagues throughout the country.

The Assessment Tool

The assessment tool is based on six of the SCONUL seven pillars of information literacy: recognizing the need for information; identifying the ways to fill this information need; constructing a search strategy; locating and accessing information; comparing and evaluating information; and, organizing and applying information (Society of College, National and University Libraries, 2007). These skills have been identified as key to the performance of undergraduate students in The University of Leeds Information Literacy Strategy, which identifies the seventh pillar—the ability to synthesize and build upon existing information, contributing to the creation of new knowledge—as a skill primarily used by research students and academic staff (Leeds University Library, 2003).

The assessment tool was designed to formatively assess student information literacy skills, with the objective of providing students, librarians, and academic staff with knowledge of the skills possessed by students at the start of each academic year. The data it provided was used to inform the development of an evidence-based information literacy curriculum redesign and thus ultimately, to promote active and independent learning in undergraduate students by enhancing their ability to engage with knowledge and research. To achieve these objectives the assessment tool was designed to provide data about:

1. the progressive development of student information literacy skills throughout the degree program, and
2. the specific strengths and weaknesses of student skills in each skill area.

The assessment consists of 24 multiple-choice questions, each assessing a component of one of the aforementioned six information literacy skills. It is recognized that these skills are not mutually exclusive, leading to the need for interpretation of some questions prior to assigning them to a particular skill. Table 4.2 identifies the information literacy knowledge and abilities assessed in each of the six areas.

To understand the progressive development of student information literacy skills throughout the degree program, the same assessment tool was used to assess students in each of the three years of study. The questions therefore address a range of issues within each of the six areas, some of which are relatively advanced skills, and are not expected to be used by students until their final year when they embark upon their independent research project.

Completion of the assessment provides the following data:

1. *The total percentage of correctly answered questions by each student across all skill areas.* When all three years of students are tested, analysis of this data identifies whether students are developing information literacy skills during their progression through the degree program.
2. *The percentage of correctly answered questions in each skill area by each student.* Analysis of this data identifies the specific strengths and weaknesses of the skills possessed by each cohort of students. Data from first-year

Table 4.2. The Assessment Tool: Specific Knowledge Assessed in Each Skill Area	
Pillars of Information Literacy	Specific Skills Assessed
(1) Recognizing an information need	• Ability to identify existing knowledge framework • Ability to define or modify the information need to achieve manageable focus • Exploring general information sources to increase familiarity with a topic
(2) Identifying ways to fill an information need	• Ability to select an appropriate search tool • Ability to select sources of information with the "best fit" for the task • Review article use
(3) Constructing a search strategy	• Keyword selection • Use of Boolean operators (OR, AND) • Use of truncation • Use of parenthesis
(4) Locating and accessing information	• Ability to implement the search strategy in an appropriate information retrieval system • Ability to identify types of information from references • Knowledge of bibliographies as a source of other related information
(5) Comparing and evaluating information	• Differentiating the quality of information provided in peer reviewed journal articles and Internet-based information • Using abstracts to evaluate whether journal articles fill the information need • Knowledge of the peer review process
(6) Organizing and applying information	• Ability to cite references • Understanding of plagiarism issues • Ability to construct a bibliography • Understanding of copyright issues

students helps to identify the specific skills already developed by incoming undergraduates, determining at what level teaching should begin. Data from second- and third-year students assists in identifying the specific skills areas in which improvements have been achieved, and therefore which aspects of the current program have been successful and which have failed.

3. *The most commonly chosen incorrect answer, for each question, by each cohort of students.* Inspection of this data identifies the common mistakes made by students, and therefore informs curriculum redesign of the teaching provided.

REFLECTING ON THE ASSESSMENT TOOL: RELIABILITY AND SENSITIVITY

Reliability

The assessment tool has now been used for several years, and data has been collected from The University of Leeds Psychology undergraduates throughout their three years of study. An appraisal of the reliability of the assessment tool was conducted to ensure that when groups of similar students are tested at different times, the data remains consistent. To achieve this appraisal, data from two successive cohorts of first-year, second-year, and third-year students were analyzed. Importantly, during the two years of data collection, the academic entrance requirements for the degree program and the information literacy teaching provided to students both remained constant. It was therefore anticipated that the two successive cohorts of students in each year of the degree program would possess similar information literacy skills.

Analysis of the total percentage of correctly answered questions from the two successive cohorts of first- , second- , and third-year students revealed no significant differences between them ($t = 0.111$, $df = 295$, $p > 0.05$; $t = -0.126$, $df = 294$, $p > 0.05$; $t = -0.488$, $df = 254$, $p > 0.05$, respectively) as demonstrated in Figure 4.1.

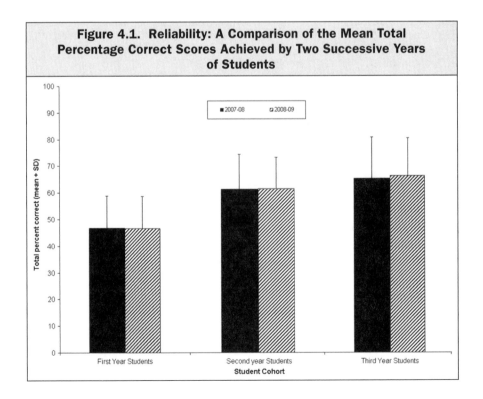

Figure 4.1. Reliability: A Comparison of the Mean Total Percentage Correct Scores Achieved by Two Successive Years of Students

Cross-Institutional Reliability

In 2006, a collaboration with Sandra Turkington of Sheffield University Library and the Centre for Inquiry-based Learning in the Arts and Social Sciences (CILASS) at The University of Sheffield provided an opportunity to test the cross-institutional reliability of the data produced by the assessment tool. The academic requirements placed on applicants to gain entry to the degree programs offered by the Department of Psychology in The University of Sheffield and the IPS in The University of Leeds are very similar, and therefore the psychology students in these institutions are likely to have very similar educational histories and experiences. It was therefore predicted that new first-year undergraduate psychology students attending each of these universities would possess similar information literacy skills.

Although there was a significant difference between the total percentage of correct scores achieved by these two groups of first-year students ($U = 2975$, $N_1 = 74$, $N_2 = 141$, $p < 0.05$), it can be seen in Table 4.3 that the data relating to specific skills highlighted similar deficits in both groups. The generally lower scores achieved by the Sheffield students are possibly the result of a low percentage of students completing the assessment ($n = 74$ in

Table 4.3. Cross-Institutional Reliability: A Comparison of the Mean Percentage Correct Scores of First-Year Psychology Students at The University of Leeds and The University of Sheffield

	Institution			
	University of Leeds		University of Sheffield	
IL Skill	**Mean % correct**	**Rank (lowest to highest)**	**Mean % correct**	**Rank (lowest to highest)**
Recognizing the need for information	64	5	50	6
Identifying the ways to fill the information need	38	2	29	2
Constructing a search strategy	44	3	38	3
Locating and accessing information	24	1	19	1
Comparing and evaluating information	67	6	47	5
Organizing and applying information	47	4	40	4

comparison to Leeds $n = 141$) and how the assessment tool was administered (Turkington, 2008).

When examining the rank order of the percentage correct scores for each skill area, it can be seen that both groups of students perform very similarly in the assessment (see Table 4.3). Close examination of this data reveals that both groups of psychology students are extremely poor at locating and accessing information, and identifying ways to fill their information need. In addition, students at Leeds and Sheffield also have difficulties in constructing search strategies, and organizing and applying information. Although students at The University of Sheffield also demonstrated limited knowledge about comparing and evaluating information and how to recognize their need for information, students at The University of Leeds performed better on questions related to these skills. Interestingly, the most commonly selected incorrect answers for each question were similar for both groups of students. This is perhaps indicative of their similar educational histories and experiences.

Sensitivity: Different Students Have Different Needs

Having established that the assessment tool produces consistent data both within and between institutions when students with similar educational backgrounds are tested, it was important to test whether the tool was sensitive to the different abilities of diverse student cohorts. The School of Healthcare at The University of Leeds provides many different degree programs with different academic entrance requirements. In 2007, Dr David Clarke in collaboration with Alison Lahlafi from the university library had recently completed an audit of information literacy teaching within the School of Healthcare. They were interested in identifying the skills possessed by students on the different programs of study within the school. This provided the opportunity for a mutually beneficial collaboration, and permitted the comparison of the performance of first-year psychology students to that of nursing students.

The two populations of students tend to have very different educational backgrounds. In England, university entrance requirements are based on academic performance of students in the A-level examinations. These exams are normally taken in the last year of school education at the age of 18. A levels are preceded, two years earlier, by another set of examinations called General Certificates of Secondary Education (GCSEs), which may also constitute part of university entrance requirements. Psychology, as one of the most popular subjects in UK higher education, has very high academic entrance requirements with students achieving A and B grades in three A-level subjects and Bs in GCSE Mathematics and two science subjects together with several other GCSE qualifications, including English. In Leeds, approximately 10 percent of psychology students enter with alternative qualifications but these must have a strong scientific core, and vocational qualifications are not accepted in lieu of A levels. In contrast, the entrance requirements for the nursing course are five GCSE qualifications, including English and Mathematics, at grade C or above, and two A-level passes. Furthermore, approximately 20 percent of the students on the nursing course enter with alternative qualifications, including National Vocational qualifications.

Inspection of the data in Table 4.4 reveals dramatic differences between the information literacy skills of incoming psychology and nursing students. Although both groups have little knowledge about how to locate and access information and how to construct a search strategy, their performance on the other skill areas are very different. Psychology students are reasonably competent at recognizing their need for information and comparing and evaluating information, whereas first-year nursing students have not yet developed these skills. In contrast, nursing students demonstrate better knowledge about how to fill their information need and how to organize and apply information. These differences between psychology and nursing students are probably related to their different educational histories and experiences, and clearly demonstrate the sensitivity of the assessment tool to the different abilities of diverse student cohorts.

Table 4.4. Sensitivity: A Comparison of the Mean Percentage Correct Scores of First-Year Psychology and Nursing Students at The University of Leeds				
	Degree Program			
	Psychology		Nursing	
IL Skill	Mean % correct	Rank (lowest to highest)	Mean % correct	Rank (lowest to highest)
Recognizing the need for information	66	6	39	1.5
Identifying the ways to fill the information need	40	2	55	5
Constructing a search strategy	43	3	42	3
Locating and accessing information	32	1	39	1.5
Comparing and evaluating information	64	5	44	4
Organizing and applying information	44	4	66	6

DECODING THE DATA: WHAT DOES IT MEAN?

To assess the development of students' information literacy skills as they progress through the degree program, data from a single group of students across all three years of study were analyzed. These students entered their first year of the degree program in 2005, completing their degree in 2008. To ensure that the analysis assessed the progression of skill acquisition, only those individuals who provided data at all three points of assessment (in each year of study) were used. This approach also meant that the sample of students used in the analysis had attended all of the teaching sessions provided throughout the degree program. The data could therefore also be used to assess the effectiveness of these sessions. The performance of these 58 students was representative of the larger year group to which they belonged, with similar errors and percentage correct scores being achieved by both the smaller and larger group of students.

Analysis of the total percent correct scores achieved by the 58 students revealed a significant increase in their skills during their three years of study $(F_{(2,57)} = 45.359, p < 0.05)$. This result indicates that the teaching sessions in the degree program are effective at some level, with the students improving as they progress through the degree program (see Figure 4.2). Although a substantial

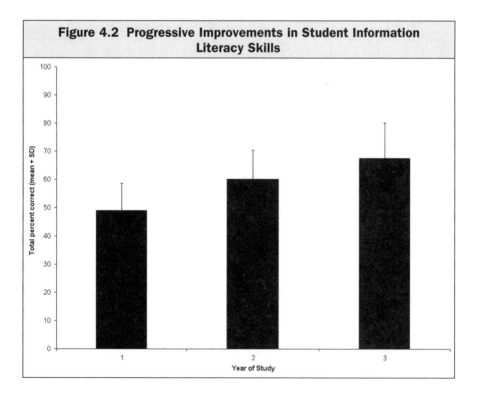

Figure 4.2 Progressive Improvements in Student Information Literacy Skills

improvement occurred between their first- and second-year scores, there is a more modest improvement between the second- and third-year scores of the students. This data suggests that the teaching for first-year students is effective, but that perhaps the third compulsory session in the students second year of study is less effective. Alternatively, the large difference between the first- and second-year data may indicate the rapid development of skills, and a familiarity with different sources of information available to students for the first time when they start university. Despite excellent access to the Internet in UK schools and colleges, students entering university for the first time are confronted by an array of new sources of academic information. Bibliographic databases, and journal and review articles, for example, are all indispensable parts of university library collections, but are unlikely to be encountered in UK schools.

A more detailed analysis of student skills was achieved by examining the data for each of the six information literacy skills assessed (see Table 4.5).

Recognizing the Need for Information

There is a significant improvement of performance in this skill area as the students progress through the degree program ($F_{(2,57)} = 5.299$, $p < 0.05$). Although performance in all years of study is good, students progressively improve in their ability to recognize the issues related to using only one source of information and to recognize that reading an introductory text can increase their familiarity with a topic.

Table 4.5. Progressive Development of Specific Information Literacy Skills			
	Year of Study (mean % correct)		
IL Skill	**First Year**	**Second Year**	**Third Year**
Recognizing the need for information	71	76	83
Identifying the ways to fill the information need	35	44	52
Constructing a search strategy	43	60	71
Locating and accessing information	24	45	43
Comparing and evaluating information	75	75	79
Organizing and applying information	50	68	74

Identifying the Ways to Fill the Information Need

Although student skills significantly improve in this specific area across the three years of study ($F_{(2,57)}$ = 10.879, $p < 0.05$), it can be seen in Table 4.5 that even in their final year, students are struggling to fill their need for information. Closer inspection of the incorrect answers provided by the students reveals that the initial preference of students to search the Internet for information in their first year develops into a preference to use recently published information from journal articles. In their final year of study, however, students continue to have difficulties in selecting an appropriate search tool and understanding the appropriate use of review articles.

Constructing a Search Strategy

Student performance on all of the questions in this category improved over time, resulting in a significant overall enhancement ($F_{(2,57)}$ = 36.282, $p < 0.05$). Many first-year students failed to recognize that their selection of keywords influences the number of sources of information found during a library catalog search, and they were also unfamiliar with the use of the Boolean operator "OR," showing a strong preference for connecting words with "AND," whether this was appropriate or not. In addition, and unsurprisingly, this group was unfamiliar with the use of truncation and parenthesis in search strategies. By their third year of study most of these deficits had been overcome, although the use of "OR" to connect synonyms during a literature search was still unfamiliar to many students.

Locating and Accessing Information

Although there is a significant improvement in locating and accessing information ($F_{(2,57)}$ = 13.034, $p < 0.05$), students in their third year continue to have considerable problems in this area. In their first year, students are unfamiliar with the library catalog, and how to find information when using this search tool. Furthermore, they do not know that bibliographies can be used to discover additional related literature. This use of bibliographies substantially increases as they progress through the degree program, although in their third year many of the students continue to have difficulties in identifying types of information from references and using the library catalog to find journal articles, all vital skills for successful undergraduate study.

Comparing and Evaluating Information

Although students perform well in comparing and evaluating information from first year onward, there is no significant improvement as they progress through the degree program ($F_{(2,57)} = 0.61$, $p > 0.05$). This lack of progression is not, however, due to a lack of room for improvement, as demonstrated by the limited number of first- and second-year students with knowledge about the peer review process and the differences in the quality of information contained in journal articles and Web sites. In their first year, students already understand that the abstracts of journal articles can be used to evaluate whether they fill an information need. Disappointingly, even in their third year of study, many of the students do not understand the peer review process.

Organizing and Applying Information

Student performance significantly improves in this area as they progress through the degree program ($F_{(2,57)} = 35.692$, $p < 0.05$). In their first year of study, it is clear that students do not know how to cite references, and are unfamiliar with copyright issues that affect the amount of photocopying they are legally permitted to do for educational purposes. They do, however, have a clear understanding of plagiarism, an encouraging aspect of a group of students new to higher education. In the second year, student knowledge about citations and bibliographies has improved, but even in their third year they remain ignorant of the copyright issues affecting their work.

In summary, first-year students preferentially search for information using the Internet; they are, not surprisingly, unfamiliar with the library catalog and other academic search tools, and some of the sophisticated search techniques that can be used in these contexts. These students also have a strong preference, or behavioral habit, possibly developed through their search experiences on the Internet, for using the Boolean operator "AND" at the expense of conducting efficient and effective literature searches using other techniques. Furthermore, they have little, if any, experience reading and using journal articles and are unfamiliar with searching for them, citing them, or understanding the quality of information contained within them.

By their second year of study, students have attended two discipline-specific information literacy teaching sessions, and show improvement in comparison to their performance in the assessment from their first year. In particular, by the second year the students search for their information from resources provided by the university library rather than the wider Internet. They also show a greater understanding of the academic information landscape, and their ineffective propensity to use the Boolean operator "AND" has been reduced, with more students using other operators correctly. However, despite attending teaching sessions about the different ways to fill their information need, and locating and accessing different types of information in their first year of study, these skills have not been adequately developed.

The students continue to develop their skills through their second year of study, and by the third year most are competent at recognizing their need for information, constructing a search strategy, comparing and evaluating information, and organizing and applying information. There are, however, some noticeable deficits in their acquired skills even at this late stage in their studies. It is disappointing that many students do not use the appropriate search tools or search strategies to locate journal articles, a vital academic skill at this level of study. Furthermore, in their final year many students do not know about their rights and responsibilities in relation to copyright laws, nor do they understand the peer review process. These skill deficits in identifying ways to fill their information need and locating and accessing information clearly demonstrate the failure of parts of the teaching program.

IS INFORMATION LITERACY RELATED TO ACADEMIC PERFORMANCE?

The data provided by the assessment tool identified deficits in students' information literacy skills and ineffective components of the teaching sessions that had been designed to address these issues. Prior to redesigning the teaching sessions, in an attempt to improve the student skills, one further question remained to be answered: Is information literacy related to academic performance?

In an attempt to address this question, correlational analyses were conducted to investigate whether students' overall performance on the information literacy assessment (total percent correct data) and their average academic performance in their first and second year of study were related. These analyses revealed significant positive correlations between the information literacy skills and academic performance of both first- and second-year students ($r = 0.349$, $n = 130$, $p < 0.05$; $r = 0.355$, $n = 118$, $p < 0.05$, respectively). Furthermore, the final degree grade achieved by students at the end of their studies is also significantly positively correlated with the total percentage correct scores they achieved at the start of their third and final year of study ($r = 0.243$, $n = 84$, $P < 0.05$). These data demonstrate a strong relationship between information literacy abilities and the academic performance of students throughout their studies. However, although it has been demonstrated that better performance on the information literacy assessment is related to better academic performance, the analysis conducted does not infer a causal relationship between these two abilities, and does not take into consideration the many other variables that may mediate students' academic achievement.

EVIDENCE-BASED INFORMATION LITERACY TEACHING: PSYCHOLOGY AND BEYOND

Armed with the knowledge that a strong relationship exists between performance on the information literacy skills assessment and students' academic performance throughout the degree program, the data provided by the assessment tool was used by the library and IPS to create a new evidence-based information literacy teaching program. The data clearly demonstrated that some parts of the previous teaching schedule were ineffective in informing and changing student behavior, and the redesigned teaching took these issues into account. The redesigned information literacy curriculum was collaboratively delivered by staff of the IPS and library. The importance of developing these skills is emphasized to students by the presence of both an academic and a librarian in all of these sessions.

The IPS identified that students required more extensive information literacy teaching in their first year of study if they were to successfully meet the academic demands of the course. A greater emphasis on providing teaching early in the degree program was achieved by scheduling four sessions for first-year students. These sessions require students to use the library catalog or bibliographic databases to find literature, or to explore the effects of using specific Boolean operators and sophisticated search strategies. In this way, a strong emphasis is placed on teaching students to select and use appropriate search tools, and how to locate and access academic information. New interactive tasks allow students to practice using and evaluating information in an academic context that is relevant to their course. One such task requires students to find and read the abstracts of several journal articles and then decide which of the articles directly addresses specific questions related to a particular essay topic. The structure of this session was designed by the library, and the specific academic content was selected by the IPS. Another new session involves discussions and tasks that are used to inform students about the journey of information from the "laboratory to the library," and to highlight important aspects of the peer review process and how this affects the quality of the information provided in journal articles. Personal experience of the academic publication process from academic staff is used to inform discussions led by the librarian with students about the varying quality of different sources of information.

In general, the new teaching schedule provides students with many more opportunities to practice, under supervision, the skills that were identified by the assessment tool as being underdeveloped in previous cohorts of students.

The previous discussion suggests that the process of justifying and creating new evidence-based information literacy curriculum interventions in the IPS is complete. However, the assessment tool continues to be used to inform and continuously improve the information literacy support provided for the undergraduate psychology students. The importance of continuous assessment of information literacy skills cannot be emphasized enough in light of the ever-changing information environment in which students study.

Our Shared Future

The success of this collaborative project at The University of Leeds has resulted in a demonstrable commitment from the university to facilitate this collaboration across all nine of its faculties. A university-funded project, initiated and run by the authors of this chapter, is now underway. The project is developing test banks of subject-specific questions through the collaboration of academic staff, including those responsible for curriculum development, directors of learning and teaching, and faculty team librarians. This partnership is an attempt to identify the information literacy skills teaching needed by students in order for them to meet the academic expectations set by their tutors. This project has already highlighted many different applications and delivery options in relation to this assessment tool; creating an electronic version, for example, will allow greater flexibility in the way in which it can be used by departments with their students. In the future it may also be used to assess student skills prior to arriving at university via the virtual learning environment, thus alerting academic staff to the needs of their incoming students, or it may be used as a formative assessment for individual students, the results of which may be discussed with academic tutors in relation to setting targets in personal development planning.

Although the creation and implementation of this assessment tool has been invaluable to the development of an evidence-based information literacy curriculum redesign, it must be acknowledged that the landscape of academic information is constantly changing, and that the skills that students require for academic success must also keep pace with these changes. It must be recognized that assessments that are "fit for purpose" today may not meet the academic needs of tomorrow's students. In the UK, for example, government-funded Research Councils increasingly require academics to make their research findings publicly accessible beyond the confines of subscription journals by placing them into open-access research repositories. (Research Councils UK, 2006) Thus, having spent many years weaning students off generic search engines and onto specialist bibliographic databases, it may be the case that in the future search engines such as Google Scholar become preferred key access points for research findings. It is therefore vitally important to recognize that students require both transient and static information literacy skills, some of which will serve them for the duration of their academic studies, and others, such as understanding the ethical issues around using information, which will be called into use beyond the lecture theater and into the world of work. Clearly, both must be addressed through degree programs in order to equip undergraduates with sufficient information literacy skills to become life-long learners. In the future, academics and librarians may want to consider how much emphasis to give to these static and transient skills at different points in the curriculum; perhaps focusing more on the transient skills as students enter university, and giving more prominence to static skills as students prepare for life as graduates.

Finally, it is also clear that to make sense of the rapid changes in the landscape of academic information, and the implications of these changes for undergraduate study, academic staff and librarians must continue to develop and deepen their working relationships, sharing the skills and knowledge necessary to produce information literate students. Sustaining successful information literacy curriculum interventions will depend on creating long-term relationships between academics and librarians similar to those described in this chapter. Where these relationships already exist, there is greater opportunity to make a valuable impact on student learning than in one-off collaborations looking for an elusive quick fix.

REFERENCES

Breivik, Patricia. S., and E. Gordon Gee, eds. 2006. *Higher Education in the Internet Age: Libraries Creating a Strategic Edge.* Westport, CT: American Council on Education and Praeger.

Julien, H., and Given, M. 2002. "Faculty-Librarian Relationships in the Information Literacy Context: A Content Analysis of Librarians' Expressed Attitudes and Experiences." *Canadian Journal of Information and Library Science* 27, no. 3: 65–87.

Leeds University Library. 2003. "Information Literacy Strategy." Available: www.leeds .ac.uk/library/strategic/ilstrategy_new.pdf (accessed September 30, 2009).

Mackenzie, Alison. 2001. "'Learning Is a Treasure That Will Follow Its Owner Everywhere' (Chinese Proverb)." *SCONUL Newsletter* 24 (Winter): 36–39. Available: www.sconul.ac.uk/publications/newsletter/24/36-39_24.pdf (accessed September 30, 2009).

Mackenzie, Alison, John Howard, Louise Makin, and Claire Ryan. 2002. "The Big Blue: Final Report. Recommendations to the JISC." Manchester, UK: Manchester Metropolitan University Library (July 2002). Available: www.library.mmu.ac.uk/bigblue/ recomendations.html (accessed September 30, 2009).

Nicholas, David, Paul Huntington, Peter Williams, and Tom Dobrowolski. 2006. "The Digital Information Consumer." In *New Directions in Human Information Behavior* (pp. 203–228), edited by Amanda Spink and Charles Cole. Dordrecht, Germany: Springer.

Quality Assurance Agency. 2007. "Subject Benchmark Statement: Psychology." London: Quality Assurance Agency (November). Available: www.qaa.ac.uk/academicinfra structure/benchmark/statements/Psychology07.asp (accessed September 30, 2009).

Research Councils UK. 2006. "Access to Research Outputs: RCUK Position on Issue of Improved Access to Research Outputs." Available: www.rcuk.ac.uk/research/outputs/access/default.htm (accessed September 30, 2009).

Secker, Jane, Debbi Boden, and Gwyneth Price. 2007. "Information Literacy Beef Bourguignon (Also Known as Information Skills Stew or Ii-skills Casserole): The Higher Education Sector." In *The Information Literacy Cookbook* (pp. 123–147), edited by Jane Secker, Debbi Boden, and Gwyneth Price. Oxford, UK: Chandos.

Society of College, National and University Libraries. 2007. "Information Skills in Higher Education: A SCONUL Position Paper." London. Available: www.sconul.ac.uk/groups/information_literacy/papers/Seven_pillars.html (accessed September 30, 2009).

Superbrands. 2008. Official Top 500 2008/09. Available: www.superbrands.uk.com/pdfs/SB10%20Official%20Top%20500.pdf (accessed September 30, 2009).

Turkington, Sandra. 2008. "Testing an Information Literacy Assessment Tool?" MSc thesis, Aberystwyth University, United Kingdom.

Watts, Nick. 2002. "Oxford Libraries Conference: 'Learner-Centred Libraries'." *SCONUL Newsletter* 25 (Spring): 102–103. Available: www.sconul.ac.uk/publications/newsletter/25/102-103_25.pdf (accessed September 30, 2009).

Chapter 5

Collaboration in Action:
Designing an Online Assessment Strategy for Adult Learners

Julie Bostock, Susan Graves, and Ruth Wilson

INTRODUCTION

Developing competent information literacy skills to support student learning is a key component in higher education. Assessment of these skills forms a crucial element of the learning experience for all students, but particularly for an adult audience, and this needs to be considered early in program design. Information literacy modules are often delivered separately by library staff as additional support sessions or, increasingly, as online tutorials. In this study an embedded approach was used that locates the development of information literacy within the curriculum. This method contextualized information literacy within subject modules with explicit links to the students' working practice. It was created by a new academic program team of library and academic staff who worked together to design and implement a different approach to delivering and assessing these skills.

This particular student cohort were studying on a Foundation Degree in Professional Development (FDA PD) designed as continuing professional development for support staff. They all work in schools and are studying part time at a university in the northwest of England. The team therefore had to consider the needs of adult learners who may have considerable professional and life experience but who may be lacking in confidence to study at a higher level. In addition, they may be challenged in terms of their technological skills. In this respect, existing traditional study and information literacy skills programs designed for first year undergraduates were not appropriate to serve the needs of this group.

This chapter addresses the challenges of academic and library staff working collaboratively to produce an information literacy module that was embedded within a subject area and included both formative and summative assessment. The discussion focuses on a module that was designed for a combination of online and face-to-face teaching. It also considers how this model may encourage self-regulated learning for a group of adult learners studying part time in a professional development program.

RELATED LITERATURE

With the foundation degree in mind, a university team utilized the concept of "andragogy" (Knowles, 1980). A learner-centered approach was employed in the design, as opposed to the more teacher-centered transmission model (Kember, 1997) commonly associated with higher-education teaching. Andragogy seeks to develop a learning environment suited to adult learners by adapting a learning strategy that takes account of learners' experiential learning. This approach views the learner not as an empty vessel to be filled with knowledge, but as presenting with a wealth of experience that can contribute to the learning process. It also draws on the work of Rogers (1969) whose experiential, self-directed approach to learning emphasizes the significance of inner autonomy when he states: "The individual who sees himself and his situation clearly and who freely takes responsibility for that self and for that situation is a very different person from the one who is simply in the grip of outside circumstances" (Rogers, 1969: 271). The aim, particularly given the rapidly changing work environment experienced by these students, is to equip them with the tools needed to develop meta-cognitive abilities, to develop their learning for life.

To use the approach described previously the team felt that developing information literacy using an embedded structure would be effective. This could then provide a bridge between the learning of information literacy skills and the prior knowledge gained from the subject module and working practice. An online information literacy and study skills program called Springboard was considered suitable for adaptation. It had been created by the university and was unique to Edge Hill. Using a modified version of this approach would provide the basis for this learning. It was adapted by linking the Springboard content to the subject module content.

Consideration was also given to the concept that using e-learning can mitigate some of the undesirable consequences of university life in the twenty-first century, such as equity of access for working students, and may improve and enhance learning outcomes for some students (Oliver, 2001). It is particularly useful in terms of students becoming independent learners (a premise of current education reforms) as it provides the conditions for them to become reflective and confident learners (Bach, Haynes, and Smith, 2007). Adopting a flexible-learning approach emphasizes students' central role in taking responsibility for their own learning and in this respect can take students on a trajectory from dependence to independence. Indeed, using an online flexible approach to learning can aid the lecturer in acknowledging that each student is at a different stage with personal levels of confidence and experience in terms of both subject and the use of technology (Bach, Haynes, and Smith, 2007).

The Springboard program embedded within the subject-specific module also provides the opportunity for self-regulated learning, which is linked to academic success (Pintrich, 2000; Winne and Perry, 2000). Self-regulated learners engage in planning, monitoring, and evaluation of their own learning and within the Springboard sessions students are given the opportunity to practice these skills while developing subject knowledge. The intention is that linking the development of academic skills to subject knowledge will motivate students and enable them to assess their own strengths and weaknesses and develop a range of strategies to overcome the latter (Perry, Phillips, and Hutchinson, 2006). It has been suggested that mature students often exhibit issues regarding self-confidence, anxiety, self-doubt and skills in directed learning (Richardson, 1995). For this reason it is important for tutors to develop modules that meet individual students' levels of competency and self-directedness in order to help them to move toward independent learning. It is also beneficial to engage students in a pre-assessment of their strengths and weaknesses and provide competency-based feedback to develop them as self-directed learners (Grow, 1991). Given our stated aim to equip students with the tools needed to develop meta-cognitive abilities, to "learn to learn" it was important for our program that we provided an active environment with opportunities for interaction in the group to enable a learning experience to be constructed relevant to the students' own experience (Knowles, 1980). In the case of Springboard, the module begins with a skills audit, offering personalized advice and interactive activities as feedback to encourage students to take responsibility for their own learning and development.

INSTITUTIONAL CONTEXT AT EDGE HILL UNIVERSITY

Edge Hill University is located in the northwest of England, with more than 9,000 students pursuing a range of degree and diploma courses and 6,000 studying professional development courses. It has a strong vision of itself as a "learning-led" university, seeking to promote inquiry-based learning using appropriate teaching and learning environments and the prior experience of the learner. A large Learning Services department offers library resources, learner support, Information and Communication Technology (ICT) user support for teaching and learning, media services, e-learning development, study skills, and dyslexia support. To assist learners in developing information literacy the Learning Services unit created Springboard in summer 2006. This online module aimed to provide students with a more flexible approach to individual academic study skills and to develop further knowledge skills and applications. Springboard was a 15-credit module that focused on enhancing skills through an eight-week online program consisting of ten units. Any university student could join the program and participants were grouped into communities using generic content and led by Learning Services facilitators.

The Faculty of Education at Edge Hill is the largest provider of secondary education initial teacher training in the United Kingdom and the faculty portfolio also includes the following:

- Initial Teacher Training (ITT) across all the age phases: Early Years, Primary, Key Stage 2/3, and Postcompulsory
- Postgraduate Professional Development (PPD) for teachers
- Professional Development for those working as part of the children's workforce, Higher-Level Teaching Assistant (HLTA) training and assessment and Early Years Professional Status (EYPS) training and assessment

Faculty programs are delivered face to face, full and part time, and increasingly using an online e-learning platform. In England there is a gradual increase in the numbers of nonteaching staff working in schools, often referred to as the wider school workforce. Along with this increase in numbers a government policy offers professional development opportunities to these staff. The faculty has been developing programs to meet this need and this has resulted in attracting more adult, nontraditional learners studying part-time for foundation degrees.

The introduction of the Foundation Degree (FD) in the UK in 2000 with its emphasis on work-based learning, employer involvement and its part-time nature is seen as part of a move toward new ways of enabling higher learning for those in work (Foundation Degree Forward, 2009). Foundation degrees are also part of the UK government's widening participation agenda that is intended to encourage a greater proportion of the population to access higher education, especially from those sectors traditionally underrepresented. Such opportunities aim to attract students who have not taken the traditional academic route into higher education. For this reason tensions often arise regarding the support of students who may find the academic work on a foundation degree particularly challenging and may require additional support in this area. The foundation degree, which is the focus of this study, was designed to address the continuing professional development needs of support staff in schools, that is, all those who work within the school environment whose primary responsibilities are not teaching and learning. This group of staff have not traditionally been required to have degree-level qualifications, but workforce reform (Department for Education and Skills, 2003) within the school sector in England is increasingly requiring higher-level skills for new and expanding support roles being created within schools.

OUR COLLABORATIVE APPROACH: INTEGRATING EDUCATIONAL THEORY AND ACADEMIC SKILLS DEVELOPMENT

Rationale

Creating an integrated module consisting of educational theory and academic skills development together with the accompanying assessment would require a team drawn from a number of specialist areas. In recognition of this, the program creator began formative discussions with the Academic Liaison Coordinator from Learning Services at an early stage in the design. This approach resulted in a wider range of specialist staff being part of the course team, assisting to create the program structure and advising on the relevant module and its assessment.

Edge Hill University has developed, over several years, a relatively sophisticated model of a new academic team, responding to the changes in teaching and learning in the twenty-first century. These changes have significantly affected the roles both of academic and support staff. E-learning has the capacity to provide opportunities for learning via new methods of creating and delivering content which can have a transformational effect on traditional modes of study. This has enabled staff to meet the challenges of widening participation and new student groups such as the foundation degree cohorts. In the course of endeavoring to meet these changes, both academic and support staff are seeking new partnerships in order to deliver high quality experiences and, by working together, growing closer in the roles they perform (Bury, Martin, and Roberts 2006). This "academic convergence" has resulted in the ability to assist in the creation of active and independent learners (Levy and Roberts, 2005).

At Edge Hill it is an institutional belief that both faculty and support staff need to collaborate to create solutions to match the requirements of the today's students. In this case study, the team consisted of academic staff, including the module leader, a learning technologist, a study skills advisor and

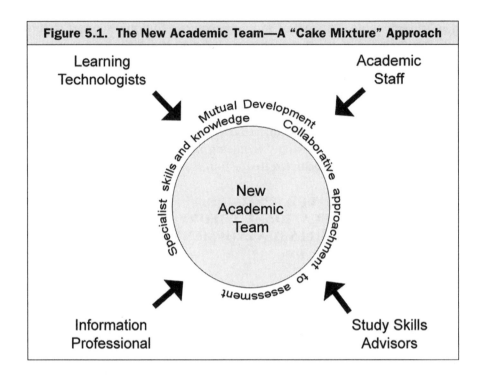

Figure 5.1.   The New Academic Team—A "Cake Mixture" Approach

Learning
Technologists

Academic
Staff

Mutual Development
knowledge
Collaborative approachment to assessment
Specialist skills and knowledge

New
Academic
Team

Information
Professional

Study Skills
Advisors

an academic liaison co-ordinator who had a background in information literacy. Working together, this group formed a "cake mixture" approach—the resultant ingredients forming the new academic team (see Figure 5.1).

The team aimed to design within the module a cohesive assessment model that would create optimum conditions for learning and that aimed to avoid the error of replicating classroom content in a digital area. As already identified, the generic online skills module that formed the basis of the structure had itself already addressed the latter issue (Roche and Martin, 2008). As the module had been developed using an embedded approach (information literacy and subject knowledge together) it was necessary to create assessment to cover the subject content as well as information literacy skills.

Benefits of Collaboration

Most examples of information literacy are focused on the summative process. The advantage of our collaboration was that the team began to view the process from a new perspective in the e-learning environment. We wanted to look at combining subject content with the Springboard skills content. The first Springboard unit had diagnostic units in four areas. It was agreed to adopt these and include a formative strand of assessment by setting tasks for each unit that matched lecture content. This process created a multilayered assessment model. Thus, the e-learning diagnostic style and the traditional information literacy summative style were augmented with formative assessment. As Forrest (2007) discusses this offers useful feedback within the module, adding to the learning experience and encouraging student reflection.

To achieve this level of complexity, the module needed to be easy to use, not overloaded with content. The very different roles and experience of the mixed professional team helped to create conditions for constructivist pedagogical learning to occur. An additional benefit discovered during the collaborative process was the appreciation and skills enhancement of all team members. Members of the mixed professional team were forced to review how they interacted with learners and how they viewed assessment as a teaching and learning tool. For the technologist it was the first opportunity to engage with any type of student assessment. The staff with library and study skills backgrounds had previously undertaken summative assessment, usually in the form of marking completed question-and-answer sheets following classroom input. This more strategic approach required them to develop their existing pedagogic practice. The tutors on the team were also confronting the need to assess e-learning through the development of formative online tasks and audits. Exactly how assessment in the e-learning context would operate was a major focus during discussions. Through the collaboration, a course design emerged that included innovation in information literacy assessment. This was based on a perception of how adult learners might interact in the e-learning environment. In this way the philosophy and structure of the course evolved as a result of individual team members' contributions that drew on their experience and background in a variety of professions.

Challenges to Collaboration

Working together across diverse specialist areas is not without its own challenges. These professionals need to understand and view the student group from the same perspective if their work is to have coherence. This can result in a need for more discussion in the early phase than may be needed in a smaller or more mature team. Time constraints were present since the design, validation, and recruitment progressed rapidly, putting pressure on the team as their module was the first in the program.

Staff also had very different background perspectives and experiences of assessment from minimal in the case of some support roles, to very extensive in the case of the academic staff. Information literacy had been subject to diagnostic audit assessment or to summative processes in other university modules. Participating in the module design would mean to a greater or lesser extent a shift in the role mind-set and some individuals would be on a journey to become comfortable in the new learning environment.

Outcomes of Collaboration

Individually, study advisors, learning technologists, and information specialists have often had success working with academic staff; however, this program offered the opportunity for the new academic team to explore the full benefit of information literacy, described by Lea "adapting to new ways of knowing, new ways of understanding, interpreting and organising knowledge" (1998: 157). Through the collaborative process, a multilayered series of assessments was constructed and the result was encouraging in terms of student engagement, producing, as it did, an embedded model that emphasized and assessed the understanding of why and how these academic skills were important in the student journey. In this sense, the collaboration had benefited from the 'mutual development' theory (Bury, Martin, and Roberts, 2006) to achieve successful outcomes.

THE CASE STUDY *SPRINGBOARD PEDAGOGY*

The course team began to plan the module with the premise of wanting to integrate a range of academic skills—ICT, study skills, and information literacy—into the content of current educational issues. The original online Springboard module offered the opportunity to move forward with a successfully evaluated generic course (McLoughlin and Martin, 2006) and embed it within a specific program of study delivered through the University Virtual Learning Environment (VLE), Blackboard. The module linked the week's input to skills development. For example, following the subject session on the changing curriculum in schools, the Springboard unit for that week incorporated information searching about the same topic.

Springboard itself has been developed with a clear focus on the social learner, not just on the online content itself. The course team took this ethos and using the social constructivist approach to pedagogic thinking (Levy and Roberts, 2005) aimed to develop participants through personal interpretive activities, bearing in mind previous individual experiences. Therefore the first of the 10 units began with diagnostic audits—ICT, time management, learning styles, and information literacy. Following the thinking of Roche and Martin (2008), the team aimed to put the learner rather than the technology at the heart of the process, acknowledging prior experience and allowing individual pace of study. To create a new style of content, traditional text-based materials on information literacy were revised and a clear, interactive content produced (see Figure 5.2). Students would work through the units sequentially, and although released each week, once available they could be revisited at any time.

Based on market research information gained during the development process, we suspected that the majority of students would be novice e-learners.

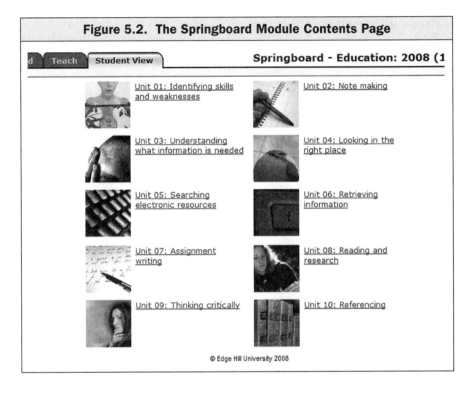

Figure 5.2. The Springboard Module Contents Page

As such, consistency of design and presentation was crucial, hence the regular pattern in the formative assessment tasks.

STUDENT ASSESSMENT MODEL

In developing an assessment strategy for the foundation degree module it was important that the assessed elements were authentic, integrated within the subject matter and contextualized in terms of work-based practice. Our aim on a wider level was to equip students to cope with the changing nature of their work and the workplace. Consequently, our goal as educators was to facilitate this change through the learning process (Rogers, 1969). There is also commitment on the program to the concept of co-learning, creating an atmosphere in the classroom of mutual inquiry between academics and students who are practitioners. In this way the teacher can become learner and vice versa, to create a spirit of mutual inquiry and support (Dewey, 1916). This also indicates to students that the "knowing how" (practice) is as valued as the "knowing that" (theory) (Brockbank and McGill, 2007). As opposed to the more didactic approach usually associated with the transmission model of higher education learning, a dialogical approach was used in the face-to-face sessions. This enabled students' experience to be explored and links made between theory and their own practice. Belenky et al. (1986) use the concept of connected and separated knowing; separated knowing uses dialogue that simply reports one's ideas, whereas connected knowing builds rapport with those in the group, connecting ideas with others to create a synergistic experience. In other words, connected knowing means suspending one's own opinion to really understand the other, and not necessarily to be persuaded or to accept the other opinion, but to gain a deeper understanding of the other perspective. Given this philosophical approach, it was important that opportunities for formative assessment of information literacy were built into the Springboard sessions through the use of self-administered audits and action planning to enable students to take control of their own progress and to direct their own learning to some extent in partnership with the lecturing staff.

Assessment is beneficial to students because improvements occur due to feedback. Learner-centered methods focus on how students perceive their progress and ask the students to identify their progress in meeting objectives (Rocco, 2007). Online activities for formative assessment can also help tutors who have limited contact time with students to continue teaching beyond the classroom. This is particularly true of literacy skills where opportunities for face-to-face contact may be limited (Forrest, 2007). In effect, the module was delivered in a blended learning form of delivery. This was chosen to assist novices in developing their skills in a supported environment. The taught module session took place for three hours and was followed by an hour of Springboard self-study in a classroom with the tutor present. Students worked through the Springboard unit alone, but the tutor was there to offer any help required and students were able to communicate with one another via the discussion forums. The result of the collaboration was the "online module," released over ten weeks whose content was linked to subject sessions and included assessment from diagnostic audit through formative tasks to summative assignment.

Each unit required the student to engage in a series of online activities to introduce them to a range of study and information literacy skills. The tasks, as they related to the week's theoretical input, were designed to encourage reflection on understanding. This could then be shared via the discussion board. As the activities were undertaken during the four-hour class time, tutor support was available, although the e-learning platform also permitted access at any time, as well as practice in using this technology that was new to many in the cohort.

One of the aims was to allow collaborative problem solving and personal identification of need to be addressed. This was to aid the completion of the summative assessment, which was in two parts as follows:

Part A   A 3,000-word assignment in which students are asked to select one particular piece of legislation, policy, or initiative to describe and evaluate both in terms of its rationale and how it is impacting on their own educational setting and role (60 percent).

Part B   A 2,000-word reflection on students' research and study approach in undertaking the above assignment, including an action plan identifying their personal development needs and potential sources of help in this area (40 percent).

When introducing the module, the aims and objectives of this integrated assessment had been explicitly stated, together with the journey to arrive at a point ready for completion. Previous attempts at our institution to offer information literacy online without related assessment were largely unsuccessful. Students either dropped out at an early stage or failed to internalize and apply the acquired skills once the particular module was completed. It was hoped that this approach would be more successful.

As the module would also need to be delivered to larger cohorts as the program expanded, it was also considered that this approach, with appropriate support, would enable tutors to deliver information literacy themselves, thus freeing themselves from staffing constraints with the Learning Services team.

Multilayered Assessment

The multilayered form of assessment allows early formative assessment and regular self-assessment of progress in the learning outcomes relating to information literacy skills (see Figure 5.3). The rationale for this multilayered assessment structure was based on the need to embed the development of information literacy skills in the first module of the foundation degree. This is because of the nature of the adult, nontraditional, part-time learners who attend the course. This group ranges in age from 25 to 60 and has a broad range of experiences of previous study and are all in full-time employment. Therefore, each weekly session of Springboard was designed to contain tasks and activities that were directly linked to their work practice and module topic for that week's session.

The first layer of assessment was the skills audit, where students were asked to self-assess their own strengths and weaknesses in various aspects of information literacy. This led them to produce an action plan of how to tackle areas of weakness. The next layer of assessment occurred at unit level as students worked through the units each week carrying out interactive tasks and assessment activities. Part of the assessment was a reflective assignment in which they had to discuss the process of developing their information literacy skills in order to produce the first part of the module assignment. This included most of the elements of Springboard—note-making, searching for information, assignment writing, thinking critically, and Harvard referencing.

The summative assessment of progress at the end occurs through the tutor-marked written assignments. In the first assignment the tutor is assessing academic writing skills alongside knowledge of the concepts taught. In the second assignment the students are self-assessing the process of developing their information literacy skills and the tutor is then assessing the development of reflective writing skills by the student.

COURSE EVALUATION

The team wanted to evaluate the progress made by the students at regular intervals during the first semester. To this end a variety of evaluative tools were employed during this period. Data were collected via the following:

- Mid-module questionnaire asking their views on Springboard as a way of learning study skills
- Online evaluation as part of the last Springboard unit—some open-ended questions
- Content analysis of the reflective assignment—students were asked to reflect on the development of their information literacy skills

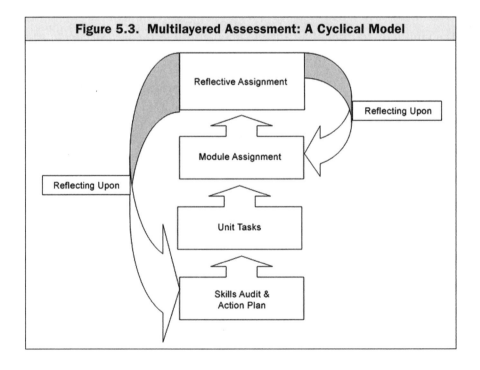

Figure 5.3. Multilayered Assessment: A Cyclical Model

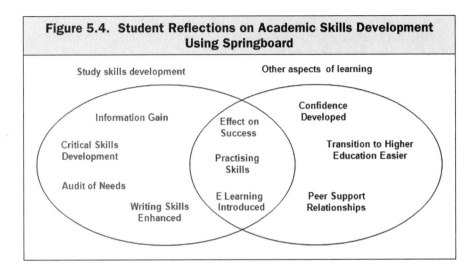

Figure 5.4. Student Reflections on Academic Skills Development Using Springboard

Thematic codes were generated from the conceptual framework of the case study and the student responses to the assignment brief. The data were scrutinized and responses categorized according to the themes. Once the data had been organized into themes, a process of reflection and interpretation was undertaken. Two broad themes were identified—reflections on study skills development and reflections on other aspects of learning. Within these, various subthemes were identified, some of which fit into both of the main categories. This is represented in Figure 5.4, which summarizes the main findings related to student reflections on their experience of using Springboard.

The following quotes illustrate student reflections within these themes and sub-themes:

- "...as a result of this Springboard unit I was able to retrieve information using credible sites via the academic subject gateways such as Intute...over the weeks I have become more effective at discriminating between a bewildering array of journals, books, and articles."
- "As a result I have developed an awareness of my particular learning style and have progressed with developing my critical analysis skills."
- "I found the task in Springboard on the subject of assignment writing extremely beneficial...it stuck in my mind when compiling the assignment so I ensured I had a printout of this to hand."
- "I felt successful and happy having completed the session."
- "Springboard has definitely increased my confidence as a learner because it helped me acknowledge skills that I already had but did not realize."
- "As the weeks progressed I began to feel more settled and confident in my ability to cope..."

- "In the beginning I was very unsure of how to go about writing a reflective account...after completing the Springboard units I felt confident enough to start planning how I would structure the assignment."
- "I now realize that this reluctance to read can partly be due to being a kinaesthetic learner, which I need to address."

These comments highlight how e-learning enabled the students to access academic resources very quickly and adapt to a relatively new way of searching for information. One result of this is the use of more academic information sources to inform their assignments. Thinking critically was also a new approach for them and they were able to evaluate sources of information instead of just accepting them. Assignment planning and writing had been a major concern for some students at the beginning of the course. For adult part-time learners there is often a lack of confidence about their academic skills and this was a central theme identified in the data. Support is also particularly important and students found that Springboard gave them another source of help via peers and tutors. Students reported a sense of success after completing the tasks and confronting their initial fear of e-learning.

Several challenges were reported by the cohort in the final evaluation. Some members of the group identified that dedicating one hour of face-to-face time to an essentially online, self-directed study module was not necessarily beneficial. Some students suggested that they would have preferred a wholly distance model as they felt this distracted from the delivery of the subject content. Face-to-face time is limited on this part-time course and dedicating part of it to online study was felt to be counter-productive in some sense. However, there was an issue of lack of confidence in using information technology for some students that could not have been resolved by using a wholly distance model. For these students the fact that they were required to use Springboard during the session did in fact have a positive impact on their confidence in this area.

As Springboard was introduced in the first sessions, late registering students did encounter problems with access. Administrative challenges prevented passwords being issued promptly and therefore students could not move forward with the tasks. Frustration was the inevitable result. This negative early experience did impact students' enthusiasm and perception of value of the module. This raises an issue for our institution's enrollment procedures and highlights the importance of a successful induction for students who are learning largely from a distance and therefore relying upon a VLE. If such problems cannot be prevented or resolved during that first teaching session on this program, it will be a whole week before these students are on campus again and they have not engaged with the online learning during that time.

CONCLUSION

The aim of the collaboration between academic and library staff was to produce an information literacy module that was embedded within a subject area on a foundation degree, and included both formative and summative assessment. This collaboration has given a new perspective on curriculum development as the multidisciplinary team offers new ways of thinking in terms of developing students' learning experiences and meeting student expectations. This is particularly important as we have moved toward a mass higher-education system that essentially involves new types of students, for example those who have no experience of studying at the higher level, and new modes of study necessitating the use of online embedded assessment models of information literacy.

The university team recognized that developing information literacy skills was essential in supporting student learning in higher education, particularly for students who, although they may have considerable professional and life experience, may not have the underpinning knowledge to enable them to access information to aid their academic study. In this case, study using an embedded approach improved student engagement and skill development at a critical point in their academic journey. It also enhanced both their confidence and their technological skills. The use of learning technologies for formative self-assessment encouraged the development of self-regulated learning and helped the students to develop as independent learners, which is important for academic success. A multilayered approach to assessment has also aided student reflection on their own skills which itself has facilitated their move to learning independence by enabling them to track their progress and take ownership of the process.

The student cohort for this module consisted of adult learners who were all in full-time work and this had the benefit of affording them the opportunity to transfer skills learned in this module to their practice. For example, it was noted that the use of learning technologies to develop information literacy skills benefited the students in the application of these skills in the workplace. This was particularly important given the nature of the cohort in terms of the widening participation agenda and bridging the gap between academic and workplace-learning. It was also concordant with the philosophical approach adopted during the course design of developing independent, self-regulated, active learners with explicit links to professional practice.

The importance of developing competent information literate students in the twenty-first century requires a willingness on the part of university staff to engage in collaborative activity by means of a new academic team. Online learning provides an environment that enables access for a wide variety of learners. Ways of developing and assessing information literacy skills, however, which are necessary for academic success, need to be embedded in program design through this collaboration. This case study supports these conclusions and demonstrates an example of collaboration in action.

BIBLIOGRAPHY

Bach, Shirley, Philip Haynes, and Jennifer Lewis Smith. 2007. *OnlineLearning and Teaching in Higher Education*. Milton Keynes, England: Open University Press.

Belenky, Mary Field, Blythe Clinchy, Nancy Goldberger, and Jill Tarule. 1986. *Women's Ways of Knowing*. New York: Basic Books.

Brockbank, Anne, and Ian McGill. 2007 *Facilitating Reflective Learning in Higher Education*, 2nd ed. Maidenhead, UK: Open University Press.

Bury, Rachel, Lindsey Martin, and Sue Roberts. 2006. "Achieving Change through Mutual Development: Supported Online-Learning and the Evolving Roles of Health and Information Professionals." *Health Information and Libraries Journal* 23 (Suppl. 1): 22–31.

Department for Education and Skills. 2003. *Raising Standards and Tackling Workload: A National Agreement*. London: HMSO.

Dewey, John. 1916. *Democracy and Education*. London: Macmillan.

Forrest, Margaret E. S. 2007. "Using Online Assessment to Support the Development of Referencing Skills." *Health Information and Libraries Journal* 24: 142–144.

Foundation Degree Forward: Innovating Workforce Development. Available: www.fdf .ac.uk (accessed September 30, 2009).

Grow, Gerald O. 1991. "Teaching Learners to Be Self-directed." *Adult Education Quarterly* 41, no. 3: 125–149.

Jacobson, Trudi E., and Thomas P. Mackey, eds. 2007. *Information Literacy Collaborations That Work*. New York: Neal-Schuman Publishers.

Kember, D. 1997. "A Reconceptualisation of the Research into University Academics Conceptions of Teaching." *Learning and Instruction* 7: 255–275.

Knowles, Malcolm S. 1980. *The Modern Practice of Adult Education: Andragogy to Pedagogy*, 2nd rev. ed. Chicago: Follett.

Lea, Mary. 1998. "Academic Literacies and Learning in Higher Education: Constructing Knowledge through Texts and Experience." *Studies in the Education of Adults* 30, no. 2: 156–172.

Levy, Philippa, and Sue Roberts, eds. 2005. *Developing the New Learning Environment: The Changing Role of the Academic Librarian*. London: Facet Publishing.

McLoughlin, Dawn, and Lindsey Martin. 2006. "Springboard: Evaluation for Faculty of Education Teaching, Learning and Assessment Committee." Unpublished paper. Ormskirk, UK: Edge Hill University.

Oliver, Ron. 2001. "Developing E-learning Environments That Support Knowledge Construction in Higher Education." In *Working for Excellence in the E-conomy* (pp. 407–416), edited by S. Stoney and J. Burn. Churchlands, Australia: We-B Centre.

Perry, Nancy E., Lynda Phillips, and Lynda Hutchinson. 2006. "Mentoring Student Teachers to Support for Self-Regulated Learning." *Elementary School Journal* 106, no. 3: 237–254.

Pintrich, Paul R. 2000. "Multiple Goals, Multiple Pathways: The Role of Goal Orientation in Learning and Achievement." *Journal of Educational Psychology* 92: 544–555.

Richardson, J. 1995. "Mature Students in Higher Education: II. An Investigation of Approaches to Studying and Academic Achievement." *Studies in Higher Education* 20: 5–17.

Rocco, Steve. 2007. "Online Assessment and Evaluation." *New Directions for Adult and Continuing Education* 113 (Spring): 75–86.

Roche, Mark, and Lindsey Martin. 2006. "Developing Academic Literacies Using E-learning." In *Current Developments in Technology-Assisted Education* (pp. 356–360), edited by A. Mendez-Vilas, A. Solano-Martin, J. Mesa Gonzalez, and J. A. Mesa Gonzalez. Badajoz, Spain: Formatex.

Roche, Mark, and Lindsey Martin, 2008. "How Can We Make Online Content Interesting?" Paper presented at the Solstice Conference, Edge Hill University, Ormskirk, England, June 5, 2008.

Rogers, Carl. 1969. *Freedom to Learn*. Columbus, Ontario: Merrill.

Winne, P. H., and N. E. Perry. 2000. "Measuring Self-Regulated Learning." In *Handbook of Self-Regulation* (pp. 531–566), edited by Paul R. Pintrich, Monique Boekaerts, and Moshe Seidner. London: Academic Press.

Part III

Humanities

SECTION INTRODUCTION

This section includes three chapters that provide assessment models related to writing courses and programs, representing both small and larger institutions. The assessments described are naturally embedded within structures that are unique to the institutions, yet elements of each approach are portable to other settings and situations. Themes that emerge within one or more of the chapters in this third part of the book include authentic assessment using existing learning goals and assignments, student self-assessments, pre- and posttests, and the critical importance of conversations between librarians and disciplinary faculty members that enable the development of in-depth assessment.

A student self-assessment project actualized through reflective writing assignments in an English course is described in the first chapter in this section, "A Model for Information Literacy Self-Assessment: Enhancing Student Learning in Writing Courses through Collaborative Teaching," by Leslie Bussert of University of Washington Bothell and Cascadia Community College and Norm Pouliot of Cascadia Community College. Students in four sections of English 102: Writing from Research, a course required for a transfer degree, were asked to undertake three (later changed to two) self-assessments connected to the information literacy components of the course. This chapter includes a rich literature review on the use of self-assessments in education and their benefits, which include increasing students' reflective thinking skills, enhancing their abilities to learn in different environments, laying the foundation for life-long learning, taking the responsibility for learning, and encouraging a positive self-concept. Bussert and Pouliot argue that self-assessment is more than an instrument to reflect on student learning because it has a practical dimension for evaluating and grading projects and assignments. The limits connected to self-assessment are also noted. The self-assessments used in the course were not graded, making them a low-stakes activity in the hope that students would be candid in their responses. The authors found that this performance-based, authentic assessment effort enhanced three components: student learning, librarian-faculty collaboration, and the visibility and relevance of the information literacy instruction program. They also detail what did not work and needed revision. Some of the suggestions for changes came from the students themselves.

Deborah B. Gaspar and Pamela S. Presser describe, in their engagingly titled chapter, "Vampires, Philosophers, and Graphic Novels: Assessing Thematic Writing Courses in *The Big Read*," the assessment connected to a first-year, theme-based writing course at The George Washington University. These are small classes, taught collaboratively by professors and librarians. *The Big Read* assessment involved the analysis of student research papers by faculty over the course of two summers. Each summer this intensive reading project focused on different course outcomes. The chapter emphasizes the assessment of their third learning outcome related to the exploration, use, and analysis of information for research. The authors highlight the need for the readers from several disciplines to develop a shared understanding of how to value elements of the papers. Although librarians were not included in the group of readers, the librarian co-author of this chapter was involved in developing the rubric for the third learning outcome. The results of this formative assessment initiative showed that the collaborative effort between librarians and faculty members was a success. This chapter explores changes that were made as a result of discussions held during the development of the rubric, including the development of shorter reflective assignments that complement larger projects. The ideas explored in this case study are especially informative for writing instructors and librarians who are interested in developing rubrics for information literacy assessment in writing programs. This model is also broadly applicable to any setting that integrates writing, literature, analysis, and critical thinking.

The closing chapter in the book, "Many Voices, One Goal: Measuring Student Success through Partnerships in the Core Curriculum," was written by Becky Canovan, Anne Marie Gruber, Mary Anne Knefel, and Michele McKinlay of University of Dubuque. The authors present a case study of a programmatic information literacy assessment model, instituted at a small private under-graduate institution. Students there participate in a core curriculum of four courses, enabling the assessment of information literacy skills to span more than one semester and one course. Assessment efforts at the University of Dubuque are outcomes-based and developed by each department, which create curriculum maps to identify learning outcomes within programmatic contexts. The library participated by creating a curriculum map, based on ACRL's information literacy standards, which includes learning outcomes for the core courses, as well as courses in history, communication, and English. This chapter is particularly valuable for the ability to see how this curriculum map spans these courses, and how the various components fit together. Both qualitative and quantitative components are used. The quantitative measure is the Tools for Real-Time Assessment of Information Literacy Skills (TRAILS) instrument, administered as a pre- and posttest in two different courses. The qualitative pieces include review of student portfolios, a student survey, and in-class components such as minute papers. One intriguing finding from the TRAILS pretest is the negative image incoming students had of librarians. Without this piece of information, librarians would not have realized the critical need to fix this image problem. The authors address the continuing conversations with core curriculum faculty members and administrators that lead to revision based on assessment findings.

These chapters all consider writing and humanities courses; however, the models they describe cover several assessment methods that could be applied in other fields. Although courses and programs are unique to particular institutions, the ideas presented in these chapters illustrate the value of better understanding student learning outcomes related to information literacy in different settings. Based on the lessons learned from these assessments, instructors can design new approaches within their own institutions. When reviewing these methodologies for your course or program, take into account the following:

- Student self-assessments of progress toward achieving information literacy goals might be included in any course with an information literacy component.
- Self-assessments provide insights and reflections to improve student learning and to influence the ways faculty and librarians work together.
- Pretests and posttests are a standard method for gauging student learning, but their use over different courses provides a twist on the traditional model that allows librarians and faculty members to determine how much learning has been retained and integrated into students' knowledge.
- External resources such as Tools for Real-Time Assessment of Information Literacy Skills (TRAILS) can be seamlessly integrated into assessment initiatives developed at the local level.
- Reading students' research papers against a rubric related to information literacy goals might be undertaken in any course that include both of these elements.
- Rubrics developed especially for one course may be adapted to other courses after the impact of this assessment strategy is understood and generalized to different contexts.

- Collaboration takes many forms and extends beyond faculty-librarian partnerships for single courses to include the work that takes place on committees with responsibility for entire programs.
- Sustainability and scalability of information literacy assessment is enhanced through faculty-librarian partnerships in the core curriculum.
- Assessment is an iterative process that continually informs course development.

A consistent element in all the chapters, not only in this section but in the entire book, is the conversations between librarians and disciplinary faculty members that were absolutely necessary for these efforts to succeed. Assessment does not occur in isolation, but is inherently intertwined with student learning objectives. Discussions both prior to and following the actual assessment efforts allowed the collaborators to revise and strengthen the selection and delivery of information literacy components and, therefore, student learning.

Chapter 6

A Model for Information Literacy Self-Assessment:

Enhancing Student Learning in Writing Courses through Collaborative Teaching

Leslie Bussert and Norm Pouliot

INTRODUCTION

The humanities librarian at the Campus Library, serving both Cascadia Community College (Cascadia) and the University of Washington Bothell, worked with faculty and students at Cascadia to assess information literacy learning in English 102: Writing from Research, a course required for a transfer degree in which information literacy instruction is closely integrated into the course content. This authentic assessment project utilized preexisting course learning goals and assignments along with student self-assessments based on a rubric to assess student information literacy learning in four sections of English 102 during the 2007–2008 academic year. This project enabled the librarian and faculty member of this multisection course to deepen their collaborative relationship, to evaluate and modify their approaches to information literacy instruction for enhanced student learning, and to gain insight into how students move through the course regarding the information literacy and related writing learning goals.

This chapter begins by reviewing the literature of self-assessment in higher education and information literacy instruction. It continues to explain how we built and conducted the self-assessments within the course, how we used the data collected from the self-assessments, and the benefits, successes, failures, and next steps under consideration for continuing the use of this assessment format within the course.

RELATED LITERATURE

Defining Self-Assessment

Self-assessments are evaluations of oneself, of one's actions and attitudes, or of one's performance at a particular job or learning task in relation to relevant objective standards. They are formative assessments in that they relate to one's development but are also authentic assessments in that they are performance-based, highly interactive, and are framed within real world contexts approximating the necessary applications of knowledge, skills, and abilities learned (Stiggins, 2003). The open-ended and engaging nature of authentic assessment requires problem solving and thoughtful responses from students, whereas its formative nature lends itself well to assessing process-based skills, such as, in our case, research and writing from sources (Knight, 2006).

History and Context of Self-Assessment in Education

The tradition of self-assessment in education dates back over 60 years (Boud, 1995). An increased interest developed in professional schools during the 1970s and later in the decade its educational value gained general recognition (Boud, 1995). By the late 1980s it became a regular part of university teaching and the use of self-assessment in higher education increased in the 1990s (Boud, 1995). Consequently, so did research on utilizing self-assessment methods in higher education and recognition of its use in student learning and cognitive development (Brew, 1995a, 1995b).

Boud (1995) highlights several key factors influencing the increased significance of self-assessment skills within higher education. He identifies macro factors such as higher education's need to prepare students to take responsibility and also the shift from traditional, authoritative curricular structures to problem-based structures in which meeting specific criteria or solving the problem is the measure of success, rather than discipline mastery. At the micro level, Boud recognizes that students rarely follow a single path of study and have fewer opportunities to discuss their work in detail with faculty. He suggests one can no longer assume graduates share the range of common skills required to be able to judge their own work (Boud, 1995). In other words, not all graduates share a common educational experience in terms of courses of study, access to and feedback from faculty, or the development of self-assessment skills allowing them to articulate their talent and knowledge. Furthermore,

Boud (1995) posits students do not enter college with these skills and that undergraduate university courses should develop self-assessments in relation to fields of study or types of knowledge.

Boud also argues that self-assessment is becoming more accepted and significant in higher education because it "enables students to become effective and responsible learners who can continue their education without the intervention of teachers or courses" (Boud, 1995: 13). Brew suggests the "rhetoric of lifelong learning" has brought about the expectation of education carrying on throughout one's life rather than being comprised of simply a "dose" of education early in one's life (Brew, 1995a: 49). This cultural expectation overflows into the professional world in which employers seek graduates with transferable skills and who are communicative, self-aware, and capable of making self-directed decisions, rather than those with specific discipline knowledge (Ball, 1990; Mayer, 1992). In other words, employers tend to seek autonomous people with the lifelong learning skills necessary to perform well in the workplace and who can identify gaps in knowledge and solve problems. Furthermore, graduates need to have self-assessment skills to articulate their talents to potential employers and to effectively evaluate their performance in the professional worlds they enter. Building self-assessment into the undergraduate university curriculum offers students opportunities to develop and refine self-assessment skills and gain the awareness and vocabulary to effectively communicate their talent and knowledge.

Benefits of Self-Assessment

Aside from developing students' skills for self-assessing and expressing their performance and knowledge, this form of assessment clearly has a wide range of benefits for enhancing student learning. For one, self-assessment fosters students' reflective thinking skills which, in turn, promote the development of critical thinking and the acquisition of expertise (Bodi, 2002; Boshuizen, Norman, and Schmidt, 1990). Hatton and Smith's (1995) research findings on reflective learning suggest a hierarchy of self-assessment and encourage instructors to offer learning opportunities that move students through it. At the lowest level of the hierarchy, students practice and refine what they call "technical reflection," or reflection on actions such as what they did or actions they took (Hatton and Smith, 1995: 34–35). On the upper end of the spectrum is "critical reflection," where one "demonstrates an awareness" that actions and events are influenced by "multiple historical, and sociological contexts" or circumstances (Hatton and Smith, 1995: 49). An example of technical reflection might be students assessing how they managed their coursework by turning in assignments on time or attending each class period. Students' critical reflection could include assessments of how they are or are not meeting specific learning goals of a course, how they are identifying skills they mastered in addition to those needing work, as well as how and where they transferred their learning into different settings such as other classes or outside the educational environment.

Self-assessments on both ends of Hatton and Smith's (1995) hierarchy may be beneficial, yet it is the ability to reflect critically upon and recognize how learning can be applied elsewhere that is another key benefit of this form of assessment. Boud posits the use of self-assessment promotes students' ability to "consolidate learning over a range of contexts," which is important for integrating learning from different academic programs of study, disciplines, or courses (Boud, 1995: 19). This skill becomes even more crucial when students graduate and enter the professional world which is by no means organized into neat disciplines or areas of knowledge. Graduates need to have developed "the capability of monitoring what they do and modifying their learning strategies appropriately" while proactively moving toward long-term development by reviewing achievements, recognizing prior learning or gaps in knowledge, and identifying courses of action to fill those gaps or to solve problems (Boud, 1995: 14). The ability to reflect upon and transfer knowledge and learning is especially important in terms of information literacy, as these skills assist in determining one's information needs or gaps in knowledge while also encouraging thoughtful and reflective inquiry into research topics, questions, or problems posed.

Brown, Bull, and Pendleburg (1997) as well as Boud (1995) advocate the ability to self-assess as key to laying the foundation for lifelong learning, or learning to learn, and they also promote self-assessment as good learning practice. In essence, self-assessments help students learn to check their learning and become realistic evaluators of their own performances and knowledge (Brown, Bull, and Pendleburg, 1997; Boud, 1995). Furthermore, Habermas's (1987) research findings suggest reflection is part of the knowledge-building process and that knowledge itself includes meta-level analysis. In other words, metacognition or awareness of one's thinking processes and strategies may be developed through reflection exercises such as self-assessments. Habermas claims it is this ability to analyze and reflect upon one's knowledge and learning that brings into one's consciousness the ways in which knowledge is constructed and enables one to move beyond it and gain new knowledge (Habermas, 1987). Essentially, the lifelong learner needs the metacognitive abilities self-assessment develops to learn how to learn by identifying and filling gaps between what is known and what is not, and also to continue ones education beyond the formal setting and into the workplace or "real world" (Candy, Crebert, and O'Leary, 1994; Justice and Marienau, 1988).

Taking responsibility for one's learning is yet another benefit to developing self-assessment skills in students. Boud argues "developing self-assessment skills is important because it is central to effective learning now and future learning and is also an essential feature of professional practice for anyone taking a responsible role in society" (1995: 15). In other words, students with self-assessment skills can identify and place merit on their achievements and learning, and thus take responsibility for their actions, judgments, and progress toward long-term academic development and later professional growth (Boud, 1995). Because self-assessment encourages students to value their learning achievements based on evidence solely from themselves rather than instructors or peers, it encourages a positive concept of self as students conceive progress in terms of their own achievement and not in relation to others (Boud, 1995). Hence, developing self-monitoring practices enables students to make necessary proactive modifications independently of their instructor or peers (Boud, 1995). In effect, students and graduates with self-assessment skills exhibit lifelong learning behaviors and responsibility for their learning and actions. Thus, one might also assert that self-assessment enhances one's information literacy because of its contribution to the development of lifelong learning abilities that are a key component of being information literate.

Uses and Limitations of Self-Assessment

The value of self-assessment goes beyond the key benefit of enhancing student learning and responsibility. It also encompasses more practical uses such as a supplement to other forms of assessment or for diagnosis and remediation. Boud and Falchikov (1989) point out self-assessment data can be as reliable as other forms of assessment if administered in low-stakes, high-trust situations, such as ungraded self-assessments. This suggests self-assessment can be useful for evaluating student products, performances, and processes, or used in tandem with other assessment methods for evaluating and grading student work. Using self-assessments as an evaluation tool can also be effective for identifying areas students need to focus on or practice (Boud, 1995). Carrying out multiple self-assessments to identify strengths, weaknesses, or problem areas at the beginning of and throughout student learning offers opportunities for both students and instructors to modify study habits and instruction. Doing so allows occasions to remediate such situations and to create optimal environments or behaviors for enhanced learning.

Of course, there are limitations to any form of assessment. Boud (1995) recommends taking into account student perceptions of the self-assessment process itself and to be clear with students about its purpose. For example, are the self-assessments used solely for learning, grading, or both? The ways in which students perceive the process may affect how they complete their self-assessments. If students feel they are "busy work," they may not thoughtfully or reflectively complete them, whereas if students know the self-assessments are not graded and are meant to enhance their learning or help the instructor's teaching, they may offer more complete and thoughtful responses. In addition, self-assessments administered within a high-stakes scenario, such as a graded assignment or test, may not garner honest or accurate responses due to the stakes involved and, as Boud and Falchikov (1989) indicate, lead one to conclude self-assessments are best used for learning rather than for summative assessments such as grades.

There is also the limitation of student self-perception. Boud and Falchikov (1989) found students' self-assessments were more accurate later in a course after more exposure or actual training in doing self-assessments. Boud (1995) indicates some evidence suggests students in introductory courses or in the early years of their program tend to overrate themselves whereas students in advanced courses or in later years of their program tend to underrate themselves. One's cultural or socioeconomic background may possibly make a difference. For example, Brown, Bull, and Pendleburg (1997) state the evidence on gender differences in self-assessment behavior is conflicting, yet it still could affect how students perceive themselves through the self-assessment process.

Information Literacy and Self-Assessment

Whereas research and evidence is found in the library and information science (LIS) literature on assessment and information literacy instruction, little exists on the specific use of self-assessment *within* information literacy instruction. Some librarians are using Personal Response Systems, or "clickers," and tutorial quizzes as self-assessment tools in information literacy instruction settings. Clickers are a useful tool for conducting classroom assessment, but can also be helpful for checking student progress and comprehension, and as a self-assessment tool (Julian and Benson, 2008). The proliferation of online information literacy tutorials also offers opportunities for students to self-assess by using quizzes as pre- and postmeasures of student understanding (Ganster and Walsh, 2008).

Most prevalent in the LIS literature is the use of the Research Readiness Self-Assessment (RRSA). The RRSA is based on the Information Literacy Competency Standards for Higher Education (Association of College and Research Libraries, 2000) and was developed over a five-year period by librarian Anne Marie Casey and psychologist Lana Ivanitskaya to assess and gather feedback on essential skills for critical thinking and lifelong learning in a variety of subject areas. This comprehensive tool measures objective or self-reported skills and knowledge but also captures beliefs strongly related to information literacy. Casey and Ivanitskaya have worked extensively with this tool. One article they published included the process of developing the tool whereas another article investigated and reported the extent of awareness college students have regarding their level of health information competency (Ivanitskaya, Laus, and Casey, 2004; Ivanitskaya and Casey, 2006). Their use of the RRSA most relevant to the project described in this chapter studied the impact of pretests on the effectiveness of information literacy instruction when graduate students are offered feedback on their pretests (Ivanitskaya et al., 2008). The RRSA was also used as a posttest and their results found students who completed the pretest with feedback did significantly better on the post-test than those who did not receive the pretest with feedback. The authors suggest offering pretest self-assessments with feedback enhances information literacy instruction and allows opportunities to explicitly compare students' actual and perceived literacy (Ivanitskaya et al., 2008).

The most relevant LIS research on self-assessment for our project is Gross and Latham's (2007) investigation into the relationship between students' library anxiety and self-assessment of their information literacy skills and actual skill levels. Despite a small sample size of freshman students, their results show no relationship between library anxiety and information literacy skill levels, but do show a difference between the information literacy skills of lower- and higher-performing students. Specifically, students who demonstrate lower-level skills demonstrate inflated views of their abilities whereas higher-level students underestimate their performance, evidence Boud (1995) also suggests and which demonstrates his and Falchikov's idea that training students to self-assess is useful and necessary (Boud and Falchikov, 1989).

The literature on self-assessment in higher education and information literacy instruction clearly offers evidence on its efficacy, making it an attractive method of assessment. The literature also illustrates the connections between the self-assessment technique and its role in developing lifelong learning skills, information literacy, and overall enhanced student learning.

INSTITUTIONAL CONTEXT AT CASCADIA COMMUNITY COLLEGE

Cascadia Community College is co-located with the University of Washington Bothell on a single campus in Bothell, Washington, a suburb about 15 miles northeast of Seattle. The Campus Library and librarians serve students and faculty at both institutions and strategically integrate information literacy instruction into core classes within the curriculum. The assessment project described here was implemented within Cascadia's English 102: Writing from Research class, a required course in their general education curriculum. With a full-time equivalent student body of nearly 1,700 and many students aiming to transfer to four-year universities after attending Cascadia, multiple sections of the English 102 course are offered year round on campus and online, requiring sustainable information literacy instruction and assessment methods.

The typical English 102 class includes traditional college students right out of high school, high school students earning college credit, adult learners just beginning or returning to college, transfer students from other institutions, and students formerly in Cascadia's English as a Second Language curriculum. As with many college writing courses, the class sizes are capped low at 24 students. This allows maximum contact between the faculty member and students as well as with the librarian working with students in the course.

Typical assignments in English 102 include introductions to and practice with:

- critical thinking,
- close reading and annotating texts,
- summary and paraphrasing,
- library research techniques and resources,
- written research proposals,
- argumentative essays,
- constructive peer review techniques, and
- rough and final draft research papers ranging anywhere from four to twelve pages in length, plus bibliographies.

English 102 instructors have no standardized or required syllabus they must adhere to, but there is an institutional Course Outcome Guide outlining learning goals that instructors must strive to meet within their course (Cascadia, 2006). During the 2005–2006 academic year, librarians provided input for revision of the English 102 learning goals and sought to reinforce information literacy outcomes within them. This process was part of Cascadia's regular Course Outcome Guide review procedure undertaken for each course in the curriculum. The humanities librarians were invited by the English faculty to contribute by participating in English faculty meetings and by working with the lead faculty member in English.

Librarians worked collaboratively with the faculty to identify the existing English 102 learning goals already including elements of critical thinking and library research. The librarians' goal was to insert specific language about the library, librarians, and collaboration. However, the faculty sought to keep the language succinct and did not want to get too prescriptive with some of the details librarians suggested. Although the librarians did not succeed entirely with their goals in terms of the language of the Course Outcome Guide, the conversations generated during the revision process were most valuable. These discussions allowed librarians and faculty to work out some common understanding about the information literacy skills and assignments appropriate for the course and strengthened the culture of instructional collaboration between English 102 faculty members and librarians.

COLLABORATION WITH ENGLISH FACULTY

Being located at a newer institution, librarians had opportunities early on to advocate for and develop integrated information literacy instruction in targeted areas of the curriculum, which encouraged a high level of collaboration between librarians and faculty. In 2000, Cascadia opened its doors as one of 12 community colleges in the United States to be accepted into the Vanguard program, which "helps community colleges develop and implement learning-centered values into their missions and curricular programs" (League for Innovation in the Community College, 2009). As such, student learning and innovation has always been at the forefront of Cascadia's culture, and their collaborative and inclusive strategic program planning processes, arising from Vanguard project values, often include librarians. Thus, the relationship between librarians and Cascadia faculty is positive and strong, especially among the faculty members teaching English 102.

Librarians integrating information literacy instruction into this course typically have anywhere from one to three class sessions (two to six hours) with the students and customize the instruction to complement each faculty member's individual approach to the English 102 syllabus and assignments.

Assessment of information literacy learning in this course began in 2006 when student work was collected into a mini portfolio and rated by librarians and English faculty against an information literacy rubric created by the humanities librarian. This assessment exercise was fruitful in bringing faculty and librarians together to discuss writing and information literacy goals and student performance in the course, and also offered librarians the opportunity to review students' final papers and bibliographies. However, the concluding data was not very useful in terms of moving forward to enhance student learning and modify learning goals or specific components of information literacy instruction within the course.

In 2007, the humanities librarian and a faculty member teaching two sections of English 102 decided to gather some qualitative data by offering students the opportunity to do an extra-credit presentation at the end of the quarter. Students were asked primarily to discuss and share their research and learning process. Most students took this opportunity, and even though many tended to also include information about their research topic, the librarian and faculty member were able to collect useful data for modifying future approaches to integrating and teaching information literacy within the course. For example, students shared the points in the research and writing process where they were most challenged or successful, while also communicating what they learned from the course and how they will apply it to other courses or their lives outside of school. The student presentations were a great attempt at obtaining qualitative data and were useful for learning about how students learn in this course; however, the humanities librarian was interested in adopting a self-assessment tool based on the information literacy rubric used in 2006 that another English faculty member experimented with previously.[1]

ASSESSING INFORMATION LITERACY LEARNING: HOW WE DID IT

The Campus Library humanities librarian selected and worked with one Cascadia faculty member teaching two sections of English 102 in 2008. This faculty member also participated in the previous assessment efforts in 2006 and 2007 and thus was familiar with the information literacy instruction program and the learning and assessment goals for the program and course. At the beginning of the quarter the faculty member asked students to give written permission to use their anonymous work and self-assessments for program and course improvement. This permission also allowed sharing the project with library and English faculty communities through various venues such as faculty meetings, workshops, or even formal regional or national conference presentations. The permission form was approved by Cascadia's Institutional Research office and there was no penalty if students did not want their work used. A few students questioned the intentions and privacy implications of consenting and the faculty member addressed their concerns by offering more context. The faculty member reinforced their anonymity and reiterated their option to deny permission without it affecting their grades while also offering examples of specific ways in which the information would be used and presented. By clarifying that the information would be used to improve the course design and teaching, and by explaining the venues in which this information would be shared, the trust of the students was earned and ultimately each student gave permission.

At the start of the quarter, the librarian and faculty member reviewed the course syllabus together to identify strategic points to offer the self-assessment to students. It was initially decided to have students complete the self-assessments three times throughout the course: once very early in the quarter before any exposure to the library or librarian; a second time after attending two information literacy instruction sessions covering Boolean searching, keywords, and source evaluation, and after completing and submitting their written research proposals; and finally, a third time following the last working computer lab session in the library and after having completed their final eight- to twelve-page research papers with bibliographies.

The self-assessments were administered during class time and were not graded. Due to the caveats involved in using self-reported data, the librarian and faculty member purposefully made the self-assessments a low-stakes activity to minimize the inflation of skills in the students' self-reporting, and to encourage honest and thoughtful responses. Each self-assessment was administered and completed in electronic format. The faculty member and librarian used a computer lab for instruction so students could conveniently access the self-assessment tool in a Microsoft Word format from their English 102 Internet research guide created by the humanities librarian (see Appendix 6.1). After completing the self-assessments students would print them out in class, put their names on them, and turn them in to the faculty member, who then provided them to the humanities librarian for review. The librarian reviewed all three rounds of the self–assessments, acknowledging trends and skills students needed more practice with and also identifying skills students already felt confident performing. The librarian shared this information with the faculty member so they could work together to make swift adjustments to the syllabus or information literacy and writing instruction as needed. As the quarter progressed and students performed their second and third self-assessments, the faculty member would provide students with their previous self-assessment forms so they could reflect, compare, and record their progress between each of the three offered throughout the course. The majority of students thoughtfully compared and documented their progress between the self-assessments and many also identified and recorded new personal learning goals or areas they needed to work on. However, some students were less thoughtful and only offered very brief or unsubstantial reflections between the three self-assessments.

OUTCOMES

There were many positive outcomes to this assessment project and it will definitely be repeated in future English 102 sections with the participating faculty member. The success of this model also generated interest among other librarians and English faculty who regularly teach the course. Some have since implemented similar assessment projects. So far four additional librarians have successfully collaborated with three other English faculty members to integrate the self-assessments and have also experienced some of the outcomes discussed here.

Enhanced Student Learning

One strong outcome and benefit of the project was the enhanced learning students demonstrated in various ways. Students exhibited stronger writing by the end of the quarter as expressed both within their self-assessments, as well as by the faculty member who administered more "A" grades than usual. By the third self-assessment, students were using language not evident in the previous self-assessments to describe their information literacy and research writing skills, such as: *stronger, confident, better, improved, strengthened, successful, capable, developed, prepared, effective,* and *comfortable.* At this point, students were also using more sophisticated vocabulary to describe their skills, which the literature suggests can result from performing regular self-assessments. The librarian and faculty member did observe some obvious inflation of abilities within the self-assessments. Interestingly enough, and as the literature indicates, students seemed much more realistic about their abilities by the second and third self-assessments, which were completed after they had gained more experience in both self-assessing and the information literacy and research skills indicated within the self-assessment tool.

Students also demonstrated and expressed enhanced metacognition and thoughtful reflection on learning. This was one outcome the librarian hoped the self-assessment tool would encourage and which the literature proposes is an advantage to doing frequent self-assessments. Having students perform regular self-assessments empowered them to take responsibility for their learning. As the learning goals of the course became transparent through the self-assessment tool, students grew aware of what was being asked and expected of them. This enabled them to internalize and set goals for themselves for meeting both the course's information literacy learning goals and their own personal learning goals.

After doing the self-assessments on the course information literacy learning goals, many students included in their responses personal goals for working toward the skills indicated within the self-assessment tool. For example, in response to the evaluating sources learning goals, one student said, "I apply evaluation criteria to some sources of information and show an awareness of the significance of the information. I need to work on applying more specific evaluation criteria and explain the audience and purpose or point of view of the information." Here the student is acknowledging perception of the current skill level while also developing the personal goal of improving upon those abilities to further meet the outlined information literacy learning goals.

The following quotes from the feedback students offered on performing the self-assessments come from just a few of many students who also expressed the benefit of transparent learning goals:

- "[The self-assessments] helped me think critically of where my skills in this class not only stood, but how they improved throughout the class."
- "I feel like I was able to track my learning because the self-assessments told us exactly what we should know how to do."

- "[By writing it down,] the information I have learned becomes engrained in my head. Therefore . . . I will be able to apply the concepts learned in this class more effectively in other classes."

In addition, students emphasized the usefulness of the information literacy instruction workshops and self-assessments in their formal course evaluations after the course ended. The faculty member was very pleased with the thorough and high quality of the rough and final drafts students produced. The faculty member also observed this sample of student work was of better quality than in previous courses even with nearly identical information literacy instruction workshops.

Enhanced Librarian-Faculty Collaboration

Another positive outcome of this project was the enhancement to the already strong librarian and faculty member collaboration. The data collected from the self-assessments allowed increased communication between all three parties (faculty, librarian, and students) in addition to accommodating flexibility and responsiveness in information literacy instruction and course planning. This entailed more frequent and in-depth conversations in person and over e-mail not only about planning the information literacy instruction sessions, but mostly about details of the students' learning as revealed through their self-assessments. The faculty member and librarian were able to identify and discuss trends in the students' reflections and immediately respond accordingly by altering lesson plans, activities, and assignments to better meet student needs.

The faculty member made it transparent to students that the librarian would be reviewing each self-assessment as well as other information literacy instruction worksheets that included reflective prompts soliciting feedback from students. During information literacy instruction sessions following the self-assessments, the librarian and faculty member were able to communicate to the students their observations from reviewing the self-assessments, and that the day's instruction session was tailored to address those specific needs students had articulated. This exchange offered students some ownership in what content was covered in class and also enforced the librarian and faculty member's intent to truly meet their learning needs.

The librarian also reviewed and commented on one worksheet from the first information literacy instruction session and the faculty member took the librarian's comments into consideration when assigning grades to the worksheets. This particular worksheet guided students through the process of identifying and developing keywords, constructing Boolean search queries and using them in an article database, and identifying two potential sources for their research. The conclusion of the worksheet asked students to reflect on what their searches were telling the database to do, the relevance of their selected sources to their topic, and most important, what they learned from the information literacy instruction, in addition to noting any remaining questions they had about the skills and tools taught.

The librarian briefly reviewed the completed worksheets to gain a sense of students' accomplishments, to make suggestions or corrections, and to take in the student responses to the reflective prompts described above. The faculty member then did the same while assigning grades to the worksheets, and also discussed the identified trends or problem areas with the librarian. Last, the faculty member distributed the worksheets to the students so they might continue their research having received feedback from both the librarian and faculty member on their topic and keyword selection, search queries, sources selected, and any questions they had. This transparent feedback loop including all three parties was found to be effective for enhancing collaboration between the librarian and faculty member, and for conveying to students the relevance of the librarian's participation in the course.

Enhanced Visibility and Relevance of Our Program

The data collected via the student self-assessments have already been useful in many arenas, especially in the ways previously discussed. The faculty member and librarian especially found the qualitative data much more useful than the quantitative data collected in previous assessment projects described earlier. The student narrative voices offered through the self-assessments provided powerful data for informing information literacy instruction at the course and program levels. In addition, the data offer evidence when communicating to campus administrators the efficacy of library instruction programs and their relevance to enhanced student learning. This information would also be useful for many other purposes such as advocating for sustained or increased funding and personnel for information literacy instruction programs or for including in budget and annual reports. Furthermore, it could be useful for faculty and librarian promotion and tenure documentation and for increasing the visibility of the library's instruction program with administrators and faculty on campus.

In terms of program planning, data gathered from the student self-assessments also reaffirm and inform the library's strategic partnering with faculty members in courses where information literacy instruction and library research skills are more critical to student success in comparison to other courses. Strategically targeting relevant courses for instruction offers increased sustainability within program resources as well as opportunities to build continuing and consistent dialog and relationships with faculty members and their respective departments. By targeting required "core" courses within programs or departments for information literacy instruction, librarians can reach the broadest number of students on campus, while also managing not to duplicate instructional content at numerous points across the curriculum which can create inconsistencies and redundancies for students. This strategic approach, rather than an "instruction on-demand" model where information literacy instruction is requested by faculty in various classes within a program, also offers increased sustainability as librarians can more easily predict and manage their instruction workload. Over time, librarians can develop enduring collaborative relationships with faculty members teaching those targeted courses while also establishing a collaborative norm for faculty new to the course, both of which foster the development of the most effective information literacy instruction strategies for the students and course at hand.

WHAT DID NOT WORK: FEEDBACK FROM THE STUDENTS

The students' third self-assessment included a brief section with prompts to collect feedback and thoughts from them on how they felt about performing the self-assessments throughout the quarter. The majority of the student feedback was overwhelmingly positive with just a few students indicating the self-assessments did not improve or alter their perception of how they learned and developed the information literacy skills taught in the course. Most indicated the self-assessments helped them keep track of their learning; better understand the course and library learning goals; and identify what skills to practice and work toward improving.

Students also offered some great suggestions for improving the self-assessment process and tool for future implementations. A few students mentioned three self-assessments for the quarter was too many. They felt there was little change in their skills between the second and third self-assessments, rendering the third one "redundant" and extraneous, which suggests the timing and administration of the second one may not have been ideal or even necessary. In response, the faculty member and librarian administered only two self-assessments during the following quarter's classes, which nonetheless offered effective data to work with and still offered enhanced student learning.

Some students indicated the language on the self-assessment tool was confusing. The tool did include small amounts of information literacy and pedagogical jargon, so for the following quarter the librarian attempted to simplify the language and included brief examples to help illustrate concepts and skills described. This may have helped some, but still warrants further attention as students in the following quarter's classes expressed the same problem in their feedback on the self-assessment process. Surprisingly, the faculty member and librarian also observed that fewer verbal or written instructions and prompts provided to the students resulted in increased data and more thoughtful responses from them in the self-assessments.

NEXT STEPS: REFINING THE TOOL AND PROCESS

There are several ways to advance this project and continue its development. First, interest exists among many English 102 faculty and librarians to try the self-assessments in their classes, and a strong possibility of incorporating it into the English 102 Course Outcome Guide, which would require all faculty members and librarians teaching the course to implement at least one self-assessment. Collecting this data across multiple sections of English 102 would create a vast library of qualitative student data and narratives for faculty and administrators to draw upon for programmatic or even college-wide assessment efforts.

A few students suggested adding proofreading and peer review skills to the self-assessment and this is an idea the librarian and faculty member will carefully consider for future iterations. Many students also lamented that the self-assessment form was "weird" to fill out electronically in a Microsoft Word document formatted with tables. In response, the librarian created and is piloting an online version using institutional Web form survey tools. Students complete the self-assessment using an online form from which the librarian and faculty member can download and save the data in various formats offering increased possibilities for use and ease of analysis. Also under consideration is finding a way to offer students feedback on their self-assessments, which the literature suggests enhances its efficacy. Last is the possibility of identifying additional programs and courses at both Cascadia and the University of Washington Bothell where this model would be effective for gathering student data in support of various assessment, curriculum development, and funding or growth initiatives.

CONCLUSION

In conclusion, this model for assessing information literacy learning was effective and fruitful in many ways. Using a self-assessment rather than other forms of assessment was beneficial to the students, as well as the librarian and faculty member teaching the course. Students were able to track their learning progress and set new goals through the process of completing the self-assessments, whereas the librarian and faculty member were able to use this data to adapt and modify instruction to address the students' learning needs and gain a stronger sense of how students progressed through the course in regard to the information literacy learning goals.

Using self-assessments enhanced student learning by echoing the benefits of using this form of assessment for learning as shown in the education and LIS literature discussed earlier in the chapter. Due to thoughtful responses within the self-assessments, students developed and practiced the metacognitive abilities necessary for learning how to learn and maintaining lifelong learning skills. The model and process described here also encouraged students to proactively take responsibility for learning through explicit exposure to the learning goals, personal goal setting, modifying study habits, and also cultivated their self-awareness and aptitude for articulating their learning and the value of their acquired skill sets.

The model fostered deeper collaboration between the librarian and faculty member as they repeatedly worked together throughout the course to adapt instruction and respond to the shifting learning needs of the students while also enhancing the feedback loop between the librarian, faculty member, and students. Furthermore, the librarian's presence and role within the course was magnified, communicating to students the significance of the library and librarians to their learning, and also increasing the visibility and relevance of information literacy instruction and library resources for their research needs.

Furthermore, this model illuminated the benefits of using self-assessments as a measure of learning and data collection tool. The qualitative data generated through the self-assessments offered valuable information for the librarian and faculty member teaching the course, but also for use in other arenas such as budget planning or program administration and assessment. Student learning data in this narrative form differs from quantitative measures in that it captures the student voice and experience of learning within the course at hand and can offer a very useful complement to quantitative or other forms of data used for such purposes.

This model contributes to the literature on self-assessment in education and LIS research by offering an approach enhancing both student learning and instruction in addition to deepening collaboration between librarians and faculty. Other institutions seeking to implement assessment projects or to enhance librarian and faculty collaboration can find here an adaptable model suitable for implementation within information literacy or other instruction and for use in assessing and collecting data on student learning in various types of courses.

NOTE

1. Thank you to Todd Lundberg, PhD, former Cascadia Community College English Faculty, for initiating the self-assessment idea and tool.

REFERENCES

Association of College and Research Libraries. 2000. "Information Literacy Competency Standards for Higher Education." Available: www.ala.org/ala/mgrps/divs/acrl/standards/informationliteracycompetency.cfm (accessed October 1, 2009).

Ball, Christopher. 1990. *More Means Different: Widening Access to Higher Education*. London: Royal Society of Arts, Industry Matters.

Bodi, Sonia. 2002. "How Do We Bridge the Gap between What We Teach and What They Do? Some Thoughts on the Place of Questions in the Process of Research." *The Journal of Academic Librarianship* 28, no.3 (May/June): 109–114.

Boshuizen, H. P. A., G. R. Norman, and H. G. Schmidt. 1990. "A Cognitive Perspective on Medical Expertise: Theory and Implications." *Academic Medicine* 65, no. 10 (October): 611–621.

Boud, David, ed. 1995. *Enhancing Learning through Self Assessment*. London: Kogan Page.

Boud, David, and Nancy Falchikov. 1989. "Student Self-Assessment in Higher Education: A Meta-Analysis." *Review of Educational Research* 59, no. 4 (Winter): 395–430.

Brew, Angela. 1995a. "What Is the Scope of Self Assessment?" In *Enhancing Learning through Self Assessment* (pp. 48–62), edited by David Boud. London: Kogan Page.

Brew, Angela.1995b. "Self Assessment in Different Domains." In *Enhancing Learning through Self Assessment* (pp. 129–154), edited by David Boud. London: Kogan Page.

Brown, George, Joanne Bull, and Malcolm Pendleburg. 1997. *Assessing Student Learning in Higher Education*. New York: Routledge.

Candy, Philip C., Gay Crebert, and Jane O'Leary. 1994. *Developing Lifelong Learners through Undergraduate Education*. National Board of Employment and Education Training (NBEET) Commissioned Report No. 28. Canberra: Australian Government Publishing Service.

Cascadia Community College. 2006. "ENGL&102 Composition II." Cascadia Community College Course Outcome Guides (2006). Available: www.cascadia.edu/class_schedules_catalogs/course_outcome_guides.aspx (accessed October 1, 2009).

Ganster, Ligaya A., and Tiffany R. Walsh. 2008. "Enhancing Library Instruction to Undergraduates: Incorporating Online Tutorials into the Curriculum." *College and Undergraduate Libraries* 15, no. 3 (Autumn): 314–333.

Gross, Melissa, and Don Latham. 2007. "Attaining Information Literacy: An Investigation of the Relationship between Skill Level, Self-Estimates of Skill, and Library Anxiety." *Library and Information Science Research* 29, no. 3 (September): 332–353.

Habermas, Jurgan. 1987. *Knowledge and Human Interests*. Cambridge, UK: Polity Press.

Hatton, Neville, and David Smith. 1995. "Reflection in Teacher Education: Towards Definition and Implementation." *Teaching and Teacher Education* 11, no. 1 (January): 33–49.

Ivanitskaya, Lana, Ryan Laus, and Anne Marie Casey. 2004. "Research Readiness Self-Assessment: Assessing Students' Research Skills and Attitudes." *Journal of Library Administration* 41, no.1/2 (January): 167–183.

Ivanitskaya, Lana, and Anne Marie Casey. 2006. "Health Information Literacy and Competencies of Information Age Students: Results from the Interactive Online Research Readiness Self-Assessment (RRSA)." *Journal of Medical Internet Research* 8, no. 2 (April). Available (with membership): www.jmir.org/2006/2/e6/HTML (accessed October 1, 2009).

Ivanitskaya, Lana, Susan DuFord, Monica Craig, and Anne Marie Casey. 2008. "How Does a Pre-Assessment of Off-Campus Students' Information Literacy Affect the Effectiveness of Library Instruction?" *Journal of Library Administration* 48, no.3/4 (October): 509–525.

Julian, Suzanne, and Kimball Benson. 2008. "Clicking Your Way to Library Instruction Assessment: Using a Personal Response System at Brigham Young University." *College & Research Libraries News* 69, no. 5 (May): 258–260.

Justice, David O., and Catherine Marienau. 1988. "Self-Assessment: Essential Skills for Adult Learners." In *Knowing and Doing: Learning through Experience* (pp. 49–62), edited by Pat Hutchings and Allen Wutzdorff. San Francisco: Jossey-Bass.

Knight, Lorrie A. 2006. "Using Rubrics to Assess Information Literacy." *Reference Services Review* 34, no. 1: 43–55.

League for Innovation in the Community College. "The Learning College Project." Available: www.league.org/league/projects/lcp/index.htm (accessed October 1, 2009).

Mayer, E. A. 1992. *Educating for Excellence: Business/Higher Education Round Table 1992 Education Surveys*. Commissioned Report No. 2. Camberwell, Victoria: Business/ Higher Education Round Table.

Stiggins, Richard, et al. 2003. "Assessment." In *Encyclopedia of Education* (pp. 123–139), edited by James W. Guthrie. New York: Macmillan Reference.

Appendix 6.1. English 102 Research and Information Literacy Self-Assessment	
Dimension 1: **Defines the topic and/or research question**	**Where am I?** **What do I need to work on?**
Often, a writer entering English 102: • Selects a broad topic rather than defining a specific topic or question (e.g. "globalization" or "globalization and society") • Identifies minimal key concepts within the topic or question • Determines the extent and nature of some of the information needed **Upon successfully completing English 102, a writer:** • Selects and defines a specific research topic or question (e.g. "effects of globalization on young women in developing countries") • Identifies many key concepts within the topic or question • Is able to determine the extent and nature of most of the information needed **An established researcher:** • Selects, defines, and clearly articulates a research topic or question with subsidiary, embedded, or implicit aspects (e.g., "gender and globalization: female labor and women's mobilization") • Identifies many key concepts and specifically addresses the topic/problem through subtopics/subquestions/multiple perspectives • Shows strong ability to determine the extent and nature of the information needed to adequately address the question/topic	
Dimension 2: **Uses various techniques and resources to access information**	**Where am I?** **What do I need to work on?**
Often, a writer entering English 102: • Demonstrates awareness, but selects inappropriate searching methods and/or information retrieval systems (e.g., only uses Google or other search engines, Wikipedia, Encarta, etc.) • Experiments with new information-seeking strategies and/or methods to learn about their research question/topic	

(Continued)

Appendix 6.1. English 102 Research and Information Literacy Self-Assessment *(Continued)*

Dimension 2: Uses various techniques and resources to access information *(Continued)*	Where am I? What do I need to work on?
Upon successfully completing English 102, a writer: • Selects appropriate information-seeking methods and/or information retrieval systems (e.g., library research databases and catalog, academic books and articles, etc.) • Applies new information-seeking strategies and/or methods to modify, update or learn about their research question/topic (e.g., Boolean searching, relevant keywords, bibliographies/ reference lists, etc.) An established researcher: • Self-consciously selects relevant and appropriate information-seeking methods and/or information retrieval systems (e.g., seeks out specific or specialized subject research databases, catalogs, people/experts, and other resources) • Applies a repertoire of creative and flexible information-seeking strategies and/or methods to modify, update, or learn about the research question/topic (e.g., citation tracking/analysis using bibliographies/reference lists, using specialized sources from related fields of study, etc.)	
Dimension 3: **Uses multiple types of sources**	**Where am I?** **What do I need to work on?**
Often, a writer entering English 102: • Distinguishes some types or formats of potential sources (e.g., Web sites, newspaper and magazine articles) • Uses a few types or formats of information Upon successfully completing English 102, a writer: • Distinguishes many types or formats of potential sources (e.g., academic journal articles, books, videos, audio clips, government reports, etc.) • Uses many types or formats of information	

(Continued)

Appendix 6.1. English 102 Research and Information Literacy Self-Assessment *(Continued)*

Dimension 3: Uses multiple types of sources *(Continued)*	Where am I? What do I need to work on?
An established researcher: • Distinguishes many appropriate types or formats of potential sources (e.g., in addition to those listed above, experts, researchers, government documents, artifacts, data, maps, institutions/organizations, primary research, etc.) • Uses many appropriate types or formats of information	
Dimension 4: **Evaluates sources for accuracy, relevancy, and bias**	**Where am I?** **What do I need to work on?**
Often, a writer entering English 102: • Articulates and/or applies evaluation criteria to some sources of information (e.g., date of publication, title of source) • Shows an awareness of the audience or purpose or point of view of information sources • Shows an awareness of the characteristics (significance, contradictions, etc.) or context of information and sources **Upon successfully completing English 102, a writer:** • Articulates and applies specific evaluation criteria to most sources of information (e.g., authorship, commercial or academic publication, relevance to topic, organization, format, appearance, etc.) • Explains the audience and purpose and point of view of information sources (e.g., audience of publication, bias, point of view of author, etc.) • Appraises explicitly the unique characteristics (significance, contradictions, etc.) or context of information and sources (e.g., understands contributions the source makes to the topic) **An established researcher:** • Articulates sophisticated evaluation criteria and consistently applies those criteria to sources of information	

(Continued)

Appendix 6.1. English 102 Research and Information Literacy Self-Assessment *(Continued)*

Dimension 4: Evaluates sources for accuracy, relevancy, and bias *(Continued)*	**Where am I?** What do I need to work on?
An established researcher *(Continued)*: • Consistently analyzes the audience, purpose, and point of view of information sources • Explains how unique characteristics (significance, contradictions, etc.) or context of information and sources affects meaning conveyed	
Dimension 5: Organizes, synthesizes, and incorporates information into knowledge base	**Where am I?** What do I need to work on?
Often, a writer entering English 102: • Minimally summarizes main ideas and/or information from sources • Establishes interrelationships among ideas and/or does little comparison of new and prior knowledge **Upon successfully completing English 102, a writer:** • Accurately summarizes main ideas and/or information in context and with detail • Establishes interrelationships among ideas and/or does some comparison of new and prior knowledge **An established researcher:** • Accurately summarizes main ideas and/or information as well as their sub-topics/sub-questions/multiple perspectives (e.g., delves deeper into all facets and perspectives on a topic) • Establishes interrelationships among ideas and/or accurately compares new and prior knowledge to construct new concepts/ideas/insights (e.g., uses new knowledge to create new ideas or ways of thinking about the topic)	
Dimension 6: Uses information ethically and responsibly	**Where am I?** What do I need to work on?
Often, a writer entering English 102: • Cites some sources appropriately (e.g., bibliography/reference list/works cited present)	

Appendix 6.1. English 102 Research and Information Literacy Self-Assessment *(Continued)*

Dimension 6: Uses information ethically and responsibly *(Continued)*	Where am I? What do I need to work on?
Often, a writer entering English 102 *(Continued)*: • Demonstrates minimal knowledge of legal or ethical standards for information use (e.g., credits quotations or excerpts from sources) **Upon successfully completing English 102, a writer:** • Cites most sources appropriately (e.g., mostly uses correct format and style for source type and parenthetical citations within text) • Demonstrates more knowledge of legal or ethical standards for information use (e.g., cites ideas/concepts as well as text quotations/excerpts from sources, aware of subtle forms of plagiarism) **An established researcher:** • Consistently cites sources appropriately (e.g., always uses proper format and style for citations in text or reference lists) • Consistently demonstrates full knowledge of legal or ethical standards	

Chapter 7

Vampires, Philosophers, and Graphic Novels:
Assessing Thematic Writing Courses in *The Big Read*

Deborah B. Gaspar and Pamela S. Presser

INTRODUCTION

A George Washington University student enrolling in a first-year writing class is offered an array of course themes to choose from. As all courses are organized around a central theme selected by the instructor, students might end up writing a research paper about topics as different from one another as graphic novels, vampires, or Alfred North Whitehead. Faculty and librarian partners collaborate to create assignments that reflect the course theme. A student might be asked to complete an original ethnographic study, write material for a community organization, reference Supreme Court arguments, evaluate exhibits at a museum, or produce a podcast. We champion this diversity while recognizing that the multiplicity of approaches imposes an intriguing set of challenges for program assessment. The University Writing Program (UWP) invited faculty and librarian participation on an assessment committee to explore methodologies that could assess student research and writing to monitor program effectiveness. The authors of this chapter are members of this committee and participated in the design and implementation of a holistic assessment project titled *The Big Read* that garnered feedback on information literacy as well as other student learning outcomes. We explain how we implemented the project, drawing on our already-existing collaboration. We discuss the impact of the project on our pedagogy, and provide a brief review of relevant literature.[1]

LITERATURE REVIEW

Information Literacy Assessment

Literature regarding assessment of Information Literacy is expanding to cover a rich diversity of formats and settings. Once ACRL approved *Information Literacy Competency Standards for Higher Education* (2000), librarians began to engage the language of the standards as learning objectives in classrooms across universities. ACRL followed with *Objectives for Information Literacy Instruction: A Model Statement for Academic Librarians* (2001) expressly so librarians could develop "objectives for an individual teaching session, or for a course, or when collaborating with a course instructor to incorporate information literacy instruction into a specific course" (ACRL, 2001: 1).

Authentic assessment strategies as embodied in learning objectives target learning behaviors, thus shifting the focus away from rote learning to student processes and transferable skills. Such assessment strategies confirm the value of information literacy learning to the broader university community (Rockman, 2002; Avery, 2003). Fiegen, Cherry, and Watson correctly assert that "the existence of the standards provides a common language from which to integrate information competence into the curriculum and courses" (2002: 309).

This review of the literature focuses on student research papers as authentic assessment and rubrics as the evaluation tool. Research papers are a common student product across universities. Tuttle and McKinzie explain "it is clear that engaging teachers and students in the process of discipline-based writing yields student products that are intrinsically valuable, give instructors another basis for genuine assessment, and deepen the student produced contribution to the conversation of enacted curriculum" (2007: 111). Their case study focuses on a three-pronged assessment: student documentation of their research process, the resulting paper, and a reflective essay. It is important to note here that *The Big Read* assessment discussed in this chapter is also but one of an array of techniques utilized by UWP. Emmons and Martin (2002) compare research papers drawn from student portfolios collected before and after the inclusion of information literacy objectives in a first year writing course. Here, too, they utilize a rubric to assess "the presence of an arguable thesis, the use of source texts to support that thesis, the overall organization of the argument, the development and coherence of paragraphs and sentences, and the control of conventional usage and mechanics" (Emmons and Martin, 2002: 549). Their process includes close reading of student papers to evaluate how well they incorporated the research into the body of the paper and a careful analysis of the sources selected.

Hutchins (2003) collaborated with political science faculty to create a rubric useful for assessing annotated bibliographies. She notes that the rubric design process was instrumental for determining student learning objectives but particularly useful for aligning disciplinary language with ACRL standards. Oakleaf (2008) surveys a variety of assessment tools, including rubrics. She advocates rubrics because they articulate agreed-upon values, structure reliable scoring, provide detailed result data, focus on standards-based learning, and are cost effective (Oakleaf, 2008: 245). Lorrie Knight (2006) utilized rubrics in a first year research and writing course, similar to GWU's first year course. She advises, "It is important to provide enough descriptive detail to ensure that students and/or alternative graders can easily grasp the content. Rubrics should avoid the use of slippery terminology" (Knight, 2006: 46). Knight's point is applicable to *The Big Read* project since construction of the rubric took time and collaborative thought in order to provide the necessary degree of detail to the readers. (See Appendix 7.2.)

WRITING PROGRAM ASSESSMENT

The literature on writing program assessment recounts a long history fraught with disagreement, yet opportunities for creative collaborations abound, and have gradually become more frequent. Michael Williamson locates the beginning of the strife within a conflict over competing models of literacy education, such as "the continuing controversy over basic skills" (1994: 59). Andrea A. Lunsford (1986) traces the origins of college writing assessment in America to entrance examinations given by Harvard in 1873, but, as she notes, such testing has always been controversial. Six years after Harvard instituted testing, the Conference of New England Colleges attempted to set regional requirements, a move that paved the way for the establishment in 1901 of the College Entrance Examinations Board. Brian Huot's (2002) analysis of Harvard's model points out that the testing was done to address a perception that students were unprepared. Huot argues, "This notion of assessment as something done because of a deficit in student training or teacher responsibility is still with us in the plethora of accountability programs at the state level" (2002: 1). As Edward White explains, the deficit approach has been responsible for the fear and loathing many teachers have expressed toward assessment (1985: 2–4). When White published *Teaching and Assessing Writing*, writing teachers and testing specialists were extremely alienated from each other and unwilling or unable to collaborate. White began his book by lamenting this breach and proposing solutions. His attempt to mediate between the two factions was influential. Huot's recent *(Re)Articulating Writing Assessment for Teaching and Learning* cites White's book as "easily the most popular" resource for writing program teachers and administrators (2002: 31). Writing teachers, observed White, were justifiably suspicious of "results...used routinely to...suggest incompetence on the part of the students, the teachers, or both" (1985: 1). Although conceding that much testing of writing was poorly done, White advocated a collaborative approach, arguing that involving teachers in the conception and execution of assessment can ameliorate such problems.

Multiple-choice testing, which attempts to identify proficiency in skills such as spelling, usage, and grammar, was developed by psychometricians and became a preferred method for large-scale assessment performed by such entities as The Educational Testing Service and The National Assessment of Educational Progress. Such a methodology privileges traditional forms of instruction, and, as Michael Williamson (2009: 67) notes, "these tests remain one of the single most important indicators of a child's future." Conversely, holistic scoring, which was the type of assessment chosen for *The Big Read*, was developed during the 1960s and early 1970s in response to what educators believed was an unnecessarily narrow focus on correctness. As Kathleen Yancey (2009: 132) states, "the last 50 years of writing assessment can be narrativized as the teacher-layperson (often successfully) challenging the psychometric expert...applying...expertise and theory located not in psychometrics, but in rhetoric...reading...hermeneutics and...writing practice."

THE GEORGE WASHINGTON UNIVERSITY

The George Washington University (GWU) is located near the White House and National Mall in Washington, DC. Enrollment currently totals around 25,000, half of which are undergraduates. Students take advantage of a wide array of opportunities associated with life in the nation's capital: internships, fellowships, and community service. University administration recognized that the demands on twenty-first-century students required GW to "pursue its goal of building greater excellence in undergraduate education by increasing academic challenge, enhancing student engagement, and fostering greater student-faculty interaction" (GWU, 2003: 7). The resulting strategic plan implemented the University Writing Program in 2003. A central goal of this new initiative was to enhance intellectual engagement for undergraduates (Nutefall and Gaspar, 2008). Students entering GWU take a theme-based writing course, University Writing 20 (UW20), which is collaboratively taught by a writing instructor and librarian. Course enrollment is capped at 15 students. In subsequent years they take two additional courses focused on writing and research protocols within their chosen major. All students must fulfill this graduation requirement.

Writing instructors and instruction librarians collaborate on the design and delivery of each UW20 course. Course themes are selected to generate interest and controversy in order to engage students in academic writing and research. Examples of recent UW20 themes include: Conspiracy Theory, Legacies of the Holocaust, Graphic Novels and Manga as Visual Argument, and Issues in College Athletics. Regardless of theme, each course focuses on five learning outcomes/goals:

1. To read, think, and write critically and analytically
2. To gain a functional grasp of rhetorical principles
3. To acquire the ability to explore, use and analyze information resources to meet research objectives
4. To demonstrate the habit and discipline of careful editing and proof-reading
5. To develop an effective writing process

Appendix 7.1 lists the five learning outcomes along with descriptions of the accompanying textual features identified by the UW20 assessment committee.

Course theme selection informs faculty and librarian practice. For example, the course looking at manga necessarily requires current and popular sources. The librarian might design a session around analyzing visual media. The Holocaust course requires historical and archival research. Fundamentals of academic writing remain the same from course to course, but the disciplinarity of the topic influences writing assignments, course readings, and research topics.

Assessment is critical to new programs and the UWP is no exception. Formative assessment is necessary to address implementation issues and guide program growth. Summative assessment chronicles successes and identifies areas for improvement. Students respond to a lengthy and detailed course evaluation when completing UW20 that includes questions regarding the classroom, assignments, and library experience. The University Office of Academic Planning and Assessment has added similar questions to the survey for graduating students to gather additional feedback. The focus of this chapter, however, is a two-year assessment initiative titled *The Big Read* (Hayes et al., 2008), which was designed by writing instructors and librarians and performed by faculty from across the university.

COLLABORATION PRACTICES

The current literature is replete with descriptions and case studies of faculty-librarian collaborations. Emmons and Martin stated that faculty-librarian collaboration at the University of New Mexico grew out of the need for a "library program that would support its emphasis on writing as an inquiry process" (2002: 546). Collaboration for the University Writing Program developed similarly: to teach students that "the epistemic and recursive nature of both writing and research are fully intertwined" (Nutefall and Ryder, 2005: 308). University libraries have embraced the collaborative model. Lynn Lampert explains the rationale of collaborative programs at California State University, "These initiatives aimed to garner support and foster a collective understanding of information literacy by providing definitions, standards, assessment practices and proactive strategies for encouraging information literacy programs" (Lampert, 2005: 7). Articulation of learning objectives is an exercise that creates fertile ground for growing collaboration (Callison, Budny, and Thomes, 2005; Fiegen, Cherry, and Watson, 2002; Raspa and Ward, 2000). Raspa and Ward advocate a fuller definition of collaboration: a "pervasive, long-term relationship in which participants recognize common goals and objectives, share more tasks, and participate in extensive planning and implementations. Collaborators share the give-and-take listening that creates the bond of belonging to a learning community" (Raspa and Ward, 2000: 5).

THE BIG READ: EDWARD WHITE'S MODEL

As mentioned previously, students enrolled in UW20 complete a lengthy course evaluation designed specifically for the course. Questions ask about course content, information literacy learning, writing improvement, and effort required to complete assignments. At the beginning of the third year of the program, members of the University Writing Program Assessment Committee met to design an authentic assessment protocol that did not rely on student perceptions. The frame utilized for this assessment was to be the five course outcomes listed in the UW20 template and the product for assessment would be student research papers. Discussions regarding process and reliability determined that detailed rubrics would provide relevant feedback and structure the reading of the papers.

Edward White has outlined six procedures to facilitate holistic scoring. The assessment model utilized during the stages of GWU's *The Big Read* closely resembled White's, but incorporated elements specifically adapted to the UWP's multidisciplinary context. Carol Hayes, former Director of First-Year Writing selected *The Big Read* title (used in previous University of California assessments), "I liked the name because it created a sense of an event: something important and exciting that was bringing together faculty from a wide range of disciplines to look at student writing." Two *Big Reads* took place, during the summers of 2006 and 2007. Different learning outcomes were assessed each time. In 2006 readers concentrated on learning outcome 2: student demonstrates a functional grasp of rhetorical principles, and learning outcome 4: student demonstrates the habit and discipline of careful editing and proofreading. In 2007 readers concentrated on learning outcome 1: student demonstrates the ability to read, think, and write critically and analytically, and learning outcome 3: student demonstrates the ability to explore, use, and analyze information resources to meet research objectives. For the purposes of this chapter we focus on learning outcome 3, and the associated rubric.

Because the instructors teaching UW20 courses tailor their assignments according to the classes' themes, the parameters of the final paper are developed accordingly. Instructors are guided by a common template created by an advisory committee as part of the university strategic plan. The template is structured enough to ensure that the five articulated goals and learning outcomes are met, yet sufficiently elastic to allow each individual instructor enough freedom to design assignments that correspond to the rhetorical strategies demanded by the course theme. The language of the template is not limited by discipline and is applicable across subject areas. Thus, the assignment prompt for the final paper might require students to perform an ethnographic study of a subculture, or to research in Gelman library's archives, or to visit museums and analyze the semiotic significance of exhibits. Recent classes have analyzed blogs, created a class wiki to capture definitions and resources relevant to the topic, or drafted an online encyclopedia to showcase student research.

Controlled reading, White's first procedure, involves bringing all readers participating in the assessment to one room where they must sit around tables and work together to establish an "interpretive community" (White, 1985: 96–97). Each discipline has particular rhetorical conventions that influence the way student work is assessed, so creating a community where everyone could ultimately agree on what textual features to value was especially crucial. Hence, Stanley Fish's (1980) conception of "interpretive community," which was central to White's philosophy of holistic scoring, was a crucial theoretical underpinning for *The Big Read*. Fish, arguably America's most pre-eminent reader-response theorist, points out that selves are social constructs "whose operations are delimited by the systems of intelligibility that inform" them. Readers thus assign value and meaning to texts according to the standards of the interpretive community to which they belong (Fish, 1980: 335). Formulating a community around the shared values expressed in the rubrics was challenging since faculty participating in *The Big Read* came from many different disciplines, including anthropology, literature, philosophy, rhetoric, and composition. Librarians did not participate as readers. Assessment was the primary goal of *The Big Read*, but a secondary purpose was faculty development aimed at all instructors involved in the writing program.

White's second procedure, scoring criteria guide, and third procedure, sample papers, are attempts to use texts to build the interpretive community of collaborative readers. A scoring criteria guide is a rubric which sets out descriptors of characteristics to be rated according to a point scale. Readers use the rubric to rate the sample papers. White emphasizes the importance of the trainer's attitude during this stage of the process, which is sometimes known as "calibration" (White, 1985: 25). The term calibration suggests that during the process, the rubric functions as a kind of tuning fork, to permit readers' minds to align with one another. Should this procedure fail, the reliability of the entire project would be in jeopardy, because readers would then be likely to produce discrepant scores. Cautioning against the temptation to present the rubric as a fait accompli, letting it stand for itself while insisting readers follow its guidance, White points out that trainers must encourage readers to interact with each other and to interrogate the rubric. This process of candid discussion can produce an atmosphere of intellectual honesty in which sensitivity to differing standards of evaluation will ultimately allow a consensus to emerge about which textual features to value.

The rubrics provided to readers and used during the 2007 *Big Read* were created by members of UWP's assessment committee, including the authors of this chapter. Committee members worked in pairs to create draft descriptions of the way students might demonstrate specific learning abilities. We then all met to discuss and revise the drafts. Committee members also collaborated to choose the sample papers, which they culled from assignments produced by their students.

The authors teamed to draft the rubric for goal 3: To acquire the ability to explore, use, and analyze information resources to meet research objectives. This goal was divided into three learning outcomes, as follows:

1. Writer shows ability to frame and investigate a research question or problem and gather evidence to find answers.
2. Writer demonstrates appropriate use of traditional library and emerging technological sources.
3. Writer cites sources with integrity and correctly according to disciplinary expectations.

The rubric format for each learning outcome was determined by the committee to maintain consistency. The rubric listed criteria for score values 5 (exceptional), 4 (strong), 3 (adequate), 2 (limited), and 1 (poor). Not only did all rubrics for all learning outcomes adhere to this five-point scale, the committee agreed on controlled language associated with each score:

- Score 5: compelling, unexpectedly apt
- Score 4: appropriate, generally
- Score 3: adequate, occasionally

- Score 2: limited, rarely
- Score 1: random, inappropriate

We met five times to complete the rubric draft. It took much discussion to determine how student papers would reflect each score of the rubric. Much of the challenge was determining which characteristics would apply to which learning outcome. Our discussions unearthed our confusion because the outcomes seemed to overlap significantly. Outcome 1 states that students should "investigate" and "gather evidence." Outcome 2 states they should "use "traditional library" and "technological sources." We determined that we would distinguish between outcomes by focusing the rubric for outcome 1 on the research question and what kind of sources it would require. We focused the rubric for outcome 2 on the actual sources selected in answer to the question.

We then worked to apply the control language to our criteria. This consistency with other rubrics would assist faculty readers to distinguish between the scoring levels and guide them to the appropriate score for each paper. It proved more difficult than we anticipated as it forced us to use terminology that we do not engage during our normal collaboration. Please see the final rubric for goal 3 learning outcomes in Appendix 7.2.

The specialized language of the rubric is often not what readers would automatically use, which makes the fourth procedure White described, checks on the reading in progress, particularly necessary. Here trainers attempt to make sure that the calibration is working, and readers are continuing to conform to the standards articulated in the rubric. The fifth procedure, multiple independent scoring, ensures that two readers rate each paper. A one-point difference in scoring is acceptable, but if the two scores vary by two or more points the paper must go to a third reader. The sixth procedure, evaluation and record keeping, is the gathering of information, which takes place after the scoring is over.

Following the spring 2007 semester, 16 volunteer readers from across the university met for six hours of training related to the learning objectives and associated rubric. One hundred and seventy-two papers were randomly selected from courses taught the previous fall. The actual readings took two days: each paper was read by two faculty members. Papers with scores diverging more than one point went to arbitration and were read a third time by another faculty member.

EXAMINATION OF ASSESSMENT RESULTS

The University Writing Program Assessment Committee was pleased "to find that the partnership between librarians and UWP faculty yielded strong results" (Hayes et al., 2008: 21) for Goal 3 learning outcomes. Seventy-four percent of the papers read during the summer of 2007 scored exceptional, strong, or adequate on learning outcome 1: Writer shows ability to frame and investigate a research question or problem and gather evidence to find answers.

Analysis of the results indicated that many UW20 students learned how to effectively utilize the broad array of resources available at Gelman Library. Seventy-five percent of student papers were scored exceptional, strong, or adequate on learning outcome 2: Writer demonstrates appropriate use of traditional library and emerging technological sources. Results for learning outcome 3 indicated that 78 percent of student papers scored exceptional, strong, or adequate regarding citations: Writer cites sources with integrity and correctly according to disciplinary expectations.

IMPACT ON COURSE PLANNING

Results from *The Big Read* validated the successful collaboration between faculty and librarians, yet conversations during the design process for the rubric stimulated ideas for changing some aspects of our practice. Gaspar and Presser had been working together on Presser's UW20 course, *Firing the American Canon: Symbolic Struggle and Cultural Wars* for several semesters prior to the planning of *The Big Read*. Our goal for the class had always been to create assignments for a theme flexible enough to accommodate the needs of the individual students in the class, yet focused enough to enable the students to form a community of scholars collaborating on related research projects. The theme of canonicity was meant to encourage students to ask such questions as: Under what circumstances does written work acquire canonical status? What kind of writing should be taught in the classroom? Should writing about film have the same cultural capital as writing in the disciplines that have been traditionally considered worthy of academic study? How do conventions of writing vary in different disciplines?

Initially the primary focus of the course was to be the American canon. In fall 2006, when a large number of students taking the class were nonnative speakers of English, we adapted the theme to allow students to draw on their own expertise to perform comparative analysis of what is considered canonical in different cultures. Although we provide some selected topics that students can modify and shape into research questions, we do not require them to choose any of these subjects and instead encourage them to pursue their own interests. Though students sometimes initially misinterpret this freedom as license "to write whatever" they want to, our flexible methodology actually ensures that they must complete a rigorous prewriting process in order to accomplish learning outcomes of goal 3.

Creating the rubric for goal 3 required us to engage in a metacognitive activity. From the beginning of our collaboration, we had always agreed about the importance of information literacy, but preparing for *The Big Read* provided us with an opportunity to create a shared vocabulary. Conceptualizing the research question occurs before the paper is actually written, but faculty readers of the assessment papers would not have access to the prewriting activities the students would have produced as they formulated their projects. We therefore had to work backward to figure out what characteristics would distinguish a paper by a writer who had demonstrated exceptional ability to frame and articulate a research question. Once we had determined what features characterized an exceptional paper, we then were able to delineate the characteristics of a paper by a writer with strong or adequate ability.

To articulate the textual features we valued in research papers, we had to analyze our own responses as readers of student texts. This self-reflexivity inspired us to rework several assignments as well as to reconceptualize the way we introduced the faculty-librarian partnership to the students. Prior to *The Big Read*, Presser would introduce Gaspar on the first day of class, immediately after handing out the course syllabus. Gaspar would then ask the students several questions about their prior exposure to information literacy instruction. Although this brief conversation was useful, many of the first-year students, who were already disconcerted by the demands of adjusting to a new environment, were often further distracted by trying to absorb the information on the syllabus. Moreover, they were sometimes unprepared to answer questions they had not been anticipating.

After *The Big Read*, we decided that a dose of the self-reflexivity that we had experienced might also be useful to our students. We devoted an entire session of the class to a conversation about information literacy and moved this discussion to the second class meeting. This change in chronology allowed Presser to prepare the class for the discussion by asking the students to write a short essay. The students, having written the essay, can now confidently participate in the conversation, which is led by Gaspar.

The essay prompt for this assignment reads:

> Dr. Debbie Gaspar will join us for a discussion of research. To prepare for this class, write a journal entry describing and analyzing one or two of the most challenging research papers or projects you have already done. What did you like and dislike about these projects? Did you feel interested in the research you did? Why or why not? What kind of research would you enjoy doing? What research skills would you like to have?

Resulting discussions have been informative but, more important, they have contributed to a sense of intellectual community between students, Gaspar, and Presser. Student responses vary widely, reflecting diversity of experience and demographics. For example, one student commented on what she wanted to learn: "I would like to learn how to pick what information is important and what is not... and know the best and quickest way of sorting through the information." Another wrote about a high school assignment: "Since I did not like the topic I was not interested in writing a paper about it. It was an assigned project and I had no choice in the matter." International students frequently note that meeting expectations for U. S. research papers is a challenging task. Student comments inform planning for the library sessions and classroom discussions.

The UW20 course outline requires three major writing assignments. Prior to *The Big Read*, the first assignment involved formulating a prescriptive argument. Each group was asked to examine the required texts for the class, choose the most appealing text and write an essay arguing that the class should concentrate on this text for the next few weeks.

This assignment did require students to develop a rhetorical stance and argue persuasively, but it did not require substantial research and thus neglected to address goal 3. We therefore decided to rethink what we wanted the assignment to accomplish. We redesigned it to optimize the course theme to introduce students to academic research. The prompt for the revised assignment now reads:

> The class will form groups of three or four. Each group will construct a canon of texts. Your canon will consist of songs, movies, TV shows, books, poems, Internet sites, artwork, or some mixture of these types of texts. Choose a theme, such as: The ten greatest movies ever made, or ten Korean works that should be translated into English, or the ten most entertaining sites on the Internet. Compose your canon. Then, write an essay explaining the reasoning behind your choices. Finally, create a presentation based on your essay.

Presser sets up the first assignment by contextualizing ways in which the definitions of canonicity have changed and by discussing how canon-formation invites particular ideas about what "good writing" is. Students are asked to justify the choices they made in selecting their own canons, which addresses goal 1: To read, think, and write critically and analytically. By asking students to make this claim of value argument, which is necessarily subjective, Presser begins a conversation about the role of rhetorical stance within research. She attempts to disrupt the binary thinking that influences many to insist that an argument is either biased or it is objective and tries to use this disruption to increase their "functional grasp of rhetorical principles." Gaspar reinforces this concept during a library session on Web evaluation and authority. She encourages students to explore the relationships between information providers and sponsors in order to interrogate bias and value. The parameters of this assignment correspond to our initial ideas about the course theme, but once we have a chance to meet the students, we incorporate their feedback so that the topics of the second and third assignments evolve organically.

The second major assignment, a collaborative project, primarily focuses on goal 3: Writer shows ability to frame and investigate a research question or problem and gather evidence to find answers. Drawing on student work from previous semesters, we provide examples of questions that seem too broad and discuss ways to set up a more compelling line of inquiry. We do not jettison the theme of canon-formation here, but we do open it up to include the subheading of the course's title, the symbolic struggle and cultural work. In order to encourage active learning, students must have a meaningful task to complete during the library session. In groups, students develop preliminary topics before the class meets with Gaspar in the library. During the instructional session Gaspar explains how the process of searching for sources can be used to narrow a topic, identify search terms, and discover topical controversies.

Because we meet in an electronic classroom, students can immediately put Gaspar's instruction to practical use. We spend the rest of the session answering the questions that arise as students work on their particular projects, finding sources to use for their proposals. Many students come to class already equipped with some research strategies. Some have used databases such as JSTOR, and we have even encountered a student who knew what a Boolean search was, but most students tend to rely on Google for their information. We discuss the rigorous standards of academic writing and research in the age of Wikipedia. Moreover, many students are unfamiliar with navigating the Gelman Library catalog.

Gelman library has three electronic classrooms. All three rooms include a smartboard so the instructor can demonstrate search strategies. One of the classrooms features desktop computer stations and the other two are wireless and students have use of laptops. The wireless rooms are flexible spaces with modular furniture. These spaces are particularly useful for group projects.

We implemented the workshop aspect of the instructional session in order to allow us to be available to mentor individual students as they search for sources, Presser was shocked to discover that many students were baffled by the prospect of finding a library book on the Gelman shelves. Presser discussed this concern with Gaspar, who designed an assignment that required the students to go into the stacks. Students are asked to locate a book in the catalog that is related to their topic. They must then go to the stacks, find the book, but also note the surrounding titles on the shelf in case another book looks more useful. This exercise is designed in part to demonstrate to the students how information is organized in the library stacks. Once they have selected a title, they are asked to analyze the source in relation to other resources and eventually to produce an annotated bibliography. This bibliography is a miniature literature review of their chosen topic and includes discussion on how they intend to utilize the source in their project.

To produce a successful proposal, students must continue to "show awareness of persuading," by responding to "expectations of various audiences." They present the proposal to the class, which then engages in peer review. Each member of the audience responds verbally to the proposal, using guidelines that Presser presents in the form of questions written on the board. The students then incorporate this feedback to further refine their research questions. Their work on the annotated bibliography gives Presser the opportunity to discuss citation practice, and concentrate on goal 4, careful editing and proofreading.

We want our students to be able to transfer the knowledge they have gained about information literacy from this project, so we hope they will continue to hone some of the same skills they worked on during the collaborative paper for the third assignment. By this time in the semester, they are more familiar with utilizing the concept of rhetorical stance to analyze sources and therefore are better prepared to work on goal 1: read, think, and write critically and analytically. When the students are generating research questions for the final paper, Presser brings in, distributes, and discusses the rubric that the assessment committee designed for this goal. Students appreciate having clear guidelines that inform their process. Some have included comments on the end-of-semester evaluations that indicate their intention to use the rubric in later courses.

ASSESSING *THE BIG READ*

It is important to remember that *The Big Read* assessed four of the five learning outcomes listed in the course template and the impact of this extensive study was reported to constituents around the university. The University Writing Program is still relatively young and information gleaned from this assessment was formative. For example, results inform ongoing faculty and librarian professional development programs. The rubrics continue to inspire conversations about student writing. Individual faculty and librarian partners have adjusted assignments and practices to better address all five learning outcomes listed in the course template.

Within First Year Writing, assessment results have prompted some partnerships to increase the number of library sessions during the semester. Others have altered the course syllabus to better inform students about learning outcomes. Some partners presented workshops showcasing their collaboration for a regional conference on the teaching of writing and rhetoric. External stakeholders used the assessment results to inform decisions and make recommendations to the university administration.

CONCLUSION

As we worked on this chapter, fall semester 2008 ended. We asked students completing the course to write essays reflecting on their experiences. Formal, formative program assessment is important, but anecdotal, student feedback is always welcome and, perhaps, equally rewarding. We were gratified to read the following comment: "I used to receive a C or D when I wrote research papers in other classes. But, now I get a B or A on research papers even in other classes such as business and history." Many students made similar statements. This may be the result of providing them with information that enables them to recognize how to successfully incorporate evidence into a persuasive argument. The rubric helps demystify the conventions of academic writing and research that many students found opaque.

Our work on *The Big Read* continues to impact our collaboration. We have integrated more short reflective writing assignments throughout the research process. For example, students working on an annotated bibliography describe their strategies after gathering preliminary source material. This encourages students to think critically as they analyze the sources' arguments while selecting and rejecting sources. Their writing enables us to monitor their progress and allows us to intervene whenever they need further instruction.

Since our work on the rubric, we have tried to retro-fit our existing course to better meet the criteria laid out in the rubric. We are currently designing a new course centered on a totally different theme: *Brain Matters: Can Science Solve the Mystery of Your Mind?* This new endeavor enables us to specifically tailor our assignments utilizing the details outlined in the rubrics. For example, course readings will be selected that can serve as models for different aspects of the learning outcomes detailed in the course template. In addition, a fresh emphasis on the interaction between primary sources and secondary sources will impact student research assignments.

The Big Read gave us the opportunity to immerse ourselves in the language of teaching, the rhetoric associated with composition, and current research on student assessment. It enabled us to build on the strengths of our existing collaboration and reflect on what practices needed improvement. By designing the rubric together we provided ourselves with a concrete tool useful to our classroom practice.

NOTE

1. We would like to acknowledge current and former members of the assessment committee: Sandie Friedman, Carol Hayes, Randi Kristensen, Derek Malone-France, Diane Matlock, Mark Mullen, Steve Salchak, Heather Schell, and Abby Wilkerson. Everyone on this committee collaborated to produce rubrics for *The Big Read*.

BIBLIOGRAPHY

Association of College and Research Libraries. 2000. *Information Literacy Competency Standards for Higher Education.* (January 18, 2000). Available: www.ala.org/ala/mgrps/divs/acrl/standards/informationliteracycompetency.cfm (accessed October 1, 2009).

Association of College and Research Libraries. 2001. *Objectives for Information Literacy Instruction: A Model Statement for Academic Librarians.* (January 2001). Available: www.ala.org/ala/mgrps/divs/acrl/standards/objectivesinformation.cfm (accessed October 1, 2009).

Avery, Elizabeth F. 2003. "Assessing Information Literacy Instruction." In *Assessing Student Learning Outcomes for Information Literacy Instruction in Academic Institutions*, edited by Elizabeth F. Avery. Chicago: Association of College and Research Libraries.

Callison, Rachel, Dan Budny, and Kate Thomes. 2005. "Library Research Project for First-Year Engineering Students: Results from Collaboration by Teaching and Library Faculty." *Reference Librarian* 43, no. 89 (January): 93–106.

Emmons, M., and W. Martin. 2002."Engaging Conversation: Evaluating the Contribution of Library Instruction to the Quality of Student Research." *College & Research Libraries* 63, no. 6: 545–560.

Fiegen, Ann M., Bennett Cherry, and Kathleen Watson. 2002. "Reflections on Collaboration: Learning Outcomes and Information Literacy Assessment in the Business Curriculum." *Reference Services Review* 30, no. 4: 307–318.

Fish, Stanley. 1980. *Is There a Text in This Class?* Cambridge, MA: Harvard University Press.

The George Washington University. 2003. *Sustaining Momentum, Maximizing Strength.* Washington, DC: The George Washington University. Available: www.gwu.edu/~academic/OfficeVicePresident/pdf/Strg_GWBook.pdf (accessed October 1, 2009).

Hayes, Carol, et al. 2008. *The Big Read Report.* Faculty Working Paper, Columbian College of Arts and Sciences, The George Washington University.

Huot, Brian. 2002. *(Re)Articulating Writing Assessment for Teaching and Learning.* Logan, UT: Utah State.

Huot, Brian, and Peggy O'Neill, eds. 2009. *Assessing Writing: A Critical Sourcebook.* Boston: Bedford/St. Martin's.

Hutchins, Elizabeth O. 2003. "Assessing Student Learning Outcomes in Political Science Classes." In *Assessing Student Learning Outcomes for Information Literacy Instruction in Academic Institutions* (pp. 172–184), edited by Elizabeth F. Avery. Chicago: Association of College and Research Libraries.

Knight, Lorrie A. 2006. "Using Rubrics to Assess Information Literacy." *Reference Services Review* 34, no. 1 (February): 43–55.

Lampert, Lynn. 2005. "'Getting Psyched' about Information Literacy: A Successful Faculty-Librarian Collaboration for Educational Psychology and Counseling." *Reference Librarian* 43, no. 89 (January): 5–23.

Lunsford, Andrea. 1986. "The Past and Future of Writing Assessment." In *Writing Assessment*, (pp. 1–12), edited by Kate Greenberg. New York: Longman.

Nutefall, Jennifer E., and Deborah Gaspar. 2008. "Raise Your Profile: Build Your Program." *Public Services Quarterly* 4, no. 2 (July): 127–135.

Nutefall, Jennifer E., and Phyllis M. Ryder. 2005. "Teaching Research Rhetorically." *Academic Exchange Quarterly* 9, no. 3: 307–311.

Oakleaf, Megan. 2008. "Dangers and Opportunities: A Conceptual Map of Information Literacy Assessment Approaches." *portal: Libraries & the Academy* 8, no. 3 (July): 233–253.

Raspa, Richard, and Dane Ward, eds. 2000. *The Collaborative Imperative: Librarians and Faculty Working Together in the Information Universe*. Chicago: Association of College and Research Libraries.

Rockman, Ilene F. 2002. "Strengthening Connections between Information Literacy, General Education, and Assessment Efforts." *Library Trends* 51, no. 2 (Fall): 185.

Schroeder, Randall, and Kimberly Babcock Mashek. 2007. "Building a Case for the Teaching Library: Using a Culture of Assessment to Reassure Converted Campus Partners While Persuading the Reluctant." *Public Services Quarterly* 3, no. 1/2 (January): 83–11.

Tuttle, J. B., and S. McKinzie. 2007. "Reconstructing the Research Project: A Case Study of Collaborative Instruction." In *Information Literacy Collaborations That Work* (pp. 109–122), edited by Trudi E. Jacobson and Thomas P. Mackey. New York: Neal-Schuman.

White, Edward. 1985. *Teaching and Assessing Writing*. San Francisco: Jossey-Bass.

Williamson, Michael. 2009. "The Worship of Efficiency: Untangling Theoretical and Practical Considerations in Writing Assessment." In *Assessing Writing: A Critical Sourcebook* (pp. 57–79), edited by Brian Huot and Peggy O'Neill. Boston: Bedford/St. Martins.

Yancy, Kathleen. 2009. "Looking Back as We Look Forward: Historicizing Writing Assessment." In *Assessing Writing: A Critical Sourcebook* (pp. 131–149), edited by Brian Huot and Peggy O'Neill. Boston: Bedford/St. Martins.

Appendix 7.1. UW20 Goals and Learning Outcomes

1. To read, think, and write critically and analytically:
   - Writer indicates capacity to examine assumptions critically.
   - Writer demonstrates ability to assess and use different kinds of evidence from a variety of genres.
   - Writer shows awareness of persuading, rather than simply informing audiences.
   - Writer demonstrates an understanding of the difference between a substantiated claim and an opinion.

2. To gain a functional grasp of rhetorical principles:
   - Writer demonstrates an understanding of the purpose and genre required for particular tasks.
   - Writer addresses audience expectations.
   - Writer arranges arguments in an appropriate structure.
   - Writer uses formats, evidence, tones, lengths, and levels of formality appropriate for a range of particular contexts.

3. To acquire the ability to explore, use, and analyze information resources to meet research objectives:
   - Writer shows ability to frame and investigate a research question or problem and gather evidence to find answers.
   - Writer demonstrates appropriate use of traditional library and emerging technological sources.
   - Writer cites sources with integrity and correctly according to disciplinary expectations.

4. To demonstrate the habit and discipline of careful editing and proofreading:
   - Writer demonstrates knowledge of usage conventions, including paragraphing, syntactic complexity, and word choices appropriate for audience and task.
   - Writer produces final revised versions essentially free of errors in grammar, mechanics, and spelling.

5. To develop an effective writing process:
   - Writer constructs sound questions or hypotheses.
   - Writer analyzes and synthesizes information pertinent to those questions.
   - Writer demonstrates a drafting process that results in coherence of main idea.

Rating Scale
5 = Exceptional   4 = Strong   3 = Adequate
2 = Limited   1 = Poor

Appendix 7.2. Goal 3 Textual Features for Information Literacy

Goal 3, Learning Outcome 1:
Writer shows ability to frame and investigate a research question or problem and gather evidence to find answers.

Score 5:
- The writer frames a compelling a line of inquiry that performs unexpectedly apt research to find answers.

Score 4:
- The writer frames a line of inquiry that is appropriate to the scope of the project and that demands the substantial gathering of sources to find answers.

Score 3:
- The writer establishes a line of inquiry that is adequate to the scope of the project and that demands basic gathering of sources to find answers.

Score 2:
- The writer's attempt to establish a line of inquiry may be too limited for the scope of the project and/or may only demand limited use of sources to find answers.

Score 1:
- The writer's handling of the line of inquiry is poor to the extent that the main research goals are incoherent.

Goal 3, Learning Outcome 2:
Writer demonstrates appropriate use of traditional library and emerging technological sources.

Score 5:
- The writer draws on an exceptionally apt selection of sources that indicates the capacity to gather traditional library and technological sources as needed.

Score 4:
- The writer draws on an appropriate selection of sources that indicates the capacity to gather traditional library and technological sources as needed.

Score 3:
- The writer draws on an adequate selection of sources, although occasional gaps may occur in the range of sources or the occasional inclusion of seemingly random research.

Score 2:
- The writer draws on a limited range of sources that are often inappropriate.

Score 1:
- The writer draws on seemingly random sources that render the paper incoherent.

(Continued)

Appendix 7.2. Goal 3 Textual Features for Information Literacy *(Continued)*
Goal 3, Learning Outcome 3: **Writer cites sources with integrity and correctly according to disciplinary expectations.** **Score 5** • The writer provides clear citations to sources, leaving no ambiguity about what is original and what is derived from the sources. • The writer stays consistent in formatting the citation style and all the relevant citation information is provided. **Score 4** • The writer generally provides clear citations to sources, rarely leaving ambiguity about what is original and what is derived from the sources. • The writer generally stays consistent in formatting the citation style and almost all the relevant citation information is provided. **Score 3** • The paper adequately cites sources, but occasionally leaves some ambiguity about what is original and what is derived from the sources. • The writer usually stays consistent in formatting the citation style, but does have some problems. The relevant citation information is usually provided, although some information may occasionally be missing. **Score 2** • The writer provides limited citations to sources, often leading to ambiguity about what is original and what is derived from the sources. • The writer's formatting for the citation style is often confused, with frequent inconsistencies, and/or the relevant citation information is frequently missing. **Score 1** • The writer provides little to no citations to sources. • The writer's citations appear random, and/or the sources are not traceable.

Chapter 8

Many Voices, One Goal:
Measuring Student Success through Partnerships in the Core Curriculum

Becky Canovan, Anne Marie Gruber,
Mary Anne Knefel, and Michele McKinlay

Universities are challenging their educators to rethink the role of assessment and its relationship to desired outcomes by asking the more difficult question, "What do I want to have happen as a result of students participating in this class?"

> — Robert Reid
> University of Dubuque Professor of Communication
> *The Four Voices of Preaching*

If reform efforts are successful, the campus, the classroom, and the library will be turned inside out.

> — Terry O'Banion
> *A Learning College for the 21st Century*

INTRODUCTION

One of the greatest challenges for academic librarians is determining the library's value to students' educational experience. Traditionally, librarians reported input and output measures such as collection size and circulation data, believing that these alone were enough to demonstrate its value. However, in the current environment of accountability, to thrive, the library must "document and measure the ways that [it] make[s] a real difference in the academic quality of life for students and faculty" (Lindauer, 1998: 546). Information literacy is a central connection between the library and student learning. Although information literacy has been robust for years, its assessment has been inconsistent (Bober and Poulin, 1995). As librarians move toward documenting and measuring the impact of information literacy, they are answering the questions central to all libraries: what impact does the library have on student learning and how is this measured?

Librarians and faculty at University of Dubuque (UD) have worked together to begin answering these questions as they relate to the core curriculum. This collaboration is a key component of the information literacy program and its assessment. What were once informal partnerships have evolved into an intentional, programmatic model with a required interdisciplinary course, Introduction to Research Writing, as its cornerstone. This unique course, developed as part of a revised core curriculum, focuses on the process of research writing, with information literacy goals as explicit learning outcomes. Librarians and faculty developed the course in partnership and continue to improve and teach the class together. In addition, they have collaborated throughout the core curriculum to deliver an information literacy program based on Association of College and Research Libraries (ACRL) learning outcomes.

This purposeful integration of information literacy (IL) instruction allows stakeholders to measure the library's impact on student learning across core courses. The IL program assessment model focuses on growth of key skills. Based on ACRL standards and informed by a curriculum-mapping process, the model includes pre- and posttests and a midpoint assessment. Quantitative IL assessment is built around *Tool for Real-Time Assessment of Information Literacy Skills*, an instrument developed at Kent State University. In addition to quantitative data, the model includes several qualitative components.

As librarians target particular IL skills identified in the curriculum map, they work with faculty to measure students' progress and together they use these data to plan appropriate pedagogical strategies. Because faculty and librarians collaborate, students hear a consistent message that information literacy is important. Both students and faculty rely on and value the IL program as it contributes to students' academic success. Librarians communicate with core curriculum faculty and administrators regularly to revise and improve the IL components in each course. Faculty provide valuable input on concepts and context for class assignments, whereas librarians provide IL outcomes and assessment results. These data provide a realistic picture of students' skills and experiences. Librarians share results with faculty teaching upper-division courses as well, and partner with them to create effective research assignments that acknowledge previous student understanding and experience. At the same time, all are discovering how to work together to improve teaching.

This chapter describes how librarians and faculty developed the information literacy assessment model for the core curriculum, including details on collaborative instruction and assessment in selected courses. It describes methods of measurement, analyzes selected quantitative and qualitative results, and evaluates the assessment model.

RELATED LITERATURE

Assessment in Higher Education

Assessment is "the systematic collection, review, and use of information... undertaken for the purpose of improving student learning and development" (Palomba and Banta, 1999: 4). It occurs at the classroom, course, program, institutional, and interinstitutional levels. Since the 1980s, the assessment movement in higher education serves two purposes: a desire to improve student learning and the need to report to external stakeholders that learning is taking place.

Interest in assessment has been driven externally by the educational accountability movement. In 1984, higher education leaders followed earlier calls for K–12 reform, encouraging colleges and universities to "design and implement a systematic program to assess the knowledge, capacities, and skills developed in students by academic and co-curricular programs" (U. S. National Institute of Education, 1984: 55). Accrediting agencies now require assessment plans as a requisite for reaccreditation. Colleges and external agencies have been especially interested in assessing core skills such as critical thinking and effective writing. In 1995, the National Assessment of College Student Learning identified a specific skill set in these areas (Jones, 1995).

Institutions have begun to examine using standardized tests such as the Collegiate Learning Assessment (CLA) to measure core skills. There has also been interest in e-portfolios, which rely on student documents as a more authentic measure of growth ("The Thrust and Parry," 2008).

Scholars believe that meaningful assessment is mission driven, process based, and locally developed (Palomba and Banta, 1999). Hutchings and Marchese suggest "assessment is best understood as *a set of questions* in which institutions ask: What is the college's contribution to student learning?... What knowledge and abilities do we intend that students acquire?.... How can the quantity and quality of student learning be improved?" (Hutchings and Marchese, 1990: 14). A successful assessment cycle requires institutions to clarify learning goals and objectives, collect data, and analyze results to improve teaching and learning (Palomba and Banta, 1999). Likewise, a successful plan uses multiple measures, is learning centered, involves faculty in all phases, and shares results with all stakeholders (Ekman and Pelletier, 2008).

Assessment in Information Literacy

In this new, evidence-based environment, the library assessment program must be clearly linked to the mission and goals of the institution and document the library's contribution to student learning. The assessment plan should provide externally focused evidence in a way that is meaningful to administrators and key decision makers (Lindauer, 1998). Information literacy instruction is a key service librarians provide to support the institutional goal of student learning. Librarians are beginning to devise outcomes-based methods to measure this service's value. Until the 1990s, literature focused less on the theoretical framework of IL assessment and more on institutional case studies and practical implementation of expanding IL programs. In 1997, Pausch and Popp (1997) commented that rigorous efforts to evaluate student learning in IL programs were few. In 2002, Merz and Mark (2002) noted that interest in IL assessment was growing; however, they also cited several obstacles to well-designed assessment, including a lack of rigorous tools.

The development of the Association of College and Research Libraries (ACRL) *Information Literacy Competency Standards for Higher Education* provided a national framework of outcomes-based standards and performance indicators. These standards call on faculty and librarians to develop "local methods for measuring student learning ... [and to] work together to develop assessment instruments and strategies" (2000: 6). Rabine and Cardwell (2000) describe the IL assessment process as a continual cycle of improvement focused on student learning through pedagogical changes. Ideal assessment is "student-centered and proactive" (Avery, 2003: 2). The ACRL Task Force on Academic Library Outcomes Assessment (1998) described this as "the ways in which library users are changed as a result of their contact with the library's resources and programs."

Iannuzzi suggests four levels of IL assessment: within the library, in the classroom, on campus, and beyond the campus. "Within the library" assessments may include any measures the library can implement independently, such as Web tutorials or self-assessments (Iannuzzi, 1999: 304–305). Authentic classroom assessment may include immediate assessments techniques such as Angelo and Cross's (1993) "minute paper," a short, open-ended reflection. It may also include tests and assignments such as annotated bibliographies, speeches, and portfolios. Librarians have recognized the critical need for valid and reliable tools to assess information literacy (Rockman and Smith, 2005). Recently, librarians have created outcomes-based IL assessment tools such as *Standardized Assessment of Information Literacy Skills* (*SAILS*) and *Tool for Real-Time Assessment of Information Literacy Skills* (*TRAILS*), both developed at Kent State

University. O'Connor, Radcliff, and Gedeon (2002) detail the development and design of *SAILS* and describe the methodology they used to ensure validity and reliability. Schloman and Gedeon (2007) report on the development and field testing of *TRAILS*. These and other tests offer librarians a variety of valid and reliable tools.

Developing programmatic assessment is a large task requiring collaboration to create meaningful measurements. Responsibility for IL assessment moves beyond library control because IL skills transcend any single discipline or department. Librarians and faculty must work together to answer: "To what degree are libraries responsible for student learning?" (Iannuzzi, 1999: 304). In practical terms, this collaboration requires that both must commit additional time to plan and implement a meaningful assessment strategy, analyze data, provide feedback, and agree to modify pedagogy based on results (Avery, 2003). The library cannot be viewed in isolation, but must be considered within the framework of institutional outcomes for student learning. To be effective, assessment of information literacy cannot be separated from course content or academic work. Iannuzzi indicates that "the most meaningful assessment models have been developed at institutions that articulate information literacy outcomes and integrate these outcomes into the campus... criteria for general educational outcomes" (1999: 305).

Core Curricula in Higher Education

Higher education curricula in America have existed on a continuum of "one education for all" to specialized graduate work. For many years, coursework consisted of classical studies. An emphasis on vocational education arose in the late 1800s, bringing about the need for a core curriculum. What was once the same education for every student became a system of specialized courses coupled with a "core set of knowledge every man must know" (Bisesi, 1982). Current general education programs range from a prescribed core curriculum to a distributional "a la carte" program. Prescribed curricula involve specific required courses designated by faculty, whereas distributional systems function on students' selecting from several courses that fulfill a requirement, usually discipline-specific.

The 1977 *Missions of the College Curriculum* and general education reform at Harvard decried the fractured nature of core programs (Boning, 2007). As a result, many institutions began to create more coherent curricula. Johnson and Ratcliff cite a 2000 national survey of academic administrators that identifies areas of continued tension, including the challenges of how to "increase curricular coherence and meaning,... address changing student and faculty needs, and... update and renew the general education program" (Johnson and Ratcliff, 2004: 86). Johnson and Ratcliff define coherence as "the extent to which students and faculty find meaning in the curriculum" (2004: 93), which opens the door to new questions: What is the distinction between finding meaning and making meaning, and giving answers as opposed to encouraging questions? Is it enough for faculty to understand the objectives of the curriculum, or must the students be aware of them as well? These questions inform the collaborative effort at UD to assess student learning in information literacy in the core curriculum.

UNIVERSITY OF DUBUQUE: A CULTURE IN CONTEXT

University of Dubuque, founded in 1852, is a private institution affiliated with the Presbyterian Church (U.S.A.) that offers undergraduate, graduate, and seminary programs. In fall 2008, the university had an FTE enrollment of 1,294 undergraduates. The focus of the undergraduate degree is professional programs with a liberal arts core. The motto, "Many Gifts, One Spirit," calls members to develop their talents and realize their potential in community.

In 1998, the University adopted a new *Mission, Values, and Action Statement.* The document called for the development of a new core curriculum: "In light of its mission, the University will continually re-examine and adjust the core curriculum to achieve an artful and purposeful blend of the arts, sciences, humanities, and theology" (University of Dubuque, 1998: 2). In 1999, faculty, students, and administrators met to envision this new core curriculum. Charged with implementing and administering the core, the Associate Dean played an instrumental role in encouraging the collaboration that emerged. By inviting a librarian to join the core committee in its second year, she ensured that librarians were at the table as the new curriculum developed. In 2001, the new core was adopted and was fully functional by spring 2006.

The new core curriculum requires students to take a prescribed sequence of four World View courses and a series of student-selected courses based on the pillars of a UD education: scholarship, spiritual growth, social development, professional preparation, aesthetic appreciation, global awareness, and stewardship. Students are expected to complete many of the core courses before fully engaging with courses in their major. The following competencies run through core courses: thinking critically, analytically, and synergistically; communicating effectively in writing and speaking; and applying technology effectively. Information literacy was not originally an explicit outcome of the new core, but it was an implicit outcome in Introduction to Research Writing. Recently, the Core Committee added information literacy as a learning outcome in the core curriculum. Previously, most faculty and administrators believed that information literacy was already included in outcomes such as critical thinking, technology, and communication. However, following discussion with librarians, the current committee decided that information literacy needed to be articulated and assessed as a distinct skill set.

Assessment at UD has shifted from an input- to an outcomes-based model more purposefully focused on student learning, partly in preparation for an HLC/NCA accreditation visit in 2005. UD has embraced the concept that ideal assessment gathers just enough data to make informed decisions at the point of need. In response to a new institutional plan, the library staff created a strategic plan, with an updated mission statement, goals, measurable objectives, and activities to meet these objectives. Information literacy is at the heart of this plan; therefore, library assessment, to a great extent, is evaluation of the IL program. Assessment consists of multiple direct and indirect measures of student learning and faculty perception. An annual report summarizes results and explains plans for instructional improvement.

Each department created program-level curriculum maps to indicate key learning outcomes and progress toward mastery. The library's curriculum map focused on IL in the core curriculum because that is where librarians are most extensively involved. The learning outcomes are based on ACRL's information literacy standards. The IL curriculum map includes learning outcomes for eight introductory courses offered in history, communication, English, and the core (see Appendix 8.1). Through mapping, librarians found that they were covering some concepts thoroughly—perhaps redundantly—but not in a planned, strategic way, and others were not taught at all. Because IL was not initially articulated as a core competency, librarians needed to justify its assessment throughout the core by linking it to other skills, usually critical thinking. The recent decision to include IL as a core competency will ensure it will be assessed as a unique skill set in the core.

Foundations in Collaboration

Faculty and librarians have collaborated on information literacy for more than 30 years. The library employs five full-time librarians, all of whom teach in an extensive IL program. Of the 487 sessions taught in 2007–2008, about two-thirds were in core courses. Faculty acknowledge librarians as educational partners who help connect concepts across the curriculum. Granted faculty status in 2008, librarians are seen as campus leaders and participate in decision making and program development. In the core, librarians and faculty collaborate most extensively in classes that share uniform outcomes and syllabi. They have also worked together in core courses that employ common readings and assignments. These shared experiences allow integration of core competencies throughout the curriculum, as well as consistent evaluation of student skills.

The campus culture encourages innovation and collaboration, and faculty are open to new ideas. For example, one librarian worked with a biology faculty member to create a template for an annotated bibliography assignment, and she evaluates students' work before the instructor grades it. Another librarian and a sociology faculty member redesigned a film analysis assignment requiring secondary sources. This created a more effective assignment and enabled the librarian to develop the film and film criticism collections to support a research project.

Instruction in the Core

The cornerstone of the information literacy program in the core curriculum is Introduction to Research Writing (RES104), a required interdisciplinary course taught by full- and part-time faculty from various departments. Students typically take this course in their second or third semester. The initial syllabus and assignments were developed by a business faculty member, librarian, and core curriculum administrator and refined and approved by the core committee.

Due to its interdisciplinary nature, the course has a unique prefix (RES) and is administered by the core rather than a specific department. Each semester, the course focuses on a different geographic region. Students write five- to seven-page research papers in each of three disciplines: social sciences, humanities, and natural and applied sciences. The learning objectives for the portfolio-based research projects include framing a research question; demonstrating effective research techniques and writing styles for each discipline; exploring and analyzing scholarly resources; writing clearly and effectively; and learning to offer and use peer critiques.

Librarians lead over 20 percent of RES104 class sessions in each of the approximately 10 sections per semester. Because the course introduces students to working with librarians, each class meets with at least three of the librarians each semester. Librarians introduce content about each discipline, help students brainstorm topic ideas for the region, and guide students in using sources to craft effective research questions. Students work closely with librarians to learn how to use the library catalog, general- and subject-specific resources, and to choose appropriate topics and sources. Faculty and librarians meet regularly during the semester to discuss teaching strategies, coordinate assignments, share insights, and plan co-curricular lectures and activities.

Several years after RES104 was introduced, faculty felt that some students were not adequately prepared for the course. They found that some students' writing skills were not at the level required for RES104. Specifically, faculty observed that some students did not understand the importance of a well-formed research question to the research and writing process. "In frustration, they would change topics, and hand in a paper full of facts either with a vague or non-existent thesis" (Gruber, Knefel, and Waelchli, 2008: 104). They were challenged when trying to identify evidence in support of an argumentative thesis. To address this issue, librarians collaborated with the Director of the Writing Center and English faculty to create a focused research writing assignment for the required prerequisite course, ENG102, Composition and Rhetoric II.

This structured unit serves as a bridge from ENG102 to RES104. All students read common scholarly articles on a controversial social issue, preselected by librarians and faculty, and begin with the same research question. Librarians introduce the concept of an effective research question and lead discussion about how to read and annotate a scholarly source. In this three-week unit, students, librarians, faculty, and Writing Center tutors work in small groups during class to identify potential evidence. Faculty then lead students in creating a common thesis and structuring an evidence-based research paper using secondary sources. Each student writes a paper using the common thesis and sources. A librarian, the Director of the Writing Center, and an English faculty member meet to discuss evaluations and changes for the next semester. Some faculty have modified the unit by substituting a detailed, full-sentence outline for the paper or also requiring an annotated bibliography.

Librarians also work with nonsequential core courses such as Basic Speech Communication (COM101), a course involving policy- and values-focused speeches. Librarians and faculty developed and refined the research components so students can be successful with these two complex assignments. In the policy speech, students persuade their classmates to take action on a pending federal bill by contacting their legislators. For the values speech, students choose recent Supreme Court cases that deal with fundamental values of American society, such as freedom of speech or search and seizure. Students persuade their classmates to consider their own beliefs about these challenging questions. Librarians help students locate bills and court cases as well as secondary resources. In addition, they work with faculty to help students understand what makes a bill or case effective for this type of speech. Recently, a faculty member has been charged with coordinating all sections, enabling more efficient communication. This faculty member and a librarian are now developing a textbook for this class, which will further embed IL concepts throughout the course.

The other two classes that are key to information literacy are World View Seminars I and II, unique, mission-based courses administered by the core. These required courses engage students in discussions about the core pillars. World View I, the first-year seminar, focuses on the theme of what constitutes the good life. It asks students to consider crucial questions about the shape of their lives, values, and religious faith. World View II, the sophomore seminar, addresses significant issues that challenge contemporary American culture, such as citizenship, sustainability, and social values.

The information literacy component of World View I serves as the introduction to the library for first-year students. It includes a self-guided, game-based tour and an introduction to scholarly versus popular resources as related to a common assignment. The most important piece of this library session is the administration of *TRAILS* as an IL skills pretest. Through discussions with core administrators, librarians integrated this instruction as a class session starting in fall 2008. Previously it was administered outside of class. While there is no specific IL objective in this course, the session is necessary to provide baseline IL skills data, and faculty and administrators of the course recognize the importance of gathering this data. Because most students complete a majority of the core requirements in their first two years, World View II is the ideal course for the *TRAILS* posttest assessment. In addition to administering *TRAILS*, librarians meet with each class for a research session to support a service learning project with a nonprofit organization.

THE PROGRAMMATIC ASSESSMENT MODEL

Librarians and faculty use assessment data, both quantitative and qualitative, to refine assignments and focus library sessions throughout the core and beyond. As librarians target particular IL skills identified in the curriculum map, they work with faculty to measure students' progress. The quantitative assessment sequence includes a pretest, midpoint assessments, and a posttest. Qualitative measures include student surveys, assignment reflections, and course-level evaluations, most of which are administered at the same time as quantitative assessments. Librarians have also piloted a faculty survey to solicit perceptions of the information literacy program.

The pre- and posttest sequence is built around *TRAILS* and provides quantitative data on students' understanding of IL concepts taught in the core curriculum. Librarians have employed this sequence for three years. In 2006, librarians considered three existing assessment tools that would allow tracking of longitudinal data: *TRAILS*, *Toolkit for Success: Information Literacy for the 21st Century Learner*, and *Information Competency Assessment Project*. Librarians chose *TRAILS* because it assessed a majority of the outcomes targeted in the IL program. Of the options provided by *TRAILS*, librarians chose the general assessment #2, which uses 30 multiple-choice questions to measure students' ability to apply IL skills (See Appendix 8.2). Although this assessment is designed for high school students, librarians determined through mapping that it closely aligns with ACRL outcomes. In addition, *TRAILS* is scalable, easy to administer, short enough to fit the testing timeframe and assessment cycle, and is available at no charge.

World View Seminars I and II serve well as a means to administer *TRAILS* because they are taken in a student's first and fourth semesters respectively.

During the first two years, librarians administered the pretest through the *TRAILS* Web site, but then transferred the questions into the campus course management system. This allows instant feedback through a familiar interface and encourages students to review results immediately.

Librarians and faculty administer midpoint IL assessments in RES104 using assignment-relevant questions from *TRAILS* and a final exam. RES104 is a logical midpoint because it is generally taken in between World View I and II, typically in a student's second or third semester. Three quizzes in RES104 assess selected *TRAILS* concepts and additional relevant skills such as locating material in the UD collection. Examining these results helps librarians and faculty remain flexible and responsive to student needs within this course and across the core.

The RES104 final exam was developed in 2007 by faculty and librarians. Although this course is focused on research and writing as a process, they agreed that there are foundational skills in discipline-specific concepts and research methods that should be assessed. Unlike the *TRAILS* assessments, this exam is graded. While the quizzes and exam provide useful data, faculty perform the most important and authentic assessment in this course. For each unit, students submit a portfolio consisting of evidence of their research and writing process, including an annotated bibliography, a formal outline, peer-evaluated paper drafts, and annotated sources. Faculty assess the portfolios using a collaboratively developed rubric to evaluate student work.

In addition to assignment- and *TRAILS*-based assessment, qualitative measures provide important data throughout the core. The first qualitative assessment component is a survey that first-year students take in World View I as a supplement to *TRAILS*; this survey solicits their previous experience with libraries and research. It includes selected questions adapted from a tool developed by the Network of Illinois Learning Resources in Community Colleges and allows for comments. The results provide a rich picture of incoming students' experiences and attitudes. Using this data and the *TRAILS* pretest results, librarians share with faculty a summary profile of first-year students' skills and perceptions.

Similar to the quantitative midpoint assessment in RES104, librarians administer a locally developed qualitative assessment at the end of this course. Questions measure student perceptions of their research skills, their interactions with librarians, and the value of the library sessions. Two of the questions measure the value of the information literacy component in ENG102. Asking these questions in this course is logical because the ENG102 unit is designed to prepare students for RES104. Initially, librarians had piloted a quantitative assessment in ENG102 but it did not provide useful data. They realized they needed to assess the impact of this unit in RES104 using a qualitative methodology that measured students' confidence. Therefore, librarians added questions to the existing RES104 evaluation. This is the only instance in the core curriculum in which assessment of one course component takes place in a different course.

There are also qualitative assessments built into other core courses. For example, the "minute paper" concept has been implemented in COM101. Librarians ask students to reflect on their research and speech preparation process, noting one concept that was difficult and one aspect that went well on their previous speech. This short assessment opens conversation during class among faculty, librarians, and students, giving students an opportunity to evaluate and improve their process for the next speech. Librarians share these comments with COM101 faculty, further encouraging conversation.

This informal dialogue about IL assessment within courses is helpful but inconsistent. Faculty often tell librarians that the IL program improves students' work. However, until recently, there was no formal structure to collect their observations and insights in part because librarians decided to focus on student assessment first. Now that the IL assessment model is in its third year, it is mature enough that faculty feedback can be meaningful. To gather this data, librarians and a core faculty member developed a pilot survey in spring 2009 and administered it to a small number of core faculty. The survey measures perceptions of the IL program's impact on student learning. This structured feedback process enables librarians to better understand faculty experiences and concerns and allows librarians to communicate a more complete picture of the information literacy program in the core to the university community.

EXPLORING QUALITATIVE RESULTS

The most important component of any assessment model is the data it provides, and the response from both faculty and students has been generally positive. Comments from the spring 2009 core faculty survey show that most enthusiastically embrace the collaboration:

- "I tell my students I wouldn't think of compiling materials for my own work without consultation with a librarian. I could not do one of these sessions by myself because, while I consider myself as familiar with the library databases as any prof, I do not know the shortcuts, the logic behind the keywords, the techniques of refining searches, and all the little subtleties that go into putting hands on source materials fast and efficiently." (*History faculty*)
- "It was not until I was attending this session that it really sunk in that you are here to be of service to our students and faculty. I know that sounds

so obvious, but I have had experiences with librarians who convey that they are more concerned about protecting their collection than about helping students find what they need!" (*Professional tutor/core faculty*)

- "By working closely with the library staff, we have been able to develop a specific set of training events that are tailored to the content and learning objectives of COM101. The result is something far superior than what is available in most textbooks. The library and library staff are often the better resource because they are the one-on-one consultants who can help the instructor resource his or her needs." (*Communication department chair*)

At the same time, a few English faculty have expressed reservations regarding the ENG102 unit. All ENG102 faculty agree the unit's goals have merit, but some dislike its design or execution. A few faculty believed it is their responsibility alone to create assignments and one in particular felt that the assignment was too difficult. Some were uncomfortable with what felt like a loss of control in the classroom. These concerns represented a small number of faculty.

Like a majority of faculty, most students are enthusiastic about the support they receive from librarian-faculty collaboration. This clearly contrasts with the experience of incoming students. In the World View I *TRAILS* supplement, they have commented as follows:

- "My librarian was a mean person, and that is being nice, so I usually never talked to her, but I already got help here a couple times and it's great, thanks."
- "I only used my library for computer use during class time. I never checked out a book during my entire high school career or talked with a librarian about a project or assignment."
- "I became familiar with my two local libraries and this helped a lot! The thing that turned me away in the beginning was that I didn't know how to use the library."
- "I never really had any experience with librarians. I always accomplished tasks on my own, and whenever I needed an answer I just did more research to find out."

These data explain many students' initial reluctance to engage with librarians. The RES104 library evaluation shows that student perceptions change. Although some are initially surprised at librarians' consistent involvement, by the end of the course most believe librarians have been helpful. Students may not consciously attribute their success to faculty-librarian collaboration because it is the norm for this class and for the core. However, the results in Figure 8.1 show that the collaboration has affected their learning.

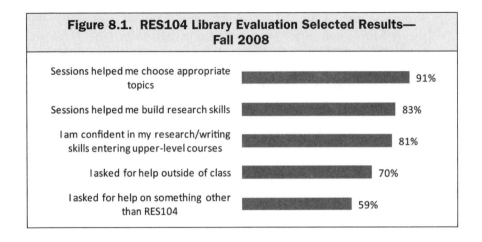

Figure 8.1. RES104 Library Evaluation Selected Results—
Fall 2008

Sessions helped me choose appropriate topics — 91%

Sessions helped me build research skills — 83%

I am confident in my research/writing skills entering upper-level courses — 81%

I asked for help outside of class — 70%

I asked for help on something other than RES104 — 59%

Comments from this evaluation have generally been positive:

- "I would never have known what I was doing my paper on without it."
- "It helped me to find an easier way to do my work, with more accurate answers."
- "I learned how to efficiently save time on a paper."
- "Every student should be able to get the info they need if you keep it up."
- "There should be another session so you can go to each individual to see if they need help."

These results, similar to previous semesters' data, show that students recognize what types of skills librarians can help them with in their research process. Most actively seek help on RES104 coursework from a librarian outside of class, and many go beyond, consulting librarians for other courses and continuing to rely on them throughout their college career. Librarians now liken reference desk hours to faculty office hours to make the concept more relatable for students. Librarians are also available in their offices, by phone, e-mail, instant messaging, and Facebook. Faculty often encourage students to meet with specific librarians. Due to increased demand, librarians staffed the reference desk 10 additional hours per week as of 2007.

EXPLORING QUANTITATIVE RESULTS

TRAILS, the key quantitative assessment instrument, also provides a rich source of data. Approximately 60 percent of World View I students during fall 2006 took the *TRAILS* pretest. In spring 2008, 82 percent of World View II students took the posttest. There were 109 students who completed the sequence, indicating they had been enrolled at UD for at least two years and suggesting they had completed most of the core. Librarians consider these students the first cohort; this model enables librarians to measure progress in IL skills throughout the core.

TRAILS Results by Student

For this cohort, the pretest average score was 72.3 percent and the posttest average score was 71.1 percent, a marginal decline. Forty-four students (40 percent) showed improvement, and 10 (9 percent) students' scores remained relatively constant (+/– no more than 2 percent). Though overall results declined, half showed improvement or remained constant (see Figure 8.2). Librarians examined results closely by evaluating data at the student and question levels. Through simple analysis of cohort results using Microsoft Excel and Access and hand-coded print copies, a noticeable pattern emerged.

Student scores appeared to fall within two subsets. Students who scored at least 75 percent on the pretest had an average score decline of 5.3 percent. However, students scoring 74 percent or below on the pretest had an average score increase of 1.6 percent (see Figure 8.3). This difference of approximately 7 percent surprised librarians. Of the 17 students in the cohort who showed a noticeable decline in posttest scores (approximately 15 percent or more), 12 had performed well on the pretest. It is likely that declines among students scoring well initially were in part responsible for the overall score decline of the cohort group.

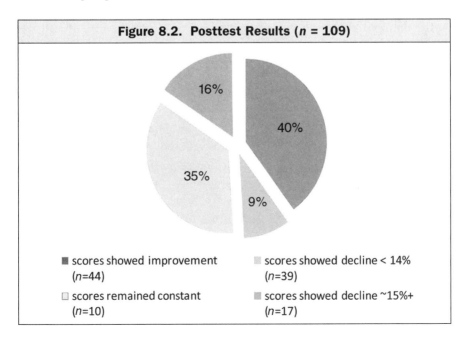

Figure 8.2. Posttest Results (*n* = 109)

16%

40%

35%

9%

■ scores showed improvement
  (*n*=44)

■ scores showed decline < 14%
  (*n*=39)

□ scores remained constant
  (*n*=10)

■ scores showed decline ~15%+
  (*n*=17)

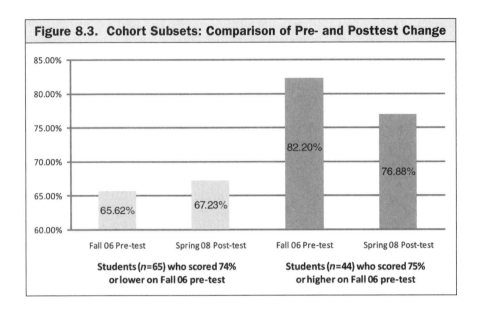

Figure 8.3. Cohort Subsets: Comparison of Pre- and Posttest Change

TRAILS Results by Question

Librarians also examined results for each *TRAILS* question to determine if particular questions could have contributed to the score decline. Limitations in data collection did not allow question-by-question analysis for just the cohort group, so librarians considered all student scores. Because overall average scores declined, mirroring the cohort scores, this information is still valuable for the IL program.

In the pre- and posttests, 27 of 32 questions were comparable; five questions were not directly comparable because the pretest was administered online and the posttest was administered via Scantron. The online version required multiple correct responses for some questions and allowed partial credit. Scantron scored these questions as completely incorrect if all correct options were not chosen. Of the 27 comparable questions, only five showed score decreases; only one of these decreased more than 5 percent. However, nine questions illustrated increases of at least 10 percent and three questions improved over 20 percent. Although not demonstrating a causal relationship between instruction and student learning, these results show that students' skills improved significantly.

In evaluating pretest scores, librarians identified eight questions of particular concern, those with pretest scores of 60 percent or below (see Appendix 8.3). On the posttest, six of these questions showed an overall score increase of 10 percent or more. In addition to the targeted eight questions, most of the other questions with relatively low pretest scores increased significantly on the posttest. This indicates that the information literacy program was successful in building students' skills in areas of particular need.

Results of Midpoint Assessment

In RES104, librarians administer three assessments with relevant *TRAILS* questions throughout the semester. These provide librarians, faculty, and students with midpoint data about student learning. In spring 2007, the first assessment indicated that students were beginning to understand the difference between scholarly and popular periodicals (four relevant questions, ranging in scores from 55–84 percent). Most could identify a valid Boolean search statement, but less than half could identify where a book with a given call number is located.

The second assessment showed that 69 percent of students could identify an encyclopedia as a valid source for background material, 75 percent could broaden and narrow a topic, 75 percent could recognize a primary source, and 83 percent could distinguish between the title of an article and the title of a journal. Sixty-five percent could identify a scholarly article when given a citation.

The third assessment showed that 74 percent could now identify an encyclopedia as a resource for beginning research and a database as a tool for finding journal articles. Sixty-eight percent could locate a book in the library by call number, 67 percent understood the difference between a journal and a magazine, and 62 percent could identify bias in a Web site. Athough students made progress, the data show that some students still have not mastered these skills.

ANALYSIS OF QUANTITATIVE DATA

Although it is too early in the assessment cycle to empirically determine the impact of the IL program, quantitative data from the first cohort indicate that student performance on targeted skills has improved. Librarians targeted instruction to address skill deficits identified by eight low-scoring *TRAILS* questions from the pretest. Using the curriculum map, they identified courses in which these concepts were introduced and reinforced. If the ACRL outcomes associated with these questions were not directly addressed, librarians added or modified content in already existing relevant library sessions. For example, two of the eight questions that were troublesome for students involved the concept of identifying source bias. This skill, ACRL outcome 3.2a, is introduced in COM101 and reinforced in World View II. It had been part of librarians' instruction previously, but assessment provided data that called librarians to more intentionally emphasize this concept.

They also introduced more uniformity of terminology, presentation, and content to library sessions across all sections of a course. This is important because different librarians teach the same IL session in different course sections. To ensure that ACRL outcomes are addressed consistently and effectively, librarians work together to prepare for each session by creating common outlines and slides for each course.

The data show that students showed greatest improvement of skills that were targeted in instruction. The analysis of this preliminary data is limited, however, as it only includes one cohort. It is also limited by the assumption that students have completed most of the relevant courses in the core by the time they take the posttest and librarians do not determine if this is true. However, because the scores for six of the eight low-scoring questions increased 10 percent or more, librarians are confident that the information literacy program has impacted student learning. For example, there was a 26.5 percent increase for a *TRAILS* question defining a database; librarians had intentionally refined their terminology and reinforced the connection between the term and the application.

Students who initially scored lower on the pretest demonstrated progress on the posttest. This indicates that those students who had the most opportunity to improve did so following interaction with librarians throughout the core curriculum. One explanation may be that students who are enrolled in RES104 and World View II at the same time see some *TRAILS* questions multiple times during that semester. This may mean that the concepts are assessed at relevant time or it may be that students simply remember the correct answers.

Librarians are unsure why scores declined steeply for 12 students who scored well on the pretest. It is possible that they were less engaged in library sessions, or may have overestimated their research skills and chose not to attend these sessions. Some may not have taken *TRAILS* seriously or were fatigued at the end of the semester, when the posttest was administered. In addition, they may have completed the research-heavy core courses their first year and had not practiced these skills recently. Although this group is a concern, librarians have not yet determined if these students share common characteristics, and, if so, how to address their needs.

Students have a wide range of experience and comfort with research, and this is apparent in the assessment results. Librarians are challenged to support students who may need extra practice while engaging those who exhibit high skill levels. Assessment data give librarians the ability to continually evaluate teaching strategies. They plan how to improve certain skills, emphasizing active learning techniques such as small group discussion and student demonstrations. They use interactive technologies including SynchronEyes, computer classroom management software, which allows them to share students' search results and encourages collaborative problem solving. Librarians introduced the student response system TurningPoint ("clickers"), which allows students to respond immediately to class content so that librarians and faculty can quickly assess student knowledge and move at an appropriate pace.

ANALYSIS OF QUALITATIVE DATA

Incoming students' perceptions gathered in the World View I *TRAILS* supplement showed that librarians were viewed negatively by many new students. This information has helped librarians realize that they first must overcome these negative images. Librarians are actively involved in student orientation in which they intentionally project the friendly and welcoming atmosphere of the library. Data from RES 104 show that students have developed more positive perceptions following librarians' involvement in core classes. One reason for this change may be that all IL instruction is tied to specific assignments. For example, in COM101, students are surprised that they are required to find pending legislation and are eager to have someone show them how to do this. In this class, students see the direct relationship between the assignment at hand and the relevant instruction librarians provide.

In addition to creative assignment-based instruction, a hallmark of the UD experience is close faculty-student relationships. The qualitative assessment in RES104 shows that students look to librarians for help. Faculty-librarian collaboration lays the groundwork for the opportunity to develop these relationships. Students see librarians as a part of their educational experience because librarians are in the classroom and work closely with faculty. Initial contact begins at orientation, encouraging students to develop relationships with librarians early in their college career. These connections are strengthened as students see librarians in the first month of World View I and continue to work with them throughout the core. These students are more likely to ask for help with other assignments, especially when faculty encourage them to meet with a specific librarian by name. Some students even routinely seek out individual librarians because they feel most comfortable with their "favorite librarian."

Because faculty and librarians work closely together, they are able to model discourse in the classroom through conversation. This introduces students to the idea that learning is an active, collaborative process. Through this dialogue, the faculty mold the IL program as it happens. For example, one history faculty member regularly prompts librarians as they teach about research tools that he feels are especially valuable. He enthusiastically reinforces the idea that databases such as JSTOR are the key to a successful paper and describes the librarians as indispensable information experts.

Preliminary qualitative assessment of faculty's response to the IL program in the core has been positive for the most part. The pilot survey of core faculty indicated that most are enthusiastic about working with librarians. They recognize the collaboration is worth their time because they do not view these process-based research sessions as taking time away from content delivery; instead, they understand this instruction improves student work. The survey also indicates that faculty convey librarians' value to their students.

The few negative comments from faculty were related to the ENG102 unit. A committee, composed of an English faculty member, the director of the Writing Center, and a librarian, meets regularly to plan, evaluate, and revise the unit. In response to faculty concerns, they made the unit more flexible. For example, some faculty now have fewer sessions with librarians and writing tutors, but some also commonly schedule more.

Unlike the student and faculty surveys, librarians' reflections on the program are informal and take place during IL librarians' planning sessions. They have observed that faculty are more aware of IL and the role librarians play in the educational process. They have also seen a change in the questions that students ask in class and at the reference desk. Qualitative data from RES104 indicate that students are confident about some IL skills, and librarians' experiences have confirmed this. They find that students are asking more in-depth questions about interpreting and understanding the information they locate. Students know they need to identify an effective research question that can be supported by quality, evidence-based material. It may be that students connect librarians with these higher-level skills because librarians reinforce the concepts using the same terminology as their faculty.

Some core faculty are now intentionally reframing assignments to target these higher-level skills. They realize when students see librarians both in and outside of class, students gradually integrate IL into other critical thinking and writing skills. As Henry Pitman, Director of Assessment, said, "Faculty can have confidence that they are assessing something that students have actually had an opportunity to learn." This also occurs in upper-division courses as library liaisons inform faculty in their departments what IL skills have been introduced in the core.

The IL program in the core has changed librarians' instruction in upper-division classes as well. Assessment allows them to know students' IL proficiency upon entering upper-division classes, making these sessions more efficient. Instead of a traditional "one-shot," librarians can offer specialized "booster shots" that briefly review the research process. For instance, students in a sociology senior seminar lead a game-based review using a "choose your own path" model (see example on Canovan's Sociology blog: www.dbq.edu/library/sociology/?p=10). These sessions can instead focus on the application of research in each discipline. An example of this occurs in a community health nursing course in which student groups consult with their librarian throughout a semester-long research project, modeling the process they will see in their careers.

EVALUATION OF ASSESSMENT

Although assessing core skills at the programmatic level is inherently difficult, incomplete, and imperfect, librarians and faculty at UD have committed to this. None of them are experts in this process, but they have had assistance from the Director of Assessment. During the first assessment cycle, they found that data need to be carefully analyzed to be meaningful. The entire process of formalizing and piloting the IL assessment model took a significant time commitment. To justify this, librarians and faculty have reframed assessment as vital to the educational mission, locating information literacy more effectively across the curriculum. As a practical, sustainable model, IL assessment at UD has strengths and weaknesses.

Discussion of the Programmatic Assessment Model

A significant limitation is the time required to prepare and administer assessments and analyze data. To create a timely feedback loop, librarians summarize and deliver data during the semester while teaching an extensive IL program and performing other duties. As additional core faculty express interest in IL instruction, librarians face the question of scalability both for instruction and assessment. They have followed the model established at UD that the ideal level of assessment is the least amount necessary to provide the most useful data. Maintaining an effective level of assessment is a challenge as the IL program grows. For example, librarians piloted an assessment in COM101, but discovered they did not have time to effectively analyze the data and were unsure they would gain useful results commensurate with the effort.

Faculty are limited by how much classroom time they can commit to IL assessment. They currently allow class time for pre- and posttesting in the World View Seminars; if this approach changes, however, the IL assessment model will be compromised. Faculty may also lack the time to use the resulting data to inform learning outcomes and teaching strategies. Others may not understand how IL connects to their teaching and therefore do not value the information that librarians provide. At the same time, librarians need to recognize that IL is only a small part of assessment in the core.

There are also some challenges with the assessment model itself. For example, librarians and faculty assume that students complete core courses their first two years. However, students in World View II may not have taken all of the research-focused core courses because the core is largely nonsequential.

Therefore, the posttest may not truly measure if a change in skills is based on IL instruction. In addition, because librarians do not see all sections of some core courses, it is not possible to immediately assess skills identified in the curriculum map for those courses. For example, although World Civilization I and II (UDHS121/122) appear in the map, librarians cannot consistently administer assessment because there is not IL instruction in all sections. They initially mapped these courses when there was consistent instruction, but when additional sections were added with new faculty, IL instruction was not included.

There is also a challenge administering the model. The course management system has made scoring and analysis easier; however, it has created extra pressure on the few available computer labs. In spring 2008, librarians gave the posttest via paper and pencil because computer labs were not available, making score comparisons labor-intensive and difficult.

Despite these limitations, the introduction of the IL assessment model over the past three years has been successful. Although the IL assessment structure was created by librarians, the actual assessment methodology and instruments have grown and changed through collaboration between faculty and librarians. For example, a faculty member, librarian, and core administrator wrote the RES104 final, which contains many IL concepts. Data generated by assessment has changed the dynamic between faculty and librarians, encouraging them to make more informed decisions about teaching strategies and course content. The IL program, including its assessment, is a cooperative venture, and faculty and librarians develop synergistic relationships as they work toward the same goals. Key administrators also contributed to the integration of information literacy in the core, particularly the Associate Dean for Academic Affairs, who supported and nurtured this process. The Director of Assessment assisted in the development of the IL model by providing a framework and outline for assessment in general and continues to consult with librarians as the model matures. The Vice President for Academic Affairs encourages community and conversation on campus, which fosters collaborative projects. In addition, he actively expresses his support of information literacy.

Although relationships are important, the programmatic model is sustainable because it is not solely based on individuals. It has thrived throughout changes in personnel and is strengthened through continual input from new contributors. The assessment model places faculty and librarians in informed conversation, and continuous assessment has allowed the program to respond to changing needs.

Discussion of *TRAILS*

TRAILS is a valuable assessment tool that is scalable and provides the librarians and faculty with meaningful data. However, no single assessment tool can meet all needs. An objective test is inherently limited in assessing process-based skills. Librarians initially attempted more authentic assessment by conducting citation analysis of RES104 papers, but found it was unsustainable. Due to extensive IL instruction, librarians could not find the time necessary to continue this assessment. This time constraint is still an issue as librarians look for assessment options that could provide richer data.

Annual changes in *TRAILS* have presented unforeseen issues with score comparability between pre- and posttests. Kent State librarians continually improve *TRAILS* by revising question wording and format, and some questions have been removed from later versions. Because of these changes, the test taken by the fall 2006 and fall 2007 cohorts was different, making empirical comparisons for selected questions impossible. To solve this, librarians chose one version to use consistently for each cohort. Using the same version of the test for all assessment, however, is also a limitation. Librarians do not use a bank of questions to assess the same outcomes. Therefore, students may become accustomed to the test and remember specific questions, so the posttest may not accurately measure knowledge of each concept. As the culture of assessment develops, students may also experience assessment fatigue.

Despite these limitations, librarians plan to continue using *TRAILS*. The assessment cycle is too new to change testing instruments. Although there are a number of other tools, *TRAILS* is available at no charge. If librarians chose a fee-based instrument, there is no guarantee the library could find stable funding necessary for longitudinal assessment. *TRAILS* provides librarians and faculty with enough data to make meaningful educational decisions.

FUTURE DIRECTIONS AND CONCLUSIONS

The assessment program has provided data demonstrating the library's vital role in the institutional mission of teaching and learning. Librarians and faculty have created a sustainable program in the core curriculum by targeting specific IL learning outcomes in selected courses. This has created both opportunities and challenges for the future.

Faculty who teach other core courses are interested in collaborating. For example, librarians and religion faculty piloted a research assignment in a required introductory course. However, developing this as a common assignment will be difficult without reexamining the existing IL program, especially as librarians commit to additional instruction, including the expanding evening and summer school offerings. In addition, as course management software is integrated in both distance and on-campus instruction, librarians are developing a variety of IL tools, tutorials, and supplemental material.

Librarians are improving communication with all faculty about students' IL skills. In 2009–2010, librarians will share posttest results with faculty so that they know what is covered in the IL program and students' level of success with basic concepts. This will give faculty teaching upper-division courses a reasonable idea what they can expect of students who have completed the core. The next step is for librarians to work with faculty to structure an IL sequence within the majors. Because of the general support of IL, this would be well received in many departments. At present, librarians are involved in upper-division classes but no major has a systematic IL component. To do this, librarians and faculty will have to replicate the process that occurred in the core, including locating IL outcomes in the majors. At minimum, additional testing could be done in World View IV, a required senior seminar in each department. Since UD is moving to an e-portfolio assessment instrument, this is a timely concern. If IL skills are adopted in departmental outcomes and assessed through students' entire careers, librarians may become responsible for some of this assessment. Faculty rather than librarians could assess competence, but any model will require a great deal of collaboration.

Another concern is the inevitability of change. At present, most core faculty enthusiastically support IL. With the model in place, librarians do not "sell" the program as much as educate new faculty about it. If there is significant turnover of faculty and administrators, librarians and core faculty might have to move from delivering the program to arguing for its existence. If assessment instruments change, either in the IL program or campus-wide, this could affect longitudinal assessment. In addition, in the dynamic environment of higher education, institutions have not come to a consensus about how long student data is meaningful.

Librarians and faculty at University of Dubuque have partnered to create a sustainable information literacy assessment model in the core curriculum. This requires balancing multiple measures of student learning with a "just-enough" and "just-in-time" philosophy. Scalable and sustainable assessment goes beyond individuals and particular class sessions, courses, or majors. Faculty contextualize information literacy in their courses and librarians link these concepts throughout the core. These roles allow librarians and faculty together to engage in meaningful assessment to improve teaching and foster student learning.

REFERENCES

Angelo, Thomas A., and K. Patricia Cross. 1993. *Classroom Assessment Techniques: A Handbook for College Teachers.* San Francisco: Jossey-Bass.

Association of College and Research Libraries. 2000. "Information Literacy Competency Standards for Higher Education." Chicago: Association of College and Research Libraries. Available: www.ala.org/ala/mgrps/divs/acrl/standards/standards.pdf (accessed October 1, 2009).

Association of College and Research Libraries. 1998. "Task Force on Academic Library Outcomes Assessment Report." Chicago: Association of College and Research Libraries (June 27, 1998). Available: www.ala.org/ala/mgrps/divs/acrl/publications/whitepapers/taskforceacademic.cfm (accessed October 1, 2009).

Avery, Elizabeth Fuseler. 2003. *Assessing Student Learning Outcomes for Information Literacy Instruction in Academic Institutions.* Chicago: Association of College and Research Libraries.

Bisesi, Michael. 1982. "Historical Developments in American Undergraduate Education: General Education and the Core Curriculum." *British Journal of Educational Studies* 30, no. 2: 199–212.

Bober, Christopher, and Sonia Poulin. 1995. "Evaluating Library Instruction in Academic Libraries: A Critical Review of the Literature, 1980–1993." *Reference Librarian* 51/52: 53–71.

Boning, Kenneth. 2007. "Coherence in General Education: A Historical Look." JGE: *The Journal of General Education* 56, no. 1 (January): 1–16.

Ekman, Richard, and Stephen Pelletier. 2008. "Student Learning: A Work in Progress." *Change: The Magazine of Higher Learning* 40, no. 4 (July/August): 15–19.

Gruber, Anne Marie, Mary Anne Knefel, and Paul Waelchli. 2008. "Modeling Scholarly Inquiry: One Article at a Time." *College & Undergraduate Libraries* 15, no. 1/2: 99–125.

Hutchings, Pat, and Ted Marchese. 1990. "Watching Assessment: Questions, Stories, Prospects." *Change: The Magazine of Higher Learning* 22, no. 5 (October/September): 12–38.

Iannuzzi, Patricia. 1999. "We Are Teaching, but Are They Learning? Accountability, Productivity, and Assessment." *Journal of Academic Librarianship* 25, no. 4 (July): 304–305.

Johnson, D. Kent, and James L. Ratcliff. 2004. "Creating Coherence: The Unfinished Agenda." *New Directions for Higher Education* 125 (Spring): 85–95.

Jones, Elizabeth A. 1995. *National Assessment of College Student Learning: Identifying College Graduates' Essential Skills in Writing, Speech and Listening, and Critical Thinking: Final Project Report.* Washington, DC: U.S. Department of Education.

Lindauer, Bonnie Gratch. 1998. "Defining and Measuring the Library's Impact on Campuswide Outcomes." *College & Research Libraries* 59, no. 6: 546–563.

Merz, Lawrie H., and Beth L. Mark. 2002. *Assessment in College Library Instruction Programs.* Chicago: College Libraries Section, Association of College and Research Libraries.

O'Connor, Lisa G., Carolyn J. Radcliff, and Julie A. Gedeon. 2002. "Applying Systems Design and Item Response Theory to the Problem of Measuring Information Literacy Skills." *College & Research Libraries* 63, no. 6: 528–543.

Palomba, Catherine A., and Trudy W. Banta. 1999. *Assessment Essentials: Planning, Implementing, and Improving Assessment in Higher Education.* San Francisco: Jossey-Bass.

Pausch, Lois, and Mary P. Popp. 1997. "Assessment of Information Literacy: Lessons from the Higher Education Assessment Movement." Chicago: American Library Association. Available: www.ala.org/ala/mgrps/divs/acrl/publications/whitepapers/nashville/pauschpopp.cfm (accessed October 1, 2009).

Rabine, Julie, and Catherine Cardwell. 2000. "Start Making Sense: Practical Approaches to Outcomes Assessment for Libraries." *Research Strategies* 17, no. 4: 319–335.

Rockman, Ilene F., and Gordon W. Smith. 2005. "Information and Communication Technology Literacy." *College & Research Libraries News* 66, no. 8: 587–589.

Schloman, Barbara F., and Julie A. Gedeon. 2007. "Creating *TRAILS*." *Knowledge Quest* 35, no. 5: 44–47.

"The Thrust and Parry of Assessment." 2008. *Academe* 94, no. 3 (May/June): 25–28.

TRAILS: Tool for Real-Time Assessment of Information Literacy Skills. 2009. Kent, OH: Kent State University Libraries & Media Services. Available: www.trails-9.org (accessed October 1, 2009).

U. S. National Institute of Education, Study Group on the Conditions of Excellence in American Higher Education. 1984. *Involvement in Learning: Realizing the Potential of American Higher Education.* Washington, DC: Government Printing Office.

University of Dubuque. 1998. *Mission, Vision, Action.* Dubuque, IA: University of Dubuque.

Appendix 8.1. Curriculum Map

ACRL Information Literacy Standards and Performance Indicators I = Introduce R = Review/ Reinforce E = Emphasize M = Mastery		WVS 101	RES 104	COM 101	WVS 201	UDHS 121/2	ENG 100	ENG 102	ENG 112
1.0.	The information literate student determines the nature and extent of the information needed.								
1.1.	The information literate student defines and articulates the need for information.	I	I/R	R	E/R	I/E/R	I	I	R
1.2.	The information literate student identifies a variety of types and formats of potential sources for information.	I	I	R	R	I	I	I	R
1.3.	The information literate student considers the costs and benefits of acquiring the needed information.		I/R			R			
1.4.	The information literate student reevaluates the nature and extent of the information need.		I/R	I					
2.0.	The information literate student accesses needed information effectively and efficiently.								
2.1.	The information literate student selects the most appropriate investigative methods or information retrieval systems for accessing the needed information.		I	I/E	I/E/R	I		I	I/R
2.2.	The information literate student constructs and implements effectively designed search strategies.		I/R	E/R	R	I/R			I/R
2.3	The information literate student retrieves information online or in person using a variety of methods.	I	I	R	I/R	R			R
2.4.	The information literate student refines the search strategy if necessary.		I/R	R	E/R	R			
2.5.	The information literate student extracts, records, and manages the information and its sources.		I/R	E		I/R			E

(Continued)

Appendix 8.1. Curriculum Map *(Continued)*

ACRL Information Literacy Standards and Performance Indicators I = Introduce R = Review/ Reinforce E = Emphasize M = Mastery	WVS 101	RES 104	COM 101	WVS 201	UDHS 121/2	ENG 100	ENG 102	ENG 112
3.0. The information Literate student evaluates information and its sources critically and incorporates selected information into his or her knowledge base and value system.								
3.1. The information literate student summarizes the main ideas to be extracted from the information gathered.		I/R	R	R	R	I	I	
3.2. The information literate student articulates and applies initial criteria for evaluating both the information and its sources.	I	I	I	R			I	
3.3. The information literate student synthesizes main ideas to construct new concepts.		I				I	I	
3.4. The information literate student compares new knowledge with prior knowledge to determine the value added, contradictions, or other unique characteristics of the information.		I/R	I/R	E/R		I	I	R
3.5. The information literate student determines whether the new knowledge has an impact on the individual's value system and takes steps to reconcile differences.			I	E				
3.6. The information literate student validates understanding and interpretation of the information through discourse with other individual, subject-area experts, and/or practitioners.		I		R		I	I	
3.7. The information literate student determines whether the initial query should be revised.		I	R	E/R	R			E/R

(Continued)

Appendix 8.1. Curriculum Map *(Continued)*								
ACRL Information Literacy Standards and Performance Indicators I = Introduce R = Review/ Reinforce E = Emphasize M = Mastery	WVS 101	RES 104	COM 101	WVS 201	UDHS 121/2	ENG 100	ENG 102	ENG 112
4.0.	**The information literate student, individually or as a member of a group, uses information effectively to accomplish a specific purpose.**							
4.1.	The information literate student applies new and prior information to the planning and creation of a particular product or performance.	I	R	R	R	I	I	
4.2.	The information literate student revises the development process for the product or performance.	I	R					
4.3.	The information literate student communicates the product or performance effectively to others.	I	I/E	E/R		R	R	
5.0.	**The information literate student understands many of the economic, legal, and social issues surrounding the use of information and accesses and uses information ethically and legally.**							
5.1.	The information literate student understands many of the ethical, legal and socio-economic issues surrounding information and information technology.	I	E					
5.2.	The information literate student follows laws, regulations, institutional polices, and etiquette related to the access and use of information resources.	I	E/R	E	E/R			
5.3.	The information literate student acknowledges the use of information sources in communicating the product or performance.							

(Continued)

Appendix 8.2. *TRAILS* Assessment Fall 2006

1. Using information from the first page of a book as given below, which of the following is the book's publisher?

> Three Nights in August
>
> *Strategy, Heartbreak, and Joy Inside the Mind of a Manager*
>
> Buzz Bissinger
>
> Houghton Mifflin Company
>
> Boston * New York * 2005

CHOOSE ONE ANSWER.

   a. Three Nights in August

   b. Three Nights in August: Strategy, Heartbreak, and Joy Inside the Mind of a Manager

   c. Buzz Bissinger

   d. Houghton Mifflin Company

2. Which information sources in the following list would help you gain an initial understanding of the Holocaust?

CHOOSE ALL THAT APPLY.

   a. a national newspaper

   b. an art museum

   c. an interview with a concentration camp survivor

   d. an encyclopedia

   e. a history book about World War II

3. It's the second week of school. Your teacher gives you an assignment to write a 10-page paper on a topic you know little about. The paper is due at the end of the grading period.

If you decide to go to the library, which of the following would be an efficient way to start?

CHOOSE ALL THAT APPLY.

   a. Ask for help.

   b. Browse the bookshelves.

   c. Find the journals and start looking through them.

   d. Use a database to find journal articles.

   e. Use a library catalog to find books.

4. The best definition for the Boolean operator "AND" is:

CHOOSE ONE ANSWER.

   a. limits the search; excludes word/phrase

   b. finds antonyms for word/phrase

   c. narrows the search; joins concepts

   d. broadens the search; results can include either word/phrase

(Continued)

Appendix 8.2. *TRAILS* Assessment Fall 2006 *(Continued)*

5. If you were using the Internet or a database, which of the following search phrases would find information on "Hurricanes" without including any information on "Florida"?

CHOOSE ONE ANSWER.

    a. Hurricanes NOT Florida   c. Hurricanes OR Florida

    b. Hurricanes AND Florida   d. Hurricanes BUT Florida

---

6. You have been given an assignment about the history of hip-hop music. You have already searched an online database for magazine articles on "hip-hop music," and you get a list of 350 articles.

If you change your search to get fewer articles, which of the following strategies would help you limit or narrow your search topic?

CHOOSE ONE ANSWER.

    a. Search for full text articles only.

    b. Search including the term "history."

    c. Search by the year of publication of the magazine.

    d. Search only for articles that have illustrations or photographs.

    e. All of the above

---

7. You've been assigned a persuasive speech on restricting the use of cell phones during school hours. Which of the following resource choices would you make?

CHOOSE ONE ANSWER.

    a. magazine article, atlas, dictionary

    b. atlas, book

    c. dictionary

    d. encyclopedia, book

    e. Web site, magazine article

---

8. When using a research database, which search is the most effective to find articles on how weight affects self-esteem?

CHOOSE ONE ANSWER.

    a. how weight affects self-esteem

    b. self-esteem

    c. weight

    d. weight and self-esteem

    e. weight or self-esteem

---

9. You need to write a paper on an event that took place two days ago. Where are you most likely to find information about the event?

CHOOSE ONE ANSWER.

    a. book   c. magazine

    b. encyclopedia   d. newspaper

(Continued)

Appendix 8.2. *TRAILS* Assessment Fall 2006 *(Continued)*

10. The following picture is from an online library catalog. If you were searching for the book, Harry Potter and the Sorcerer's Stone, which search type would you choose?

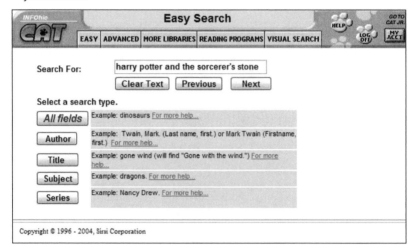

Copyright © 1996 - 2004, Sirsi Corporation

CHOOSE ONE ANSWER.

    a. All fields   c. Title   e. Series
    b. Author   d. Subject

11. Which one of these resources would most likely have a current article on steroid use in professional baseball?

CHOOSE ONE ANSWER.

a. a school library catalog
b. a science database such as Access Science
c. a newspaper and magazine database such as EBSCOhost
d. biography database such as Gale Biography Resource Center
e. a biography database such as American National Biography

12. What is the term for an online resource that shows what materials a library owns?

CHOOSE ONE ANSWER.

    a. bibliography   d. research database
    b. keyword   e. subject heading
    c. library catalog

13. If you want to find good periodical articles on a specific topic, which of these is the best way to start?

CHOOSE ONE ANSWER.

    a. Flip through periodicals.   c. Use a Web search engine.
    b. Use a research database.   d. Use the library catalog.

(Continued)

Appendix 8.2. *TRAILS* Assessment Fall 2006 *(Continued)*

14. If you want to find books that Charlotte Brontë wrote, which search would you do?

CHOOSE ONE ANSWER.
    a. author search on: brontë   c. title search on: brontë
    b. subject search on: brontë

15. If you wanted to find books about the American poet Maya Angelou, which search would you do?

CHOOSE ONE ANSWER.
    a. author search on: angelou   c. title search on: angelou
    b. subject search on: angelou

16. If you need to know what chapters are in a book, which part of the book provides the best information?

CHOOSE ONE ANSWER.
    a. cover of the book   c. introduction
    b. glossary   d. table of contents

17. Read the following quotation from the Web site of the organization known as Beef International.

"Mad Cow disease occurs in animals located in small, defined areas. Government measures to restrict the movement of cattle or even to destroy those in a larger region are not necessary and limit a farmer's freedom to make his own decisions. Farmers are able to handle problems within their own herds."

Which of the following should you consider in deciding whether this is a credible source?

CHOOSE ONE ANSWER.
    a. This is a credible source because it is from the Beef International Web site.
    b. This is a credible source because the information is written as a quote, indicating this is an expert opinion.
    c. This is not a credible source because the organization is likely to be biased about this issue.
    d. This is not a credible source because it does not support government policy.

18. You need to find reliable information about treatments available for headaches and plan to use an article from the periodical Pain-Free Living as your source. What should you think about as you decide whether this is a good source?

CHOOSE ALL THAT APPLY.
    a. Does the article refer to medical research?
    b. Is the article short?
    c. What experience does the author of the article have?
    d. Who publishes the periodical?
    e. All of the above

(Continued)

Appendix 8.2. *TRAILS* Assessment Fall 2006 *(Continued)*

19. You are assigned a report for your social studies class on a speech given by the U.S. Secretary of the Interior four days ago. What research tools would be most helpful in finding information about the speech?

CHOOSE ALL THAT APPLY.

a. Search for articles in Yahoo News Directory (online).
b. Search for articles in a newspaper database (online).
c. Search for books in your library's catalog.

---

20. Which term means lack of bias or prejudice?

CHOOSE ONE ANSWER.

a. coverage
b. objectivity
c. currency
d. accuracy
e. authority

---

21. Contemporary and up-to-date refer to:

CHOOSE ONE ANSWER.

a. coverage
b. objectivity
c. currency
d. accuracy
e. authority

---

22. You are responsible for writing a paper on the production of electricity in your state. Which resource is least likely to have biased information:

CHOOSE ONE ANSWER.

a. Environmental Protection Agency (http://www.epa.gov)
b. Freetheplanet.org
c. The Greenworks Gazette
d. a newsletter written by an electric company
e. Sierra Club

---

23. Does the excerpt below illustrate fact, opinion, or bias?

"According to the U.S. Department of Justice, 39 percent of adults say they have a gun at home and an additional 2 percent say they have a gun somewhere else on the property or in a car or truck."

CHOOSE ONE ANSWER.

a. bias
b. fact
c. opinion

---

24. Which of the following are considered primary sources in history?

CHOOSE ALL THAT APPLY.

a. bibliographies
b. book reviews
c. lab reports
d. letters
e. personal diaries

(Continued)

Appendix 8.2. *TRAILS* **Assessment Fall 2006** *(Continued)*

25. What is the best definition of censorship?

CHOOSE ONE ANSWER.
  a. the right of every individual to both seek and receive information from all points of view without restriction
  b. the prevention of cheating by students
  c. the encouragement of open and public sharing of ideas
  d. the limiting of access to ideas and information that some people find objectionable or dangerous
  e. the support of the Bill of Rights

26. Plagiarism means:

CHOOSE ONE ANSWER.
  a. quoting someone else's work
  b. writing a short story
  c. the use of another's original words or ideas as though they were your own
  d. developing a handbook on copyright laws

27. Is it legal for you to use images created by another person on your own Web page?

CHOOSE ONE ANSWER.
  a. Yes, if the creator gives permission.
  b. Yes, if you scan the image yourself.
  c. Yes, if you alter the image.
  d. No, it is not legal for you to use images created by another person on your own web page.

28. Jeffrey, Nancy. "Are Tanning Beds Unsafe for Teens?" *People* 63(19), 5/16/2005: 153–154.

Using the MLA-style citation above, the last numbers, 153–154, refer to what?

CHOOSE ONE ANSWER.
  a. volume number   c. page number
  b. issue number   e. date

29. The citation below refers to what?

Gertz, Bill. *Business Cycles in the United States Economy.* New York: Viking, 1999.

CHOOSE ONE ANSWER.
  a. book   d. newspaper article
  b. chapter within a book   e. periodical article
  c. encyclopedia article

(Continued)

Appendix 8.2. *TRAILS* **Assessment Fall 2006** *(Continued)*
30–32. Three students have been given topics for research papers. They have decided to change their topics to make their papers better. Read their original topics and read their revised topics. **Decide if the revised topic is broader (less specific) or narrower (more specific) than the original topic.**
30. Initial Topic: Describe the elements needed in an auditorium to reduce echoes. Revised Topic: Describe the elements needed in an auditorium for good sound quality. CHOOSE ONE ANSWER. a. Revised topic *broader* than Initial topic b. Revised topic *narrower* than Initial topic
31. Initial Topic: What are the effects of plate tectonics on California? Revised Topic: What are the effects of the 1994 earthquake on Los Angeles? CHOOSE ONE ANSWER. a. Revised topic *broader* than Initial topic b. Revised topic *narrower* than Initial topic
32. Initial Topic: How have recycling programs in the U.S. been successful in reducing the amount of waste? Revised Topic: How do recycling programs compare to landfills in terms of the effect of waste on the environment? CHOOSE ONE ANSWER. a Revised topic *broader* than Initial topic b. Revised topic *narrower* than Initial topic
Source: TRAILS questions (general assessment #2, Fall 2006 version). Copyrighted Kent State University Libraries.

Appendix 8.3. Pretest Questions of Concern			
TRAILS Question	Fall 06 Average (%)	Spring 08 Average (%)	% Change
If you want to find good periodical articles on a specific topic, which of these is the best way to start?	41.50	68.00	26.50
Contemporary and up-to-date refer to:	36.10	58.50	22.40
You are writing an essay about how Maya Angelou's life has influenced her writing. If you wanted to find books about the American poet Maya Angelou, which search would you perform?	40.20	58.00	17.80
You are responsible for writing a paper on the production of electricity in your state. Which resource is least likely to have biased information?	41.10	53.00	11.90
Read the following quotation from the Web site of the organization known as Cattle Producers International. Which of the following best reflects the credibility of this source?	54.80	66.50	11.70
The best definition for the Boolean operator "AND" is:	36.50	46.50	10.00
You consult a bibliography to get ideas for resources to write your paper. Within the bibliography you find the citation below. In order to know where in your library to look, you must determine what type of resource this is. Citation: Gertz, Bill. Business Cycles in the United States Economy. New York: Viking, 1999.	59.80	64.00	4.20
Three students have been given topics for research papers. They have decided to change their topics to make their papers better. Read their original topics and read their revised topics. Decide if the revised topic is broader (less specific) or narrower (more specific) than the original topic: recycling topic.	52.70	54.50	1.80

Afterword

In her Foreword to this book Debra Gilchrist compared the assessment cycle with the synergy of ecosystems and the ability to carefully listen. When we first read her response to our book, we were both at different points on the map, teaching in the United States and traveling to a conference in Europe. Through e-mail, the images and sounds Debra described at Vashon Island, Washington, rippled to Albany, New York, and Brussels, Belgium, and we both thought—this works—this is exactly how we see it. Assessments are carefully developed over time, providing us with a systematic means to observe and to improve teaching and learning in a continuous, iterative process.

During this past year we have been in dialogue with faculty-librarian author teams from the United States, the United Kingdom, and New Zealand. We gained insights about information literacy assessment from this international perspective, reinforcing the universal need for improving critical thinking to engage with the increasingly complex information environment. The central tenets of information literacy—searching, locating, evaluating, synthesizing, and using information-constitute a necessary skill set for all lifelong learners.

As we have seen, the authors in this book represent multiple disciplines, describing innovative assessment models in business, finance, political science, psychology, education, and humanities. These teams explored assessment strategies at the undergraduate level, in an adult education program, in the core curriculum and for departmental requirements and foundation degrees. We helped shape a path for these writings, which collectively argue for the development of faculty-librarian partnerships to design effective assessment efforts. By working together, faculty and librarians expand the disciplinary influence of information literacy and help to provide students with practical and theoretical knowledge for success in academic pursuits and throughout one's life.

We know that collaboration is not easy and that faculty-librarian partnerships are not fully supported or developed at all institutions. There are many real barriers to developing successful collaborations between faculty and librarians and the incentives to encourage working together may be lacking. The author teams in this book and in our previous two publications, however, show that information literacy collaborations work, and that student experience is always enhanced by these endeavors.

This book examines information literacy assessment through a case study approach that is essential to learning about this topic from those who are leading the way in the classroom and online. Rather than present a single methodology, we offer varied pathways, demonstrating that more than one model is relevant and that knowledge is created through dialogue with others. We were impressed with the many ways that our chapter authors overcame some of the practical and institutional barriers to working together to carefully reflect on student learning through original assessment strategies. This multiple case study approach is also instructive when exploring the varied tools for assessment. As we have seen, some of the instruments for assessment include:

- citation analysis,
- written reports,
- annotated bibliographies,
- observation,
- self-assessments,
- multiple instruction sessions,
- surveys,
- online modules,
- multiple-choice questions,
- research and writing rubrics, and
- *TRAILS* pre- and posttests.

These tools were developed by faculty and librarian teams that focused on ways to integrate and embed these resources into the curriculum. These diverse approaches demonstrated the fact that no one owns these tools and that assessments defined as formative or summative can be applied beyond the bounds of any particular disciplinary perspective. One of the central lessons of this book is that multiple tools are possible in a range of disciplines and that what happens at the local level really matters. All assessment strategies, even those that are mandated, require input from instructors who are closely involved in the design and delivery of courses.

Based on our experience editing this book, we expect that the future of information literacy assessment will necessarily involve faculty-librarian collaboration. The tools will continue to be refined based on the needs of particular courses and programs and through the ongoing analysis of learning outcomes. This work will be done in teaching and learning teams, and these partnerships may expand to include other stakeholders such as instructional technologists, student and academic support professionals, and administrators. As trends in open and online learning expand, many of these instruments may become available in a variety of Web-based delivery modes as well, to be shared in an information literacy commons.

In closing, we are certain that faculty and librarians will continue to lead these initiatives and we hope they will receive the institutional support they need to experiment and innovate. As this book demonstrates, the shift in emphasis to learning outcomes is realized through collaborative practice. It is encouraging to know that we are listening to our students in a new way.

About the Editors and Contributors

Thomas P. Mackey, PhD, is the Associate Dean at the Center for Distance Learning at SUNY Empire State College in Saratoga Springs, New York. His teaching and research interests include information literacy, blended and distance learning, social networking and Web 2.0, Web-based multimedia, and social and community informatics. He has published two co-edited books with Trudi E. Jacobson for Neal-Schuman Publishers, *Using Technology to Teach Information Literacy* (2008) and *Information Literacy Collaborations That Work* (2007). His research articles have been published in *Computers & Education, The Journal of General Education, College Teaching, Rhizomes, The Journal of Information Science, The Journal of Education for Library and Information Science*, and the *Journal of the Library Administration and Management Section (JLAMS)* of the New York Library Association. Tom was a member of the Advisory Panel on Information Literacy for the Middle States Commission on Higher Education (MSCHE) and contributed to a guidebook on information literacy titled *Developing Research & Communication Skills: Guidelines for Information Literacy in the Curriculum* (2003). He may be contacted by e-mail at Tom.Mackey@esc.edu.

Trudi E. Jacobson, MLS, MA, is the Head of User Education Programs at the University at Albany, SUNY. She coordinates and teaches in the undergraduate Information Literacy course program. Her interests include the use of critical thinking and active learning activities in the classroom. She is the co-author, with Lijuan Xu, of *Motivating Students in Information Literacy Classes* (2004), and co-editor, with Thomas P. Mackey, of *Using Technology to Teach Information Literacy* (2008) and *Information Literacy Collaborations That Work* (2007). She also co-edited or edited *Teaching the New Library to Today's Users* (2000), *Teaching Information Literacy Concepts: Activities and Frameworks from the Field* (2001) and *Critical Thinking and the Web: Teaching Users to Evaluate Internet Resources* (2000). She has published articles in a number of journals, including *The Journal of*

General Education, College & Research Libraries, portal, Journal of Academic Librarianship, Research Strategies, College Teaching, and *The Teaching Professor.* She is the editor of Public Services Quarterly. In 2009, Trudi won the Association of College and Research Libraries Instruction Section's Miriam Dudley Instruction Librarian Award. She may be contacted by e-mail at tjacobson@uamail. albany.edu.

* * *

Julie Bostock, BSc (Hons) PGCert, is Senior Lecturer in Education at Edge Hill University where she is Course Leader for PGCE Psychology (teacher training). Her research interests include the professional development of the wider school workforce and the psychology of education. She is a member of the British Psychological Society, including the Division for Teachers and Researchers, and a member of the Association of Psychology Teachers. She may be reached via e-mail at julie.bostock@edgehill.ac.uk.

Leslie Bussert, MLIS, is Acting Head of Instruction Services and Literature and Humanities Reference and Instruction Librarian at the University of Washington Bothell and Cascadia Community College Campus Library. She has worked in academic libraries for nearly 10 years, first as a library technician, then as a librarian for five years. Her research and writing interests include assessment, information literacy, learning and social networking technologies, and comic books and graphic novels. She may be contacted by e-mail at lbussert@uwb.edu.

Becky Canovan, MA-LIS, is Reference and Instruction Librarian at Charles C. Myers Library, University of Dubuque in Dubuque, Iowa. A recent graduate of the School of Library and Information Studies at the University of Wisconsin-Madison, her research interests include collaborative learning and the reading and study habits of college students. She may be contacted at bcanovan@ dbq.edu.

Douglas G. Carrie, PhD, is Director, Bachelor of Business and Information Management degree program, at the University of Auckland in New Zealand. A Canadian by birth, Doug's professional background includes management and consulting experience in Canada, Taiwan, and the UK. Doug's educational background in the academic discipline of marketing is equally international, with a Bachelor of Commerce from Canada, an MBA from the United States, and a PhD from London Business School in the United Kingdom. His research interests involve teaching and learning in tertiary business education, and media planning in advertising and marketing communications. Doug is a two-time recipient of the University of Auckland Distinguished Teaching Award. He may be contacted by e-mail at d.carrie@auckland.ac.nz.

Deborah B. Gaspar, EdD, is currently an instructional librarian at The George Washington University where she provides instruction sessions for undergraduate and graduate courses. Her primary task is to collaborate with writing instructors to embed information literacy learning in University Writing Program courses. Before moving to higher education, she worked as a high school librarian and was active in curriculum design, strategic planning, and technology initiatives. She advocated for information literacy learning across curricula, increased staffing for district libraries, and wrote several successful grants to facilitate student learning through the library. She may be contacted via e-mail at dgaspar@gwu.edu.

Christopher P. Gilbert, PhD, is Professor of Political Science at Gustavus Adolphus College in St. Peter, Minnesota. He teaches courses in American politics and research methods. He has written extensively on Minnesota politics, third parties in the United States, and the religious dimensions of American political behavior. He may be contacted via e-mail at cgilbert@gustavus.edu.

Julie K. Gilbert, MA, MLIS, is Assistant Professor and Academic Librarian at the Folke Bernadotte Memorial Library, Gustavus Adolphus College in St. Peter, Minnesota. She earned her library science degree at Dominican University, Lake Forest, Illinois; she also earned a Master of Arts degree from St. John's University, Collegeville, Minnesota. At Gustavus, Julie participates extensively in the instruction and reference programs. She also oversees the library's integrated library system. Julie's research interests include information literacy, promotion of recreational reading in academic libraries and workflow analysis practices in technical services. She may be contacted via e-mail at jgilber2@gustavus.edu.

Susan Graves, MA, BA (Hons), Cert Ed, is Principal Lecturer in the Faculty of Education at Edge Hill University, Ormskirk, Lancashire, England. Sue teaches on programs and professional development courses for those in nonteaching roles within schools and also on the master's degree program for teachers in schools. Her research interests include developing the wider school workforce, using action learning, developing reflective practice, developing learner identity, and e-learning to improve access to learning. She can be contacted at gravess@edgehill.ac.uk.

Anne Marie Gruber, MA-LIS, is Assistant Director for Library Instruction & Public Services at Charles C. Myers Library, University of Dubuque in Dubuque,

Iowa. She earned her MA from University of Iowa School of Library and Information Science. She has published and presented on collaborative information literacy models, game-based learning, and issues of interest to new librarians. Her research interests include active learning techniques and creative faculty-librarian collaborations. She may be contacted at amgruber@dbq.edu.

Amanda A. Harrison, PhD, is Senior Lecturer in Behavioural Neuroscience in the Institute of Psychological Sciences at the University of Leeds. She teaches courses in biological psychology, neuropsychology and drug addiction. Her research interests include the neurobiology of drug addiction, depression and impulsive behavior, and the creation of evidence-based information literacy teaching. The latter has led to several conference and invited presentations about the assessment of information literacy. She is the recent recipient of a University of Leeds Teaching Fellowship Award. She may be contacted at a.a.harrison@leeds.ac.uk.

Mary Anne Knefel, MLS, MBA, is Library Director, Charles C. Myers Library, University of Dubuque in Dubuque, Iowa. She received her MLS from the University of Illinois at Urbana-Champaign and her MBA from the University of Dubuque. She has taught information literacy skills to students from first grade to graduate school and has published and presented on a collaborative information literacy unit. She may be contacted at mknefel@dbq.edu.

Casey M. Long, MLIS, is currently the User Education Librarian at Agnes Scott College in Decatur, Georgia, and previously worked at Georgia State University as a Business Liaison Librarian. Her active pursuit of establishing a business information literacy program at Georgia State University earned her the honor of being named to the *Library Journal*'s annual Movers and Shakers list in 2009. She has been invited by several organizations in Georgia to speak about information literacy teaching techniques and is the co-recipient of two teaching awards given at Georgia State University. She may be contacted at clong@agnesscott.edu.

Michele McKinlay, MA, is Teaching Specialist Faculty in English and Core Curriculum at the University of Dubuque in Dubuque, Iowa. She received her master's in English Literature from the University of Northern Iowa. Among the courses she teaches are Introduction to Research Writing, Modern Grammar, Composition & Rhetoric, and World View Seminars. Her interests include acting and directing in regional theatre. She may be contacted at mmckinla@dbq.edu.

Lynne M. Mitchell, PG Diploma of the New Zealand Library School and Diploma of Teaching, has been a business librarian at the University of Auckland for nearly 10 years. She is the program librarian for the Bachelor of Business and Information Management (BBIM) and the Master of Business Administration degrees. In particular, Lynne has worked closely with BBIM colleagues to encourage teaching integration and the embedding of information literacy capabilities within that program. Her professional interests include encouraging librarian-faculty teaching collaboration, providing librarian support for issues of plagiarism and academic honesty, and developing resources such as library course pages to support student learning. Lynne has co-written and presented a number of conference papers with academic teaching colleagues on information literacy initiatives. She may be contacted by e-mail at lm.mitchell@auckland.ac.nz.

Angela Newton, MA, MCLIP, is Faculty Team Librarian in Science and Engineering at the University of Leeds, with a particular interest in connecting people with collections through information literacy. Her work on information literacy initiatives for students and researchers is dependent on developing high quality relationships with academic staff, and a commitment to continual professional development in learning and teaching. Angela is an active committee member of the Cilip (Chartered Institute of Library and Information Professionals) CSG Information Literacy Group. Formed in 2004, the group has rapidly advanced the information literacy agenda, through the creation of the Lilac conference, awareness-raising publications, and through the Web site, www.informationliteracy.org.uk. Angela is also a member of the Higher Education Academy. She may be reached by e-mail at a.j.newton@leeds.ac.uk.

Norm Pouliot, MA, in English, is Senior Associate Professor of English at Cascadia Community College with more than 30 years' experience teaching English at the high school level in three different states before moving into college teaching in 2002. His particular interest lies with the creation and implementation of strategies designed to address the learning challenges faced by today's learners. Norm regularly teaches Composition and Writing from Research courses at Cascadia and values collaborating with librarians to enhance the role of information literacy in the English curriculum. He may be reached by e-mail at npouliot@cascadia.edu.

Pamela S. Presser, PhD, is currently a writing instructor in the University Writing Program at The George Washington University, where she has taught for 17 years. Dr. Presser consults on interdisciplinary projects outside of academia. She coordinated a pilot writing program for the Health Effects Division of the Environmental Protection Agency and has served as a technical writing consultant for the chair of the outreach committee of the District of Columbia Board of Real Property Assessments and Appeals. She has been researching, writing about, and presenting papers on composition pedagogy since 1993. She is particularly interested in exploring methodologies that train student writers to use the arguments of theorists to analyze portrayals of science in the media. She may be reached by e-mail at ppresser@gwu.edu.

Milind M. Shrikhande, PhD, is Associate Professor of Finance in the J. Mack Robinson College of Business at Georgia State University. He has a strong interest in pedagogical issues, which has led him to publish and present on information literacy and teaching styles. He is the co-recipient of the J. Mack Robinson College of Business Harvey Brightman Award for Innovative Instruction and the Georgia State University Instructional Effectiveness Award. He may be contacted at mshrikhande@gsu.edu.

Ruth Wilson, MA, PG Diploma in Librarianship, PG Certificate in Teaching & Learning in Higher Education, is Information & Research Development Coordinator within Learning Services at Edge Hill University, Ormskirk, UK, where she co-ordinates all information literacy developments for the Faculty of Education. She has published on changing learner support roles in information environments and the emergence of the new academic team. Her current research interests include the development and growth of academic partnerships, supporting outreach and part time students and information literacy in the widening participation agenda. She may be contacted by e-mail at wilsonr@edgehill.ac.uk.

Index